Business Leadership and the Lessons from Sport

BUSINESS LEADERSHIP
and the Lessons from Sport

Hans Westerbeek

and

Aaron Smith

palgrave
macmillan

First published 2005 by
PALGRAVE MACMILLAN
Houndmills, Basingstoke, Hampshire RG21 6XS and
175 Fifth Avenue, New York, N. Y. 10010
Companies and representatives throughout the world

PALGRAVE MACMILLAN is the global academic imprint of the Palgrave Macmillan division of St. Martin's Press, LLC and of Palgrave Macmillan Ltd. Macmillan® is a registered trademark in the United States, United Kingdom and other countries. Palgrave is a registered trademark in the European Union and other countries.

ISBN-13: 978–1–4039–4716–1
ISBN-10: 1–4039–4716–3

This book is printed on paper suitable for recycling and made from fully managed and sustained forest sources.

A catalogue record for this book is available from the British Library.

A catalog record for this book is available from the Library of Congress.

10 9 8 7 6 5 4 3 2 1
14 13 12 11 10 09 08 07 06 05

Printed and bound in Great Britain by
Creative Print & Design (Wales), Ebbw Vale

Contents

List of Figures and Tables

Figures

Tables

Acknowledgements

We would like to express our appreciation to Colin Smith for his immense contribution to this book, in both its conceptual development and practical application.

We are also grateful to Loes and Clare for their unending support.

Hans Westerbeek
Aaron Smith

CHAPTER 1

Introduction: The Sport of Leadership

Bad luck does not exist. (ENZO FERRARI)

From the Front

An era in Formula One motor racing is currently being forged by a handful of some of the most capable leaders in the world of sport. With six constructor's and five consecutive driver's championships to its name from the last half-dozen seasons of Formula One, Ferrari has muscled its way onto the podium as a contender for the greatest ever sporting team. In any successful organization leadership lessons are available. But perhaps some of the characteristics of sport leadership can offer a richer source of information; a metaphor for leadership action in business that goes beyond the tired sporting clichés of commitment, dedication, and aggression.

Jean Todt, the French team director of Ferrari, nicknamed by some as Napoleon for his uncompromising leadership style, once described his world champion driver and close friend Michael Schumacher as a sweetheart, an emotional softie. And yet, the media personification of Schumacher is almost the opposite. What the public sees is a leader with ice running through his veins; logical, capable, strong, brilliant. Great leadership is not always what is seems from the outside.

After a blistering youth spent mastering karts, Schumacher was offered a seat in a Formula Koenig (Ford). His first season returned nine wins in ten starts, and propelled the German into Formula 3, where he finished third in his initial season and won the championship the following year. Graduating to the Sauber team behind the wheel of a sports car, Schumacher again distinguished himself enough to attract the attention of Eddie Jordan, principal of the Formula One team bearing his surname.

Schumacher was hastily signed, but legal complications sneaked their way in and Schumacher unexpectedly found himself at Benetton by the end of the season. Schumacher's first Grand Prix was a taste of what was to come, however, qualifying seventh and racing aggressively before a forced retirement.

At only 23, Schumacher made it to his first full Formula One season in 1992. It was a promising start. On 11 occasions, Schumacher finished in the points, and by the end of the season he had even collected his maiden Grand Prix victory. The following season offered a similar story, Schumacher competitive, but subservient to some of the best drivers of the time, including Prost, Hill, and Senna. However, by the 1994 season, only his third in Formula One, disaster struck, but not for Schumacher. Championship favorite Ayrton Senna crashed out of a race at San Marino and was killed after violently hitting a wall. In the mourning and shadow of Senna's death, Schumacher collected his first world championship, a feat he repeated the following year.

Moving to Ferrari in 1996 Schumacher endured the frustration of being close but not close enough. Then, after the mixed fortunes of 1999, when Schumacher broke his leg, but Ferrari managed to win the constructor's title, the records began to fall. Five driver's championships later, Schumacher has broken just about every record there is to break in Formula One, including the most driver's championships and Grand Prix victories. It's easy to assume that Schumacher is the guiding force leading the Ferrari team. But, in fact, according to the team director Jean Todt, although Schumacher provides infectious motivation, technical expertise, a natural authority, and a point of reference, he plays no strategic or managerial role in the team. The reality is that Schumacher's contribution is just the phalanx of an immensely deep leadership team.

When professional athletes and teams compete, the resulting contest has a dynamism that is unpredictable at its core, despite being bound by specific rules. For example, one knows what to expect from a football match compared to a wrestling bout. However, the exact way in which a contest unfolds – regardless of the sport – is impossible to anticipate or control. From the chaos that is on-field play emerge some of the most exhilarating moments of human experience. From the melee of a Grand Prix race start, Schumacher can mold a race of precision and, at times, flawlessness. For the sport fan, these passages of aesthetic wonder are like fleeting glimpses of an effortless perfection. They represent a kind of spontaneous innovation, founded upon countless hours of training, but realized in one string of critical activities that run together like a scripted performance. From the uncertainty of the contest emerges a winner: the team or individual capable of converting complexity to innovation, chaos to control, choice to opportunity and, perhaps most importantly, indecision to leadership.

Sport offers a unique metaphor for critically examining business; the two share some common ground. Both are fast, complex, and at times unpredictable. Both demand professional training, benefit from the experience that accompanies performance and aim to inspire loyalty from their consumers. And both are at their best when they transfer knowledge from specialists to the front line, find the balance between chaos and the desire for control, discern opportunity from deception, and confer importance to leadership rather than management. This book is about the lessons for business leadership that can be found on the sporting field of play. It is not intended as a recipe book offering quick, "bake at home" solutions, but it is built upon the premise that while leadership is complex, its execution can benefit from new ways of thinking about and looking at the subject. The nature of sport offers such a view.

> The car was good today and the backmarkers did a good job of keeping out of the way. *(Michael Schumacher after a race)*

Parallax

When someone scans an object with only one eye open and then only the other, it appears to have moved. This apparent displacement is known as the "parallax effect". This book uses sport as a vehicle to achieve this effect in viewing leadership in the business world. It does not shirk the responsibility of presenting the genuine challenges associated with leadership, nor does it conflate the solution to a single or simple behavior or activity. It does, however, take an innovative approach to discussing leadership by utilizing international, professional sport as a metaphor. And to get us rolling, few other sporting cases are as plentiful in example as that of Ferrari.

Ferrari is the only team that has competed in the Formula One World Championship since its inception in 1951 when the series was contested by private athletes racing under national colors. In stark contrast, the current world championship involves 10 teams competing in 18 Grand Prix races spanning Europe, Asia, Australia and North and South America, generating an estimated US$1 billion in broadcasting rights alone and a cumulative audience of seven billion across over 200 countries. Formula

One Administration Limited, founded and managed by Bernie Ecclestone, holds the exclusive commercial rights to the FIA (Fédération Internationale de L'Automobile) Formula One World Championship, and is not shy about exploiting those rights. In fact, doing so has made Bernie Ecclestone's personal fortune amount to US$4500 million. He owns roughly 25 percent of companies involved in the management of Formula One. In this frenzy of capitalism, Ferrari boasts the largest annual budget and employee numbers of any Formula One team, approximately US$300 million and 800 respectively. It also commands the performance of the highest paid athlete in the world, Michael Schumacher, who earns US$80 million per year including endorsements to drive a 900 horsepower vehicle up to 350 kilometers an hour using technology that NASA would be proud of.[1]

> Money makes the world go around and in Formula One it greases the wheels too. *(Roger Horton, motor racing journalist and commentator)*

To look at any organization like Ferrari that has sustained high performances over time suggests "best-practice" lessons. Undoubtedly, there is no shortage of suggestions offered by academics, consultants, and even business leaders themselves as to what leadership best practice entails. Typically, leadership best practice is represented by a set of dimensions, characteristics or qualities. A brief trawl through the internet provides an immediate feel for the volume of different views. Somewhat appropriately, Jay Cross in his internet article *The Last Word: The Changing Nature of Leadership*, makes the point with some much needed cynicism:

> Books teach you leadership's 108 skills, 101 Innovative Ways, 30 Marine Management Principles, 22 Vital Traits, 21 Indispensable Qualities, 21 Irrefutable Laws, 21 Most Powerful Minutes, 18 Workshops, 17 Indisputable Laws, 17 Principles, 15 Secrets, 11 Lessons, 12 Principles, 10 Traits, Ten Keys, Nine Keys, 7 Acts of Courage, Seven Habits, Six Fail-safe Strategies, Six Strategic Principles, Five Temptations, Five Giant Steps, Five Decision Styles, Five Practices, Four Disciplines, Four Practical Revolutions, Three Keys, One Minute, and the Other 90%.[2]

> In theory, there is no difference between theory and practice. But, in practice, there is. *(Jan L.A. van de Snepscheut, former Professor of Computing Science, California Institute of Technology)*

Unfortunately, despite the volume of rhetoric on leadership, there is not necessarily much consensus about any of it, although the gap is probably most distinct between descriptive, academic theories of leadership and prescriptive, popular approaches. Academic versions tend, to their credit, to emphasize precision and empirical data. As a result, they also tend to tell us what we already know: that "good" leadership is neither describable in universal terms nor is it definable in a common way.

The truth about leadership from those who study it seriously for a living is that it is complex, uncertain, and powerfully affected by inescapable but unpredictable contextual variables like the composition of followers, the type of organization and its goals, as well as the idiosyncrasies of the environment at the time. Add to this the fact that empirical data remind us that completely different approaches to leadership can be effective in the same situations. To put it another way, leadership for business is a lot like leadership for sport, except for the fact that the vagaries of sport leadership seem to be far better accepted. We all accept that former England rugby coach Sir Clive Woodward and basketball coach Phil Jackson employ fundamentally different approaches to leadership. The research data would encourage us to accept this as an axiom of business leadership. The popular literature, on the other hand, would try to convince us that there are secrets to leadership that will be exposed in a handful of chapters if only we buy the book. With this in mind, we will not be offering another leadership panacea, but we do begin with the premise that it can be profitable to look at business leadership from another perspective, in this case from the viewpoint of successful sport.

> What has instructed all of the world's builders of safe, efficient cars? Auto racing. Any theory, any laboratory experiment needs practical support, and only the race can offer it because during the race the driver submits the car and its parts to intense, unpredictable, unthinkable testing. *(Enzo Ferrari)*

Most popular approaches draw certain elements from different theoretical bases of leadership in order to best suit their needs. These needs range from selling books, educational programs or people. We would immediately recommend to the reader some caution, in that while such approaches can elicit useful information, they are frequently flimsy in content, even when they are, on the surface at least, very appealing. They use exciting language and seem to make sense of events that shape the corporate and personal worlds in which we live. For example, some leaders such as

Rudolph Giuliani, Colin Powell, and Jack Welch have capitalized on personal credibility and defining events to present their own views on leadership. Some of these personal accounts can be enlightening, and while it does not mean that they represent the only way to lead, sometimes they contain some useful lessons.

> The country is full of good coaches. What it takes to win is a bunch of interested players. *(Don Coryell, former coach, San Diego Chargers)*

Leadership Lessons

Perhaps the most profound leadership lessons of the Ferrari case can be found in the life of the founder himself, Enzo Ferrari. The son of a metal worker, Enzo Ferrari led an undistinguished and underprivileged life first punctuated by action when called up to serve in the Italian army in 1917, although he ended up spending most of his time shoeing mules. A decade later, Ferrari was effectively running Alfa Romeo's racing operations, three decades later, he presided over his car's first Grand Prix victory, and four decades later, the world champion driver was sitting behind the wheel of a car adorned with Ferrari's name.

But it was a humiliating start for Enzo Ferrari. With a letter of discharge from the army in his pocket, Ferrari presented at Fiat for an interview, only to discover that he was destined to be among the unlucky ones in a labour market bloated with ex-servicemen. Gifted with a sense of foresight and planning, Ferrari spent time expanding and massaging his network of contacts, which eventually culminated in a job offer with car manufacturer CMN. The connection was fortuitous, allowing Ferrari to seize upon the opportunity to race. Within three years of being discharged from the army, Ferrari took an Alfa Romeo to a second place finish in the Targa Florio. A love of racing was kindled, and the early foundations of his personal leadership journey were also laid in place. Ferrari's approach to leadership was to be poignantly expressed in a symbol that has become one of the most recognized logos in the world.

Racing for Alfa Romeo in 1923 on the Savio at Revenna circuit, Ferrari won convincingly despite driving a comparatively underpowered car. After the race, Ferrari was approached by the father of Francesco Baracca, the famous World War I fighter pilot. Baracca senior was so impressed with Ferarri's boldness behind the wheel that he presented a badge to Ferrari emblazoned with the prancing horse of his son's squadron. The same symbol is carried by every Ferrari made today, and has become the most famous automobile logo ever applied to a hood or bonnet.

Throughout the 1920s, Ferrari built a network of contacts in Alfa Romeo, many of whom would work with him for decades. Meanwhile, Ferrari secured a degree of notoriety from success on the track, albeit in an Alfa Romeo. His performances nevertheless delivered awards and titles, including "Commendatore," a high distinction that Ferrari dismissed with a characteristic but increasingly unpredictable charisma that would feature in his leadership style for the rest of his career.

> That which is yet to be won. *(Enzo Ferrari, when asked which race victory was the most important the team had achieved)*
>
> That which is yet to be built. *(Enzo Ferrari, when asked which Ferrari model he liked the most)*

Deciding to step away from a formal affiliation with Alfa Romeo, and retiring from racing in 1929, Ferrari formed his own team in Modena, which, although operating under the name Scuderia Ferrari, still fielded a conventional Alfa Romeo. Of note was Ferrari's astute decision to share ownership with the wealthy Caniato brothers, whose early financial clout helped to establish what effectively became a semi-autonomous entity within Alfa Romeo. Scuderia Ferrari grew to become a professional racing outfit, led by the increasingly ambitious Ferrari. By 1939 the team had enjoyed substantial success, having won a number of important Grand Prix events, and having defeated the larger teams with less powerful vehicles. But by this time, Ferrari had had enough of clashing with Alfa Romeo's director and engineers, a tension that reached a climax with the giant manufacturer's intention to reabsorb the Scuderia Ferrari's racing operation, along with its intellectual and design property. The event provided a catalyst for Ferrari to manufacture, by 1940, several eight cylinder cars, which later that year raced under no specific designation, but which have come to be regarded as the first genuine Ferrari cars.

Despite a serious downturn during World War II that forced Ferrari to focus his company's efforts on specialist machine tool work, the team survived and continued to manufacture in its original Modena premises, establishing what is still considered an infamous hub of high-performance automobile engineering. After the war, Ferrari's team raced a 1.5 liter V12 car with some success, but it was not until 1948 that the new supercharged Ferrari 125 had its first outing in the Italian Grand Prix, in what was the first world championship. Ferrari's team took the driver's championship in 1952, 1953 and again in 1956 with Juan Fangio at the wheel. Two years later, the world's first British world champion was driving a Ferrari.

As in many success stories, great leaders are more important in times of difficulty rather than triumph. Such was the case with Ferrari during a long dry patch that yielded only one championship in 15 years. The period was intense and frustrating. Mechanical innovation and a string of creditable drivers simply could not break the success of the larger teams. In many ways, it was the emergence of another leader, this time on the track, that provided Ferrari with an injection of energy. A young Austrian driver, Niki Lauda, showed great promise in his first season with Ferrari in 1974, and won the title brilliantly in 1975. Lauda could have made it back-to-back championships but suffered a horrendous accident at Nurburgring in Germany that left him with serious burns. In fact, he was so badly injured that he was administered the last rites, a fact made more remarkable by Lauda's return to competition within a few races, only to lose the championship by a single point. Extraordinarily, Lauda reclaimed his title in 1977, and Ferrari enjoyed success again in 1979 with Jody Scheckter driving the prancing horse. But it was going to be another period in the wilderness – this time 21 years – before Ferrari was to win another driver's championship, despite signing some of the best talent available, including Alain Prost, Jean Alesi, and Nigel Mansell. The fact was that Enzo Ferrari, for all his charisma and focus, was growing old, and his death at 90 in 1988 left the team with a leadership vacuum and in desperate need of re-invigoration. What had worked in the past was no longer yielding success. The Ferrari leadership formula needed a change.

> Aerodynamics is for those who cannot manufacture good engines. (*Enzo Ferrari*)

The Leadership Formula

One of the most significant issues facing leadership is the lack of an accepted formula. There is no such thing as an accepted model or approach. Further, many sound approaches to leadership tend to be one-dimensional, driven by a single idea or focused on a small part of the puzzle. It is clear from the outset, therefore, that leaders tend to be faced with the prospect of positioning themselves as either champions of a certain approach, or selecting from a menu containing diverse and perhaps

*multi dimensional*

even incompatible approaches. This is not to suggest that several different approaches cannot be used successfully together, nor has the ineffectiveness of empirical leadership research discouraged leaders from attempting to fill the gaps themselves. Indeed, there is a current push that suggests methodology that has been used in scientifically based models is not providing results that can be applied by practitioners; methodology that is grounded in organizations and businesses rather than from the transposition of psychological and quantitative survey methods upon businesses. For example, Parry and Meindel's recent book *Grounding Leadership Theory and Research* provides a perspective of leadership, grounded in organizations, and developed through the study of organizations.[3] Recently, approaches to leadership have begun to focus more directly on events and the changing nature of leadership for different settings. This assumption is a core feature of sport, and one of the ongoing themes of this book. It is also apparent to anyone who has ever studied a case like that of Ferrari, in detail.

Of course many approaches to leadership are grounded in the experience of commercial, business organizations. If, as is commonly the case, these approaches are published as books, they often tell a good story, and make sense to those working in organizations like the one described. A good example is *The Oz Principle*,[4] a leadership book based around the story line of *The Wizard of Oz*, complete with the leadership pathway, which naturally enough is a "yellow brick road." This makes for an easily understandable and at times entertaining read, but is limited in its ability to communicate the principles of leadership. Most approaches to leadership tend to assume that leaders (and the implementation of their decisions) make a difference in organizations. However, the essence of what makes that difference changes depending upon the approach. Thus, a successful leadership approach should be multidimensional and should take a broad focus of where leaders influence an organization. We shall argue that the sport metaphor helps in this ambition.

> You need to know Spa to savour Senna, the steepness of the descent to Eau Rouge, the strange ferocity of the left-right kink at the bottom; you need to know that Eau Rouge is to be taken at high speed, balls to the wall. *(Christopher Hilton in Ayrton Senna – The Hard Edge of Genius)*[5]

A convergence of appointments was responsible for the Ferrari rebuilding. At the top, former team manager Luca di Montezemolo stepped into the space left by Enzo Ferrari. As chairman and chief executive of

Ferrari, Luca di Montezemolo has largely been credited with the company's reinvigoration over the last decade as well as the turnaround of their subsidiary Maserati. Montezemolo's focus has been on developing a new generation of technologically advanced racing cars to complement their existing engineering superiority. In addition to research and development, at an operational level, Montezemolo has also revised the product lines, downsized the workforce and changed manufacturing practices. These strategies have been heavily driven by the investments he has made in the Formula One racing team, a marketplace battering ram which has returned handsome dividends. Montezemolo has also taken Ferrari to a successful public float, with the backing of their principal owner, the Fiat group, which also own the automotive company of the same name among other enterprises. It is easy to forget in the midst of Ferrari's record-breaking dominance that it was languishing at a historic low when Montezemolo assumed the leadership in 1991. Even then, success had to be relearnt. It was not until 1993 that the foundations of the racing team were created.

One of Montezemolo's key moves was to secure Jean Todt as team manager with the design and engineering expertise of Ross Brawn and Rory Byrne added to the portfolio shortly afterwards. Of course, the changes culminated in the acquisition of double world champion Michael Schumacher in 1996. Schumacher was immediately competitive, and came tantalizingly close to taking the title in 1997 and 1998, with Eddie Irvine as a solid second driver. Things got worse in 1999, however, when Schumacher broke his leg at Silverstone, leaving Irvine to battle on, ultimately coming close to winning the driver's title. It was enough, however, to clinch the constructor's title. But in 2000, Irvine was dissatisfied with having to play the second driver to Schumacher, after stepping into the top role during the previous season. The team was unambiguous though; Schumacher was to remain the top man, and Irvine left to be replaced by Rubens Barrichello.

The prancing horse regained the driver's championship after 21 years in 2000, and has never seriously looked to be challenged since. After no less than nine Grand Prix victories, Schumacher won the title, bolstered admirably by an improving Barrichello who also secured his first Grand Prix victory during the season. Another nine race wins in 2001 were enough for Schumacher to secure the championship again, as the most consistent performer in the field. Ferrari has not relinquished its control of the world championship since, Schumacher taking 11 Grand Prix victories in 2002, a new record for the most in any one season, and delivering him a fifth driver's championship, equaling Juan Fangio's achievements of the 1950s. Barrichello finished second, accumulating four Grand Prix wins of his own.

Sport Thinking

We are not advocating sport itself as a leadership tool. Playing sport won't help. Nor do we advocate treating business as a sport, but we do believe that looking at business from a sport frame of mind is helpful in dealing with the dynamics of contemporary business. Kevin Roberts, chairman and CEO of Saatchi Worldwide commented:

> don't look to great companies for inspiration. Instead look to the world's greatest sports teams. Sport is the most relevant model for peak performance in business. Sport is about teamwork, inclusion and empowerment. It's about passion, fun, excitement, making magic, winning and being part of a dream.[6]

There is precedent, of course, for looking at business this way. For example, David Parkin, a successful coach in Australian Rules football, co-wrote *Perform – Or Else!*, which offers commentary regarding how managers and leaders can learn about business strategy, tactics, and leadership from sport.[7] *Peak Performance*[8] (by Gilson et al.) analyzes successful sport teams in a series of case studies, attempting to illuminate the strategies behind their success and suggest how business leaders can learn from these. Another notable example is *The Business Playbook: Leadership Lessons From the World of Sports*[9] by Brandon Steiner whose suggestions can be summarized as: "Start with a road map; Find your niche; Wake up nervous!; Know your purpose; Go the extra mile; You never know; Get focused!; Nothing changes if nothing changes; It's not what happens, it's what you do with what happens; and See success as a habit." This book, *Business Leadership and the Lessons from Sport,* unlike Steiner's, is not so much about attitudes and habits as systems and practices. Like Holland's *Red Zone Management*[10] which uses the red zone (the last twenty yards in American football before a touchdown) as a metaphor for critical moments in an organization, *Business Leadership and the Lessons from Sport* views some conditions in sport as consistent with those pivotal times in business where the manager (or leader) must introduce innovations, competitive strategy, mergers, culture changes, and put his or her best players (the team) on the field (or in the game).

As sport and business can overlap in practical and metaphorical ways, leaders in business might benefit from a better appreciation of the principles employed in leading sport, from wresting order from chaos, to the nuances of coaching.[11] It is noteworthy, however, that most of the evidence suggests that good leadership is hard to come by in any organization and context, including sport. For example, Pamm Kellett showed in her research that the popular ascriptions of leadership are not all that familiar to coaches in professional sport.[12] In other words, either these professional coaches do not think that the stereotypical descriptions of what leaders are supposed to do are accurate, or that their experiences of actual leadership are of a different nature. Of course, another interpretation is that professional coaches perform managerial and operational roles more than they do leadership tasks. In this sense, coaches might be like most people in leadership roles – average. Perhaps, though, there is the chance that professional coaches perform some tasks that are pivotal to their leadership contribution, and the popular leadership literature simply does not accurately distil what it is that leaders really should do. Sport is useful in this way because it helps to tease out the hidden activities – like the relationships formed with athletes – that are part of the foundations of good leadership and teamwork, but are not high profile enough for anyone to link to the charismatic roles that the popular literature has brainwashed us into thinking is normal.

Gideon Haigh arrives at a similar conclusion, albeit from another angle entirely.[13] He suggests that the cult of the CEO is responsible for elevating them to superhero status where their acting ability is as much a factor in their perceived leadership performance as anything else. In the cult, it is assumed that the CEO is the sole author of a company's future, dependent largely upon their celebrity leadership status, which, unhelpfully, can be elevated by paying them ridiculous salaries. There is little doubt that marketing leaders is a critical aspect of contemporary business, and of the leadership function itself, but as in sport, leaders need to be able to demonstrate that their performance is worthy of the price. Moreover, as in sport, there are a series of key leaders in any team, and many of them receive very little exposure or credit.

> Experience is a hard teacher because she gives
> the test first, the lesson afterward.
>
> Some people are so busy learning the tricks of
> the trade that they never learn the trade.
> (Vernon Law, former pitcher, Pittsburgh Pirates)

A New Vision

A key leader in the Ferrari camp is undoubtedly Jean Todt, who has presided over the last five consecutive championship victories as the director of the racing team. Jean Todt has enjoyed a varied set of experiences in motor sport, beginning with a brief stint of rally driving, before realizing he was better suited to navigation. After a number of years of success, he moved to the international scene where he partnered a number of top drivers, eventually gravitating to Talbot Sunbeam Lotus, a team that won the 1981 World Rally manufacturer's title. Todt subsequently retired to manage the development of the Peugeot Talbot Sport team competing in the world rally championships. The team was competitive in 1984 and took the title along with the driver's honors in 1985 and 1986. Peugeot turned away from world championship rallying shortly afterward, but Todt led the team into other events, winning the world's premier endurance rally, the Paris–Dakar four times, as well as the infamous Pike's Peak hill climb. Peugeot changed its focus again in 1990, this time to sports cars. Todt again proved to be the right man at the helm, guiding the team to the 1992 World Sports Car Championship and the 1992 Le Mans 24-hour race. He surpassed this achievement in 1993 with an extraordinary clean sweep of the podium for Peugeot at Le Mans. However, the success was not enough to enable Todt to convince Peugeot management to enter Formula One, so he moved across to take up the reigns in Ferrari's Formula One motor racing team.

Todt's arrival at Ferrari constituted a major new leadership presence in a team that was struggling to come to terms with its identity in a post-Enzo Ferrari era. While Montezemolo had his hands full with the manufacturing efforts of the company, the focus was on Todt's first contribution, bringing the racing team together under new standards of organization and planning toward the achievement of a world championship. By 1994 Ferrari was again competitive, finishing third, an achievement replicated in 1995. The following year proved decisive, in that Todt managed to secure the services of twice world champion Michael Schumacher, along with Eddie Irvine as his number two. Todt's strategy was straightforward; there could be no substitute for the best driver, so Ferrari had to have him, irrespective of the cost. It was also a significant year, in that it heralded the acquisition of Ross Brawn, the race strategy wizard, and Rory Byrne, a leader in racing car design engineering. The new composition of the team proved effective, although close seasons in 1997 and 1998 relegated Ferrari to second place in both years.

Todt would have engineered the dream season in 1999, but for the accident in which Schumacher broke his leg and was forced to relegate his seniority to Irvine. The mantle was grasped firmly by Irvine who almost delivered the goods, but eventually finished second in the driver's championship. The effort, however, was enough to get the team over the line as constructor's champions, and half of Todt's vision was realized, to be completed in the dream season that was 2000. It had taken seven years of

Todt's leadership – focus, vision, thoroughness, and bold innovation – but the rewards finally arrived. Todt has since been awarded the Chevalier de la Légion d' Honneur, which is the French equivalent to a British knighthood. Recently, Todt was named as the new director general of the Ferrari company, but will retain his responsibilities as chief of the racing team.

Perhaps Todt's most admirable leadership quality is his ability to draw a high-potential team together and lead them to new levels of collaboration in a sport where innovation and precision in a team setting are serious competitive advantages. Notably, Michael Schumacher's arrival at Ferrari coincided with Todt's broader restructuring which brought the new chief designer Rory Byrne to the team along with Schumacher's long time collaborator, team manager Ross Brawn. Byrne had designed Ayrton Senna's chassis in 1986 as well as Schumacher's championship winning Benettons of 1994 and 1995. Lured out of retirement to work for Ferrari, Byrne has designed the last five successive world championship winning cars, a feat that has confirmed his position as the most senior designer in Formula One. Similarly, Brawn had already marked his performance with a track record carved out at Williams as an engineer and designer and with Benetton in its championship winning days as a technical director.

> If we are the best in the world, it is because we have the best staff in the world, you World Champions. *(Jean Todt addressing the Ferrari racing team)*

It has not all been smooth sailing for Todt. There was the vacuum after Schumacher's effective departure from the season with a broken leg in 1999 and the incident at the European Grand Prix where Mika Salo, driving in Schumacher's place, made a pit stop unexpectedly during a period of radio malfunction immediately ahead of Irvine's scheduled stop, delaying him severely. The Italian press were wild with speculation that Todt's head should roll. And then, during the 2003 season, Ferrari became mired in a controversy which went to the heart of what it means to compete in sport. In the final moments of the Austrian Grand Prix in which Barrichello was leading ahead of Schumacher, he moved aside on team orders to allow the German to win. Adding to the controversy, Schumacher pushed Barrichello up to the top of the podium during the award ceremony, an action that revealed as much as the race footage. Ferrari was fined US$1 million by the FIA over the incident, deemed to have brought the sport into disrepute.

Although certainly unpopular with Formula One aficionados who proclaimed the loss of uncertainty over a race's outcome as a blow to the very heart of what sport stands for, the incident is somewhat banal when viewed from a business perspective. After all, Ferrari is a team and its collective best interests were best served by the action, which was conducted quite overtly, not unlike the support the top rider receives from his or her team during a road cycling event. But that was not the way some fans viewed the team orders, seeing it more like a professional foul in football than a legitimate strategy for maximizing team success. Indeed, the FIA has introduced a new rule banning team orders, although in reality it will more likely result in strategic maneuvering in its application. The fact is that sometimes sport gives a different view of good leadership compared with business. The purpose of this book is to consider these and evaluate their usefulness to the business leader.

Think Differently Through Sport

This chapter explains the advantages of taking a sporting view of leadership. For example, leaders cannot control organizations comprising people in the same way that an operator can control a machine made of moving, but inanimate parts. This means that it might be more effective for leaders and managers to define the parameters of the business, but remain less involved in the operational conduct of the business, trusting it to those on the "field of play." Indeed, it might be dangerous for leaders to make decisions based upon linear assumptions about where they think the organization should head or is heading. Sport illustrates the importance of understanding that cause and effect is complex, and the field of play, whether sporting or business, is unpredictable. As a result, the assumption that strict policies lead to high levels of control does not always hold because linear causality does not always hold. For example, excessive rules to help employees solve problems can communicate that they are considered incapable of solving problems, and can lead to a workforce averse to thinking for themselves and initiating innovative solutions. Who wants players who can't think for themselves? Change leads to unplanned consequences and high-pressure situations. Great athletes and teams 'thrive on chaos' because they have embraced the fact that success in the sporting arena is as much about opportunity and innovation as it is about command and control.

> I skate to where the puck is going to be, not to where it has been.
> (Wayne Gretzky, former National Hockey League player)

For our purposes, a leader is someone either charged with the responsibility, or who assumes the responsibility, for coordinating the efforts of others toward a predetermined end goal. Within this are the dual issues of how they get there, and whether they get there. Sport tends to iron this out in favor of whether the goals are achieved. The leader in sport is the one responsible for winning. This is the platform from which we work in this book.

What are the chief characteristics of sport that are useful to embrace from a business leadership viewpoint? In the first instance, sport clearly has a symbolic intensity and emotional dimension that is rarely found in the business setting. Passion adds a new facet. Sport followers not only develop steel bonds to their favorite clubs and players, but also gain endless pleasure from their sport participation and watching experiences. Because sport engenders such high levels of loyalty, the identification that fans have with sports and teams can also spin off into their relationships with family, friends, their sporting heroes, and their heroes' behavior. Sport arouses energy, the intensity of which is infrequently discharged in commercial business. Sport and business therefore often operate within different behavioral parameters. While commercial businesses would like to stimulate strong emotional loyalty from their employees, their overriding concerns tend to be efficiency, productivity, and market conditions. Sport, however, is consumed by attachments that penetrate commercial exploitation, and are powerfully linked to the past through nostalgia and tradition as well as the future through a sense of hope for success. The Ferrari Formula One team may operate unashamedly as a business but it is hard to believe that either the team members or its supporters view it merely as a job.

Perhaps one of most noteworthy differences between professional competitive sport organizations and business is the way in which they respectively measure performance. Sport is one of the few products or services that depends on unpredictability for its success. Indeed, it is well known that attendances at sporting contests are higher where the outcome is considered uncertain, compared to games where results seem predictable. Indeed, the domination of Ferrari has caused a drop in Formula One television ratings. The difficulty for sport is that its inherent lack of predictability encourages enormous variability in the quality of sporting performances, exacerbated by variables such as the weather, player injuries, the location of the venue, the position of opponents in the competition season, the proximity of the scores, whether the game is being televised, and even the size of the crowd. By contrast, in business, most products and services have relatively little variability in their quality, and are prized when achieved. Although sport needs unpredictability to prosper, it is hardly the goal of any sport leaders other than league administrators. In fact, the unpredictability of sport has forced sport leaders to develop more comprehensive performance measurement systems than in any other industry. For the best sport organizations like Ferrari, performance is monitored at a level that makes business approaches look quite sloppy. It is also transmitted into training and development faster and more smoothly than the corporate world would imagine possible. Given the much discussed escalation in the speed of market change in business, the role of the leader in monitoring performance would seem vital.

> My jump was imperfect, my run-in was too short and my hands were too far back at takeoff. When I manage to iron out these faults, I am sure I can improve. *(Sergei Bubka, pole vaulter)*

The sporting world is nevertheless full of contradictions. While fans will sometimes go to great lengths to preserve traditional practices or symbols, there are other situations where sport fans have a high tolerance for changes in personnel and product quality. The emotive glue that joins members and fans to their clubs means that they will endure countless changes to the personnel of their club if it means a greater chance of success. Part of this acceptance revolves around an awareness of what is core to the sport business.

Ferrari's Competitive Advantage

Ferrari's dominance, as we have demonstrated so far, has stretched beyond its historical limitations and the skills of its individual members. What makes the team so extraordinary is the way in which it has leveraged its collective skills. Ferrari's competencies as a team confer upon them significant competitive advantages for success in the astonishingly fast-paced world in which they operate. In this sense, Ferrari embodies the key sport lessons for business that we intend to explore in the subsequent chapters. All the chapters engage ten leadership themes or metaphors to a greater or lesser degree, depending on the topic and objectives of the chapter. These themes and the chief metaphors that can be derived from them are briefly described below, and in so doing, we answer the question: What can business leaders learn from sport generally, and Ferrari specifically?

1. "Surfing the edge of chaos" and capitalizing on complexity and ambiguity

Few sports change and improve at the rate Formula One has; its competitive environment is cutthroat. In many sports, to perform at the same level as the previous year will bring about a similar result, but in Formula One such a performance will relegate a team to certain failure. The ability of Jean Todt to progress performance through ongoing change and periodic crises, including the constant introduction of new technologies and the certain turnover of employees, has been critical to its success. In particular, success in Formula One leadership requires a certain philosophical mindset where comfort with rapid change is a distinct advantage. With races spaced frequently during the season, the Ferrari team scarcely has time to celebrate its victories. The team's race begins the moment they touch down in a new location and lasts until its drivers cross the finishing line. There are thousands of variables to consider, and hundreds of decisions to be made in an instant. The edge of chaos is a constant companion, but it is also the Ferrari way.

For the business leader, Ferrari teaches the counterintuitive notion that control is not necessarily the same thing as stability. The most successful leaders in the next generation of market-dominating companies will be the ones who not only constantly evaluate the environment and trends, but will also assume the mindset that everything is temporary. The edge of chaos rules. Innovation is born in the Ferrari-like leadership philosophy that not only accepts change but thrives on it.

2. Emergent leadership

More than in business, sport demonstrates the potential for emergent leadership; leadership emanating from the bottom up rather than just the top down. Sport is one of the few products in the world (in addition to the entertainment industry) where those delivering the key services at the "coal face" are considered the most important individuals in the organization, and are compensated accordingly. Ferrari demonstrates this principle admirably through the performance of Michael Schumacher and Rubens Barrichello. In sport it does not seem unusual to see leadership from athletes and players, but they are the equivalent of the teller in a bank or the customer service officer in an insurance company. Sport simply exposes the fact that all people engaged in a service or product delivery can add leadership value.

In Ferrari, emergent leadership has occurred in all levels of the team. While Schumacher and Barrichello receive the accolades of the public, their vehicles are the outcome of innovation produced by hundreds of talented mechanics and engineers. What would become of Ferrari if only the line managers were allowed to display leadership? No one individual, no matter how gifted, is capable of sustained insight beyond the collective contribution of the rest of a team. This holds true in Ferrari for the drivers, designers, engineers, mechanics, strategists, tire specialists, marketers, and managers. The business leadership lesson from Ferrari and other successful sport teams is the reminder that there is always potential for leadership to emerge from unexpected locations in the hierarchy.

3. Training and practice

Few would argue that the sport product is bolstered by more practice and training than any other product in the world. In fact, performance in sport represents only a fraction of the time taken in preparation. What few people realize is that Ferrari never ceases its development activities. When the drivers take a break after the season, the cars do not sit dormant in a garage. Instead, test drivers work furiously with new features while the engineers collect vast amounts of data. Simply watching a Ferrari pit stop should be enough for leaders in business to see the outcome of dedication to training. For Ferrari it is more than just a dedication; it is a complete commitment to perfection.

Sport thinking encourages business leaders to think more systematically about training as part of both a long-term plan and regular, operational activities. Practicing pit stops every day is second nature for the Ferrari team, even if it is only for 15 or 20 minutes. How many businesses take the same amount of time daily to polish their skills? No sport leader would ever consider bringing about serious change without supporting it with substantial training preparation. More importantly, sport teaches us that training should not be for preparation only, but should be a standard part of everyday business life.

4. Importance of relationships

Teams are built on the relationships between members. Schumacher, Brawn, Byrne and Todt are the key leaders in Ferrari and have developed close working relationships with each other as well as the other team members. It is not an exaggeration to say that each of the team members spends far more time with each other than they do with their marriage partners. Work time can be 60 or 70 hours a week, and more during race weeks. In between races, if the team members are not working or catching whatever sleep they can, they are on the road toward the next race destination. A team that spends so much time together under such pressure cannot be successful unless it has built strong relationships.

Like those in Ferrari, other sport leaders are acutely aware of the importance of the relationship between leaders and followers, especially where they interact in team situations and where the role of leader and follower can be fluid. In business, leaders tend to stay in leadership positions, rarely taking a subservient role even if the circumstances might demand it. Sport thinking can draw attention to the importance of coaching, mentoring, teamwork, collaboration, and communication while reinforcing flexible ideas about leadership positions. Teams like Ferrari can also highlight the way close working relationships under pressure and adversity, which also yield success, can develop the strongest relationships, where team loyalty is intense.

5. Personal development

An athlete more committed to personal improvement than Michael Schumacher would be difficult to find. Schumacher is the epitome of professionalism, and like all athletes who have worked their way to the top of their sport, stands as a role model for what can be achieved through raw talent, hard work, and a commitment to personal development. For example, although already well known for his exemplary fitness and arduous physical training regime, Schumacher spends hours in front of computer race simulations that match the tracks perfectly. As the most experienced driver in Formula One, Schumacher probably already knows each track better than any other driver, but he continues to strive to engrain the perfect lap in his mind, accounting for inches around walls and braking markers.

More than in business, sport confers the responsibility for personal improvement and development upon the individual and team in equal measures. Because sport exposes vulnerabilities in a team climate, sport thinking encourages leaders to find ways to facilitate personal development. In addition, although perhaps a cliché, sport offers a consistent way for individuals and teams to be confronted unambiguously with their own performance and success. In business this objective assessment of performance is often hidden. Individuals and teams in business have fewer opportunities to further their own development as a result. Sometimes an external and potentially confronting assessment of performance is the most precious for personal development.

6. Long-term sustainability

Of all the characteristics that set Ferrari apart from the competition, its unprecedented, long-term success is perhaps the most impressive. This, it has achieved in arguably the world's most difficult, competitive, and resource-intensive sport. While the other nine themes mentioned in this section go a long way to explaining why Ferrari has enjoyed such longevity at the top, part of the explanation can also be found in its attitude to sustainability in the first place. This is the legacy of both Ferrari himself and his successor Montezemolo. Both have proven absolutely committed to long-term success. That meant there could be no shortcuts and quality was paramount. For example, Montezemolo recognized that for the brand to hold its position on the pedestal, the Formula One team had to perform. To Montezemolo, this did not mean that the team had to do reasonably well, it had to win, and Montezemolo was prepared to make the decisions and commit the resources in order to do just that.

While in hindsight, it might seem to have been a straightforward decision to hire Todt and acquire the best driver in the world, in reality, the decision must have taken a great deal of fortitude and vision. Other teams scoffed at Ferrari for paying Schumacher such exorbitant sums. Commentators cautioned that Todt would never be able to hold together for a long period the egos and personalities of the key team members who were poached from competitors. But what both Montezemolo and Todt realized was that in acquiring the best, they were also acquiring people with an uncommon commitment to long-term performance. For these team members, to perform well was not a desire or even a goal, but a part of their life they could not live without. Montezemolo spent vast sums ensuring that the team would be built in a way that would allow it to sustain its dominance. He saw a decade ahead, and took action accordingly. That philosophy has been embedded in the culture of Ferrari.

Business takes for granted the need for sustainable success. In sport, in contrast, genuine sustainable performance is quite rare and celebrated. Because the sport environment is so competitive, sport leaders invest considerable thought into the nature of sustainability. Indeed, the measure of greatness in sport is long-term success. Given the increasing competitiveness and changeability of business markets, sport thinking helps business leaders to reconsider the prerequisites of sustainability, which frequently demand different strategy and leadership than short-term performance.

7. Commitment to knowledge

It is hard to imagine any sport more obsessed with innovation and the development of new knowledge than Formula One. In Ferrari no detail is too small, from the precision engineering of engine components to the software systems used to compile and analyze data. Every possible angle for enhanced performance is explored. Sometimes, even Ferrari goes too far, as when the cockpit of the car was lowered too far and the heat from friction across the track burnt through to the driver's skin, causing blisters in a most inconvenient location.

While Schumacher is the racing face of Ferrari, one of the reasons that the team stays ahead of the competition is that all its key members are dedicated to improving their knowledge and performance. On planes they study engineering specifications and try to imagine new ways of doing things that will give the car an advantage while staying within the rigid structures of the rules. In the office, marketing executives benchmark other professional sports to find new ways of servicing sponsors. The team has developed a critical mass of activity that has kept it ahead of the competition for several years. The leaders of Ferrari have cultivated an atmosphere where members are committed to innovation and knowledge that will give the team a competitive advantage.

Sport leaders are obsessed with knowledge in an attempt to find new opportunities and advantages. This typically includes nutritional supplements, novel training methods, and even drugs. For the business leader, this commitment to knowledge for competitive advantage is an important lesson that Ferrari leaders have shown delivers success. In the business world of leadership, strategy has received a great deal of attention, but one of the most salient lessons from sport comes from the way its leaders value knowledge as a vehicle for innovation.

8. Constant measurement and evaluation

Ferrari studies, measures, and records every aspect of racing from the nuances and preferences of other team's drivers and their cars, to the impact of a one-tenth of a degree change in track temperature on the performance of tires. Not only is no other product in the world subject to such intense measurement and scrutiny as sporting performance, but Formula One makes all other sports performance evaluation methods look simplistic. For every second of time on the practice or race track, hundreds of different measures are taken about the performance of the car and engine. This vast supply of data is used to make minute changes in aero-dynamic down force, tire selection, gear ratios, fuel quantity, and engine torque. The commitment Ferrari has to studying performance is stag-gering, and if business leaders were to adopt its philosophy to even a tiny degree, it would mean a substantial change in the measurement and evalu-ation of companies.

Although business has embraced performance management as a funda-mental aspect of leadership, the comprehensive approach to measurement demonstrated in professional sport offers a reminder to business leaders of the depth and frequency with which a performance can be assessed. This can extend to all parts of leadership and the organization.

9. Passion and spiritual connection

If nothing else, Ferrari's history and experiences presented in this chapter illustrate a furious and unyielding passion for motor sport. From Enzo Ferrari's consuming obsession for creating the flawless racing vehicle to Todt's Napoleonic, unifying charisma, Ferrari shows the lengths that people will go to succeed in sport precisely because it holds an almost spiritual importance to it. The passion associated with sport is a model for business leaders to pursue. An emotional commitment to the organization from both customers and employees is an ideal that many sport leaders cultivate and exploit.

10. Clear focus on the right goal

Although controversial at times, Ferrari has demonstrated a clarity of purpose second to none in sport. From a leadership viewpoint, the team has never wavered from its goals. Team instructions for the finishing order for the two Ferrari drivers have been contentious, but are really just reflec-tive of its focus on the bigger picture. As a team with clear goals, team orders make sense. Although such orders have been outlawed, it remains obvious that Ferrari uses its two cars to leverage each other's performance. Sport thinking like that demonstrated by Ferrari encourages clarity of

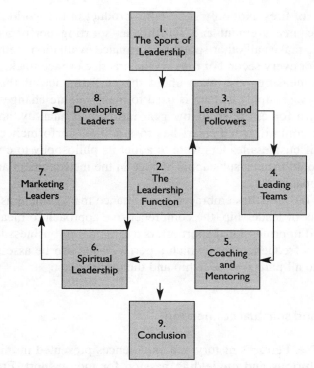

Figure 1.1 Structure of *Business Leadership and the Lessons from Sport*

focus on core business issues and meeting core business goals without distraction. In the case of Ferrari, this is particularly impressive, given the immense opportunity for distraction that the nature of competition in Formula One presents.

These themes are contained in each of the chapters which deal with specific aspects of leadership. The structure of this book is illustrated in Figure 1.1.

> Every car is a prototype at all times. *(Martin Brundle, former Formula One driver and now commentator)*

In Chapter 2, Playing to Win: The Leadership Function, we turn our attention to the key activities that leaders undertake. However, we do not take a conventional approach to this. Instead, we note that the great power of sport is in channeling a leader's focus into what might be called its "core business". While the concept of core business is well known in business literature, the actual process of determining what is core business is more troublesome. Our starting point is that sport thinking helps to distinguish between activities that reflect the core of a business, say, in sport terms, merchandise, and those that are core *to* the business, like the cultivation of player talent. On the surface, this may seem to be a pedantic distinction, but the reality is that there is a significant difference between the two approaches.

The advantage of sport thinking, in our estimation, is that it reveals unambiguously the 'core to' business activities. For example, it is clear that actual performance is core to the sport business, whereas merchandise is critical for revenue, but remains a means to an end rather than the end in itself. Similarly, business leaders can benefit from thinking about their organizations in terms of the sport metaphor. In other words, what is their equivalent of the sporting performance? The ability to do this, we believe, is instrumental to the success of a business leader. Chapter 2 also explores the role that the business leader plays in orchestrating change. In this way, the leader is a change agent, in a way comparable to a captain of a sporting team. With this aspect of leadership in mind, the chapter highlights the importance of the leader in performance management and measurement.

The business 'captain' is charged, of course, with leading all of his or her 'players'. In Chapter 3, Fair Game: Leaders and Followers, the importance of the follower is considered. Drawing from the sport metaphor, we examine the roles of individuals throughout the sport organization, from the humble fan to the chairman of the club. Our central argument is that the commitment of followers is central to organizational success. Moreover, successful sport leaders show the ability to engender intense levels of commitment from followers by emphasizing personal identity, ownership, and involvement. The chapter also aims to equip business leaders with a better understanding of the role of personality, charisma, and tribal identity in organized followership.

Building on this understanding, Chapter 4, Team of Champions or a Champion Team?: Leading Teams, ventures further into the value of meaning as a currency of team success. The chapter illustrates how great teams in sport demonstrate emergence, where the sum of their parts is subservient to the synergy of the team as a whole. Sport illuminates several central aspects of team leadership, including its approach to membership, where team composition is more important than individual talent, the sense of belonging it can provoke, the precision of its structures and accountability of roles, and its depth of ritualization. We use these characteristics of sport to examine what constitutes great teams, and we draw heavily on some of the greatest sporting teams of all time for inspiration.

From the team side of the leadership equation, we turn to some of the more individualized aspects of leadership. In Chapter 5, From the Sidelines: Coaching and Mentoring, we identify the place of coaching and mentoring in the leadership development cycle, emphasizing the pivotal contribution to performance that coaches (managers) make in sport. In so doing, this chapter explores how competencies can be transmitted through leadership coaching. Whilst coaching and mentoring in business are familiar terms and, in many cases, popular managerial practices, their use in business has not been built upon a thorough understanding of how they are used in sport, and exactly what they mean in sport. More than any other relationship between organizational members, coaches are mentors for players, and in many sports encourage a holistic player welfare approach to managing life and sport performance. Coaches are required to manage all elements that might impact upon player performance. This includes finance, relationships and sport-related issues. This mentoring approach, with an emphasis on a player's welfare, recognizes that leaders off the field need to nurture those at the coal face, sometimes in a spiritual and emotional way as much as physically.

Chapter 6, The Flow State: Spiritual Leadership, explores the importance of personal development and readiness as a function of leadership development and performance. It provides a discussion of the psychological mechanisms necessary for individuals to develop "spiritually" and emotionally as a platform for a leadership contribution. Traditionally, there have been few educational pathways for coaches, resulting in their need to develop some of their skills through self-development and reflection. Although the importance of professional management training for both coaches and business managers is undisputed, one advantage that coaches have acquired is more flexibility in their work environment to employ different approaches to developing players, particularly on an individual basis rather than one exclusively based on organizational standards and rules. Sport has long been viewed as a character-building pursuit, but this assumption has been undermined recently, particularly with the abundance of ill-tempered sporting superstars. Nevertheless, it is impossible to argue with the fact that sport stars are attuned to perform under high pressure and have the ability to manage their emotions in critical situations on the field. The chapter specifies how to employ the correct emotional perspective in developing leaders and how to cultivate the most effective transmission of leadership messages. Ultimately, this translates to a situation that in sport is also described as "the flow state" or "being in the zone." It is at those moments when successful leadership translates into peak performance: playing for the championship, going for gold, establishing that merger or successfully floating the organization on the stock exchange.

The success of leaders is not always a matter of what they actually achieve quietly, but what they manage to convince others they have achieved. Chapter 7, Thinking Outside the Ball Park: Marketing Leaders, takes up this issue. It explains the role of perception in the leadership equation and the importance of selling leaders and their messages. It begins by examining the nature of leadership in business, and by using a sport analogy, begins to develop a set of usable marketing tools. This chapter illustrates that transformational leadership and charisma are a function of leadership marketing that can be mobilized by any leader at any level. The chapter reviews the aspects of hero building associated with sport, the marketing techniques used to highlight the performance of on-field leaders, and the lessons business leaders can learn from high-profile sporting personalities. Bend it like Beckham becomes sell it like Beckham.

Chapter 8, Staying Ahead of the Game: Developing Leaders for the Future, examines the future of work, sport, and society and provides the basis for organizations to understand the essential aspects of leadership in the future. Sport thinking helps to encourage leaders to be comfortable in uncertain environments. If the right management philosophy is in place, there is more room for experimentation and the potential emergence of genuine innovation that could not have been forced or prescribed. The sport metaphor also demonstrates the importance of training and practice as a key to success, even when training time far exceeds that spent in actual performance. The chapter also highlights how sport is at the fore-front of technology and innovation, in order to stay ahead of the game.

In the modern business environment, stability can signify slowdown and even organizational death. Leaders cannot be successful simply by instilling prescriptive working conditions; the very nature of business is far more dynamic than in the past. Chapter 9, Conclusion: Leadership in Sport, shows how sport offers the opportunity to take a perspective on leadership that encourages innovation, flexibility, training, coaching, performance measurement, and thinking about the future; qualities that we have emphasized in this chapter's commentary on Ferrari.

Post Game

Although Schumacher's end to the 2004 season at the Brazilian Grand Prix failed to yield yet another win – after crashing in a practice session and incurring a ten-place penalty for changing engines and starting in 18th place on the grid – he still managed to finish a creditable seventh. For Ferrari it brought to an end a season of 15 wins from 18 races, as well as its sixth constructor's championship and Schumacher's fifth successive driver's title. In Formula One, the achievements of Ferrari in 2004 are benchmarked only against their own 15 wins from 17 races in 2002 and McLaren's 15 wins from 16 races in 1988. It also, arguably, solidifies its place as the greatest Formula One team of all time and, perhaps, even as one of the greatest sporting teams of all time. So, with the sport metaphor in mind, let us start to tackle the conundrum of the leadership role and function, which is exactly where we intend to begin in Chapter 2.

> Ideas and tenacity are our strength. *(Enzo Ferrari)*

Notes

1   D. Denison and J. Henderson (2003), *The Ferrari Renaissance*, International Institute for Management Development, Lausanne, Switzerland.

2   Jay Cross's internet article *The Last Word: The Changing Nature of Leadership*, can be found at: http://www.linezine.com/6.2/articles/jccnol.htm.

3   K. Parry and J. Meindel (2002), *Grounding Leadership Theory and Research: Issues and Perspectives*, Information Age Publishing, Greenwich, GT.

4   R. Connors, T. Smith and C. Hickman (2004), *The Oz Principle*, Penguin Putnam, New York.

5   C. Hilton (1994) *The Hard Edge of Genius*, Motorbooks International, Osceola, WI.

6   Summary of speech by Kevin Roberts delivered at the Makati Business Club, Hotel Intercontinental, Makati City, Philippines, 12 August, 1999.

7   D. Parkin, P. Bourke and R. Gleeson (1999), *Perform – Or Else!* Information Australia, Melbourne, Australia.

8   C. Gilson, M. Pratt, K. Roberts and E. Weymes (2001), *Peak Performance: Business Lessons from the World's Top Sports Organizations*, Profile Books, London.

9   B. Steiner (2003), *The Business Playbook: Leadership Lessons from the World of Sports*, Entrepreneur Press, Irvine, CA.

10   D. Holland (2001), *Red Zone Management: Changing Rules for Pivotal Times*, Dearborn Financial Publishing, Chicago, Il.

11   C. Gordon (1995), "Management Skills for the Next Millennia", *Management* (March), pp. 5–7; J.B. Miller and P.B. Brown (1993), *The Corporate Coach*, Bookman Press, Melbourne, Australia; C.D. Orth, H.E. Wilkinson and R.C. Benfari (1987), "The Manager's Role as Coach and Mentor", *Organizational Dynamics*, 15(4): 66–74.

12   P. Kellett (1999), "Organizational Leadership: Lessons from Professional Coaches", *Sport Management Review*, **2**: 150–71.

13   G. Haigh (2004), *Quarterly Essay 10 – Bad Company: The Cult of the CEO*, Black Inc., Melbourne, Australia.

CHAPTER 2

Playing to Win:
The Leadership Function

If somebody told weightlifters they could lift an extra five pounds by munching Brillo pads, there wouldn't be a clean pot within three miles of any gym in this country. (MARK CAMERON, WEIGHTLIFTER)

Like business, professional sport organizations may have many imperatives placed upon them. However, sometimes, unlike business, they have less difficulty in understanding where their core business lies. Moreover, they recognize the significant difference between activities that reflect the core of the business (like providing sporting merchandise for sales), versus those that are core *to* the business (like developing player talent). This chapter explains the importance of understanding an organization's core business and the impact that leadership has on driving success in the "right" areas. It places leadership in the context of wider organizational change and explains the role of the leader as a change agent, in a similar manner to a team's captain.

In addition, we consider the importance of performance management in leadership and development by discussing measurement techniques used to feedback upon performance. Moreover, we demonstrate how the roles of leaders change during different phases of organizational life, in particular those that are intense and dynamic, and suggest a path for organizations to cultivate leaders ready for crisis situations.

Lastly, this chapter shows the importance of leadership and coaches as part of leadership development beyond the organization (and sport) and in the community, by looking at some leaders who are considered to be at the forefront of society. It can be argued that there is a significant role and opportunity for athletes and sport organizations to work with non-sport organizations in the spirit of excellent corporate sport citizenship.

The Core Business

> For every pass I ever caught in a game, I caught a thousand in practice.
> *(Don Hutson, National Football League, offensive end)*

Although we have just said that, unlike business, sport teams have less difficulty in understanding where their core business lies, we could play devil's advocate and take issue with our own statement. Firstly, we need to define what is meant by "core business." The problem here is that theorists often confuse three separate but interrelated concepts: those of "core business," "core competency," and "core to the business." Generically, we may describe core business as the main business of an enterprise as opposed to any ancillary business it generates. It is the activity from which a business derives its greatest income. Thus, for example, it might be argued that the core business of Toyota is making cars, of Coca-Cola, soft drinks, and of Manchester United, playing (and winning) soccer games.

It's an apparently sound theory, but, in our role as devil's advocate, we might argue that, like so many management and leadership theories, reality comes in many shades of gray. In reality, we might suggest that the core business of all organizations, whether in business or sport, is simply to stay in business. And to achieve this, an organization must make money. Fail to make money, and no matter how successful you may be, the organization will ultimately fail. Take, for example, the Siddeley Armstrong motorcar, an excellent automobile by all accounts, but a product of an organization no longer in business. Or Accrington Football Club, which, on joining on 17 April 1888, became one of the 12 founding members of the football league in England. In the 1892/93 season they finished 15th, second from bottom, a relegation position, and resigned from the league rather than play in the newly formed Division Two. Shortly afterwards, Accrington FC became prey to financial problems which led to their demise in 1896. Fail to make money, and you go out of business!

Some business writers associate core business with successful competitive advantage. Zook and Allen, for instance, suggest that having a clear sense and definition of the core is the foundation of growth strategy.[1] Having undertaken an analysis of companies that have been financially successful such as Dell, EMC, and General Electric, the authors contend that to identify a core business, there must be a clear understanding and definition of the set of products, customer segments, and technologies with which a company can build the greatest competitive advantage. Then, having defined the core business, a firm can further identify their sources of differentiation that will continue to create market power, as well as explore new territories ancillary to the core.

Implied in Zook and Allen's discussion of core business is the concept of "core competency." This may be defined as the one or more things that a company can do better than its competitors and may include anything from a better product to the capability of an organization's personnel. If the core competency is transitory, it may provide only a short-term competitive advantage. However, if the core competency yields long-term advantage it may be considered a sustainable competitive advantage.

The concept of core competency was initially developed by C. K. Prahalad and Gary Hamel in their 1990 *Harvard Business Review* article, "The Core Competence of the Corporation."[2] As examples of core competency, they suggested Honda's expertise in engines which allowed Honda to develop successful engines for everything from heavy vehicles to lawn mowers, and Canon's proficiency in laser systems and subsystems. Prahalad and Hamel suggested that a core competence has the characteristics of:

1. Providing potential access to a wide variety of markets
2. Increasing perceived customer benefits
3. Being harder for competitors to imitate.

Although a number of writers since Prahalad and Hamel have refined the concept of core competency, its definition around the concept of being areas which differentiate a company strategically has remained fairly constant.

"Core to the business" is a term that is generally employed when discussing outsourcing. By having outside resources undertake a range of business processes there is a belief that the focus on the core business can be maximized and costs minimized. But this depends, of course, on ensuring that activities that are outsourced can be undertaken more effectively and with greater efficiency by the organization to which they are outsourced. Many of the critical functions in an organization are core to the business, while others may be considered necessary but not core. This concept of relating "core to the business" together with business processes is, in our belief, far too narrow in its vision. We would rather believe that there are areas which are core to the business which are not viewed as a business process in the traditional way and which cannot be outsourced. These may include, say, a reputation for cleanliness as with some drug companies or a brand name for excitement, as with the World Wrestling Entertainment. It may also simply include activities like developing player talent within a sports club.

> **The Rope a Dope would not have existed without the Big Dope.**
> *(George Foreman, commenting on his role in the rumble in the jungle)*

So, how do the terms interrelate? Let us take as an example Glaxo-SmithKline (GSK), a drug company giant. We might suggest that GSK's core business is selling drugs. It is the activity from which the organization derives the greatest income. Its core competency, however, that which gives it sustainable competitive advantage, is the development of new drugs and bringing them from inception to the marketplace. What is core to the business for GSK, however, is its reputation for reliable and effective drugs.

Let us return to our principal discussion in this segment, that of core business. It is, as we stated earlier, the activity from which the organization derives its greatest income and it is often totally different from what is superficially apparent. As an example, consider the case of Real Madrid football club. Over the past few years, Florentino Pérez, president of the club, has bought many of the superstars of the game including Luis Figo of Portugal, for whom Real paid a then world record price of €59.8 million (then US$56 million), and then the French star Zinedine Zidane at a new world record price of €75.5 million (then US$85 million). Close on their heels came Ronaldo and English star, David Beckham. Pérez's aim was not simply to have a first-rate soccer team but to turn Real Madrid into a global brand, with revenue spin-offs from sponsorships to merchandising. Pérez claims that the 29-times Spanish league champion is approaching Manchester United in marketing power and he plans to make the club's brand name the most valuable in the world.

According to Pérez, it was only

> a few years ago [that] Manchester United was the club which sold most throughout the world for the simple fact that its marketing policies were 10 years ahead of everyone else. That's no longer the case ...right now the global rise of the Real Madrid brand has no comparison.[3]

Pérez said income from Real's merchandise sales this year – €138 million (US$171 million) – would be greater than the club's total earnings four years ago when he took over as president. As a result, unlike Manchester United, whose main revenue still comes from gate money, Real's main income will come from commercial revenues. Real's dominance in commercial branding may not last long. Manchester United has hired Andy Anson, a former Walt Disney executive who was responsible for marketing the Mighty Ducks ice hockey team, as its first commercial director. According to Manchester United Chief Executive David Gill, creating the post of commercial director was "critical to delivering our strategies of converting more fans to customers and leveraging the club's brand through global commercial activities."[4]

It is not only in sport that core business is changing shape. Movie companies like Disney no longer earn their major income from films but from the music, video and game spin-offs, and merchandise. Even a number of major car companies make a loss on the manufacture of cars, making their income on less generously priced car parts.

There is a general belief in industry that focusing purely on a company's core business is the best way to achieve growth. While this concept has much to commend it, a rigid pursuit of the core business can result in the loss of promising new opportunities. For example, the decision by many US NFL teams not to play in a proposed Asian tournament may result in the loss of Asian customers. Equally, however, a strong core business can provide excellent opportunities to move into a profitable adjacent business, as with Real Madrid and merchandising. The problem here, however, is that by then concentrating on non-core activities, the company can lose focus. The balancing act between core and non-core business requires companies to have a clearly defined core before looking for opportunities that fit in with a company's core competencies – its competitive differentiation and advantage over competitors.

Two points of importance need to be borne in mind. Sometimes it is necessary for an organization to fundamentally redefine its core business and, when considering core business, it is necessary to consider also the requirements of one's customer. Take, for example, Starbucks, which has just started opening coffee shops with music-listening stations equipped with CD-burning facilities; a capability attractive to its customers. Or consider the case with Nike. Until 1995, Nike's core business was in making sports shoes, yet, in that year, Nike branched out from shoes to golf apparel, balls, and equipment. By securing the endorsement of a leading athlete like Tiger Woods, whose US$100 million deal in 1996 gave Nike the visibility it needed, Nike totally redefined its core business and satisfied customers' requirement for the swoosh, its legendary logo. Now Nike's core business is marketing.

Leadership for Change

> If you're a positive person, you're an automatic motivator. You can get people to do things you don't think they're capable of.
> *(Cotton Fitzsimmons, Kansas City Kings coach)*

While it is the leadership of an organization that generally determines its core business and drives success in the "right" areas, there are other factors which impinge on organizational effectiveness. James Weese has suggested that while leaders impact the culture of their respective organizations through their words and actions,[5] organizational effectiveness can also be determined by a variety of factors, many of which fall beyond the scope of the leader's influence or the culture of the organization.[6] These factors may include the financial viability of a company, the strength of its core competencies, the economic health and turbulence within the market, the capability of leaders from competing organizations, and customer expectations. This suggests that while leaders may seek to drive success or change the vision, external factors may preclude that success or that change in vision.

Recognized theory suggests that successful change management requires one or more of the following to occur:

1. The development of a vision and strategy by the leader, the ability to align relevant people behind those strategies, and the empowerment of individuals to make the vision happen, despite obstacles.[7]
2. The ability of the leader to clearly enunciate the change required, explain everyone's part in the change, and convey a correct sense of direction and purpose.
3. For the leader to understand the level of risk in any change project and have a plan to deal with that risk.
4. For the leader to lead the change process by example, while fostering collaboration and consultation with key individuals.
5. For the leader to determine realistic measures of success and gather and celebrate early victories in the change process.
6. The motivation, the ability and the opportunity to change.
7. Resources sufficient to drive the change.

Robert Denhardt, from Arizona State University, in his book *The Pursuit of Significance* profiled a number of important public sector leaders in several countries seeking to establish the characteristics of successful "revolutionary" public managers. He identified five common characteristics among these change leaders – a commitment to values, service to the public, empowerment and shared leadership, "pragmatic incrementalism," and a dedication to public service.[8] In a follow-up to his book, Denhardt suggests that the traditional view of a change leader as one who comes up with the ideas, decides on a course of action and exerts influence to move everyone in that direction appears to have changed. In its place are leaders who help the organization understand their needs and potential, articulate that vision and act as a trigger for group action.[9]

There are clearly a number of requirements for successful change management to occur. The development of a vision and the ability to have a majority within the organization motivated sufficiently to accept and pursue that vision are vital. Whether the vision stems solely from the leader or whether it is the organization's vision is debatable and will probably differ depending on the circumstances as well as the personality and ego of the leader. Whether the vision belongs to one person or stems from the organization, it requires a leader to have excellent interpersonal skills and the ability to convince followers that the vision can be achieved. There is also a necessity to ensure that sufficient resources and skills are available. Effective training leads to personal growth and confidence.

> The secret of managing is to keep the guys who hate you away from the guys who are undecided. *(Casey Stengel, former manager, Brooklyn Dodgers, Boston Braves, New York Yankees, New York Mets)*

The one common factor in successful change management is the role of the leader. The leader need not be the formal head within an organization. Rather, he or she may be the individual perceived by the remainder of the group as the person of influence or power in the organization. Unless the leader is committed to the change, prepared to drive that change, and is capable of selling that change, then change is unlikely to occur. The actual process of change may be led by a surrogate for the leader, but without total and visible leadership support success is unlikely. One of the vital strengths of a good leader is their ability to lead the change while still overseeing and understanding everything else that is going on. Watch David Beckham (Real Madrid) or Tim Duncan (San Antonio Spurs) when they play. They understand the game plan, can follow it, and can change from offence to defense in a moment through being totally aware of everything else that is happening on the field of play. Lesser players become so involved in the game that they lose sight of the game plan. A good leader is like Beckham or Duncan. They remain focused on the end result while still leading the team.

Keeping to our sporting analogy, good change management requires good teamwork. In business, good leaders select individuals for roles that display their strengths. In sport, teams operate in the same manner. Operating in a team environment usually means that elitism and individual competition is discouraged. Yet in many team sports, elitism is paramount. Players at clubs like the New York Yankees or Arsenal are paid vastly different salaries depending on the view of the leader as to their worth to the team. Theoretically, one would assume that this would create divisiveness, yet somehow it seems to work and teams remain totally bonded.

An excellent example of a successful change management leader is Pat Bowlen, president and chief executive of the Denver Broncos. For over 20 years, Bowlen has presided over a franchise that is considered one of the jewels of the NFL. Since he assumed majority ownership of the club in 1984, Bowlen's leadership has earned him the reputation of being a dynamic and visionary leader and under his control the Broncos have had 11 play-off appearances, winning the Super Bowl in 1998 and 1999. From an average club, Bowlen has guided Denver's first major league football franchise to the best home record in football over the past 30 years and in all the years he has been in charge every home game has been a sell-out. In addition to being the owner of the Broncos, Bowlen has become a key figure in many of the higher NFL committees, being chair of the NFL Broadcast Committee which secured the NFL's current US$18 billion TV contract. Bowlen's success has not been automatic. When he took over the Broncos he provided a vision of a club that had two aims: sporting leadership on the field and financial leadership off the field. That vision was sold to the coach and the citizens of Denver. He gave the coach the funds to find new players and provided him with first-rate assistant positional coaches. He spoke to every player and every individual on the Broncos' payroll and converted them to his vision. In addition to bringing the fans within Denver on board, Pat Bowlen traveled Colorado, exhorting the entire state to join him and the team. Most did.

Good leaders can often overcome tremendous obstacles thus driving success along previously defined paths. Sometimes, it is their vision or charisma which underlies their success, while at other times it may be their experience or simply having the "right" set of subordinates. On occasions, however, luck becomes a major partner in the change process. Consider the case with Florentino Pérez. Pérez's stated aim was to make Real Madrid the foremost soccer team in the world. But when he took over as president of the club, Real was in debt to the tune of around €250 million

(US$310 million). In his first term as president, Pérez negotiated a deal under which he sold a Real training ground to the city authorities, after it was first reclassified as prime building land. The money obtained from the sale enabled the club to pay off its debt and launch its enormous player spending spree. Without the good fortune of having the training ground reclassified, the sale might not have taken place and certainly would not have drawn such a fine sum. And without the money, Pérez would have had profound difficulty in achieving his vision.

Undoubtedly, the strongest obstruction to successful change management comes from middle managers who often feel that proposed change may not be to their benefit. Such obstruction must, and can, be overcome, either by persuading the recalcitrant individuals of the benefit of the change and thus bringing them aboard, or by bypassing them. Bypassing is frequently a successful tactic in change management. It follows Ted Turner's dictum of "lead, follow, or get out of the way." Sports leaders are less regulated than normal businesses by workplace regulations and laws. As a consequence, they are usually far more willing to remove individuals who provide obstacles to change.

Often, vision, charisma, experience, and luck need a helping hand, although a little cleverness and aggression do not go astray. Recall the case of José Mourinho, who stated before even formally taking over at Chelsea FC, that "when I arrive, I will be ready for a change in the football organization and method."[10] Chelsea's backroom staff, he stated, would have two weeks to prove themselves. In saying this, he was demonstrating that any changes he proposed would either have the backing of middle and coal face management or opponents to the change might be looking elsewhere for a job. Mourinho made it equally clear to Chelsea's players that they must work with his methods or face the axe. In the event, there were a number of high-profile departures and new arrivals.

Performance Parameters

> The two basic coaching differences between sport and business are lack of imperative and lack of frequent and precise measurement in the latter.
> *(Ric Charlesworth, Australian hockey coach)*

According to Marcus Caton, performance indicators are best used to assist managers in their decision making, ensuring that performance levels over time may be compared.[11] Effective performance indicators can highlight areas that are performing well in terms of objectives, effectiveness and efficiency, as well as areas that are encountering problems. Good indicators can also determine and analyse trends over a continuing period, and, where appropriate, may identify areas where improvements may be made. An initial key to obtaining successful data is ensuring that any measurement which takes place compares "like with like." In business, performance indicators have often been used to measure "hard numbers," that is, material used, output figures, time, wastage, and so on. Equally, performance indicators traditionally have been used to compare financial data such as profit and loss. More recently, however, companies have measured "softer" data such as employee morale and customer loyalty. The difficulty, here, is that measurement is more subjective and, consequently, less reliable. One of the major functions of measurement is to allow for the comparison of performance levels with similar organizations both within the same country and overseas. This allows a company to benchmark itself against competitors. Despite the fact that good performance measures are available to most organizations, public and private, many organizations lack robust performance measurement and make limited use of performance indicators.

There is a trend, however, towards the use of more effective performance indicators. The strength of this trend owes much to technology which allows access to more timely, accurate, and relevant information than ever before. This provides a significant competitive advantage for companies that understand and embrace performance measurement and particularly for those who use such measurement as a basis for continuous improvement. An awareness of how performance is improving over time can demonstrate to both internal and external partners and stakeholders that continuous improvement is being achieved and targets are being met. Conversely, of course, such performance measurement may also indicate continuing problems.

In sport, benchmarking is undertaken in much the same manner as in business, but the benchmark is usually easier to identify. Personal best times, national records, Olympic and world records are known to all athletes in their individual track and field event or in sports such as swimming. Sport tends to involve performance measurement at the most minute levels. The men's 100 meter sprint world record, for example, stands at 9.79 seconds, besting the previous record of 9.84 seconds, yet the difference of just 0.05 seconds is considered by competitors to be immense.

Individual athletes and their coaches use established frameworks for measuring progress, understanding that the emphasis must be on constant improvement. That framework may be formal or informal but is documented on a regular or even daily basis. Some team sports use a combination of formal and more intuitive assessments. Birmingham City FC manager Steve Bruce assesses his team by comparing their position in the league, goals scored and given away, and points obtained during certain periods in the football season, and by comparison to the previous year's statistics at the same time. He assesses the progress of individual players, however, by constant benchmarking. During the game, Bruce measures a constantly fluctuating number of performance indicators. They include the number of corners and free kicks, the amount of time spent in attack and defense, the length of time the ball is held by Birmingham players, and a variety of data on individual players. Rather than wait until the game is over to review performance, Bruce constantly adjusts his strategy, based on those indicators, while the game is in play. In Australian Rules football, the data collected during a game is so extensive that the coach employs runners to continually enter the field of play to convey information to players and adjust team tactics.

> When you are playing for the national championship, it's not a matter of life or death. It's more important than that. *(Duffy Daugherty, Michigan state football coach)*

In most organizations, it will take a number of indicators to adequately measure performance. In deciding which indicators will be most effective there are several questions which need to be considered, the most important of which will relate to the reasons for measuring performance. Are the results simply for internal distribution, or is there a need to convey the information obtained to a wider audience? Where, and how, and by whom will the performance indicators be used? While there have been a number of discussions in the academic literature concerning this issue, in a document designed to help local sports authorities instigate reliable performance measurement, Sport England suggested that:

1. What gets measured gets done.
2. If you don't measure results, you can't tell success from failure.
3. If you can't see success, you can't reward it.
4. If you can't reward success, you're probably rewarding failure.
5. If you can't see success, you can't learn from it.
6. If you can't recognize failure, you can't correct it.
7. If you can demonstrate results, you can win support.[12]

To assist Sport England, the British Audit Commission determined six underlying principles of performance measurement:

- *Clarity of purpose.* It is important to understand who will use the information and how and why it will be used, that is, is it for the general public, a partner organization, or customers? Is it to justify a resource or show that a service is cost-effective?
- *Focus.* Performance information should be focused on the priorities of the organization, that is, the information sought should be identified either in, or as part of, the corporate strategy.
- *Alignment.* The performance measurement system should be aligned with the objective setting and performance review processes of the organization. Performance indicators used for operational purposes should link to those used to monitor corporate performance.
- *Balance.* The overall set of performance indicators should give a balanced picture of the organization's performance.
- *Regular refinement.* The performance indicators should be kept up to date to meet changing circumstances, whilst balancing the needs for consistency over time.
- *Robust performance indicators.* The performance indicators used should be sufficiently robust and intelligible for their intended use.[13]

To these six principles we might add the need to ensure that the links between measures are continually validated and statistically reliable. It is not sufficient to simply collect and collate the data obtained from the indicators. On their own, data have doubtful value. Interpreted correctly, however, and taken in consideration with information provided by other areas of the organization, the data obtained can be of immeasurable value and can correlate the resources used against the outcomes of the organization. This is always providing, of course, that the data are reported to the appropriate individual or audience and that the individual or group have the authority to act on the information obtained.

A number of writers have commented that good performance measures made available to employees often sufficiently stimulate them to take ownership of their actions rather than wait for management. This is understandable in an age of empowerment and participatory management. The corollary here is that employees may easily misinterpret the information obtained or may act in isolation to the rest of the organization.

Having made, hopefully, a strong case for performance measurement, it needs to be stated that there are limitations to its use. The first of these is that while performance indicators act as signposts to things that are being undertaken well or problems that may be occurring, they do not detail the underpinning reasons why things are performing well or poorly. Thus, they cannot indicate the extent to which the activity caused the measured results. Performance indicators often raise questions but seldom provide the answers. The second limitation is that in some circumstances, performance measures may not reflect reality. How a soldier trains during an exercise or an athlete performs on a training field may be completely different to performance under real or competitive conditions. It is difficult to simulate during training neurological and physiological responses caused by stress and other factors. A third limitation is that performance measures rarely tell the full story and should be considered only as part of the information required to make decisions. Performance measures by themselves are not a replacement for good management and leadership. Poorly applied, performance measures can be manipulated to make either individual managers or the entire organization look either good or bad.

Crisis and "Accidental Leaders"

> One of the most reliable indicators and predictors of true leadership is an individual's ability to find meaning in negative events and to learn from even the most trying circumstances. (Warren Bennis and Robert Thomas)[14]

Misfortune can build team spirit as was shown in the tragic World Trade Center attack. One story which emerged in the aftermath of the attack concerned the Marsh and McLennan group of companies which occupied floors 93 to 100, the floors directly in the path of the first hijacked airliner to hit the buildings. On that fateful day 1908 people were working in or visiting Marsh and McLennan. Of these, 294 people were killed and many more were badly injured. One further employee was a passenger on one of the planes involved in the attack. In a moving article, the CEO Jeffrey Greenberg tells the story of how the terrorist attacks brought out the best in his employees and how many of them gave up or delayed their opportunity to escape the horror in both successful and vain attempts to help workmates.[15] As the extent of the disaster became clear and the casualties mounted, many individuals pitched in to give what aid they could. They demonstrated that in a crisis, people often grow stronger and willingly face situations they would prefer to avoid.

Thankfully, in business, such extreme times are rare. Yet, many businesses do face crisis times and at such times leaders must take the opportunities offered to change the organization or the culture. Indeed, as the pace of change within the business world accelerates, the need for leadership becomes more critical. Failure to respond to change may itself lead to crisis. It must also be remembered that response to change is not just the responsibility of senior management but of all managers. Crisis times do not occur solely in business, however, as can be seen from history. One case that comes readily to mind is the story of Ernest Shackleton during his 1914 expedition to be the first to reach the south pole. Shackleton, faced with some of the worst weather on record, never made the pole, yet succeeded in a far greater objective, that of keeping his expedition members alive during more than a year of relative hell. After camping on the ice for five months, Shackleton made two open boat journeys, one of which – an 800-hundred mile ocean crossing to the island of South Georgia – is now considered remarkable. With only two companions he then trekked across the mountains of South Georgia and, on reaching the island's whaling station, organized a rescue team for the men he had left behind. He was a good leader who became a great leader under extreme adversity.

In their article, "Crucibles of Leadership,"[16] Warren Bennis and Robert Thomas suggest that a traumatic event will force a profound redefinition of the self. They believe that the skills used in adversity are the same skills that make for extraordinary leaders. Certainly, that was the case with Shackleton who encouraged his men to embrace his beliefs using clearly visible symbols and behavior. Shackleton's skill was in constantly emphasizing teamwork and insisting that all members of the expedition would live or die as one. He instilled an exceptional degree of self-confidence in his men and convinced them never to give up hope. Perhaps, more importantly, he led by example.

> Victory or defeat is not determined at the moment of crisis, but rather in the long and unspectacular period of preparation. *(Unknown)*

Emergence

Leaders may sometimes appear as a response to a crisis. The University of Leicester's Sir Norman Chester Centre for Football Research provides excellent examples in its fact sheet – *Racism and Football*.[17] Racism in and around football has been evident since the 1970s. Indeed, even back in the 1930s, Dixie Dean, Everton's dark-skinned center forward, was abused as he left the field. By the late 1980s the abuse had increased and Liverpool's John Barnes, for example, was pelted with bananas as the team warmed up. Such racism was not confined to Britain. Abuse of ethnic minority players was widespread in countries such as the Netherlands, Belgium, Spain, Germany, Italy, and France. In the United States, too, African-American footballers and basketball players were for many years constantly derided and treated as second-class citizens. In Australia, a country proud of its multiculturism, Aboriginal athletes have also been racially abused. Sadly, few great Australian indigenous footballers were given the opportunity to play at the highest levels before the 1960s.

One Aboriginal player who became a formidable leader for his cause was "Pastor" Doug Nicholls, a Fitzroy FC superstar who went on to become governor of South Australia. He also paved the way for such great indigenous footballers as Geelong's Polly Farmer, north Melbourne's brother combination of Jim and Phil Krakouer, and St. Kilda's Nicky Winmar who, after being been subjected to racial abuse by sections of the crowd, famously lifted his jumper and pointed to his skin after St. Kilda beat Collingwood in 1993. The response to racism has been the emergence of a number of popular counter-movements often led by individual club managers and players. Ruud Gullit and Aaron Winter, two black Dutch players, have spoken out about racist behavior and under their leadership a day of action was declared on 13 December 1992, with the slogan *No al razzimo!* (No to racism) being paraded by all players in the two Italian professional league divisions, Serie A and Serie B. Leadership under such circumstances often takes a great deal of courage. Ask Paul Ince, who became the first black footballer to captain England, or Hope Powell, the first black coach of the England women's football team, or Australia's Aboriginal Olympic gold medal winner, Kathy Freeman, who stood up to years of being poorly treated until her warmth, charm, and obvious ability eventually gained her such great acceptance. These individuals may never have sought leadership positions, but leadership still sought them.

Like the World Trade Center attack, the onset of a crisis can be swift and the results devastating. The Manchester United air disaster on 6 February 1958 was such an incident. Among the 24 who died that night were some of the greatest soccer players in Britain at that time. One who did survive was Bobby Charlton, a 20-year-old forward who was thrown 40 yards clear of the wreckage and escaped with a cut head. With the Manchester United team all but non-existent and Matt Busby, the manager, hospitalized for many months, the task of rebuilding the shattered team fell, off the field, on Jimmy Murphy, the assistant coach, and, on the field, on young Bobby Charlton. Within two months of the Munich tragedy, Charlton had fully assumed leadership responsibility for the team and had been rewarded by being chosen for England, scoring in the defeat of Scotland at Hampden Park. A month later, United reached the FA Cup final with a side made up of young reserve players, new signings and only a couple of players from the original pre-Munich team. Although they lost to Bolton Wanderers by two goals to one, no one could doubt that the crisis leadership team of Murphy and Charlton had restored pride and passion back to United. For Bobby Charlton, however, the Munich air disaster had an enormous effect, and he became a quiet, somewhat introspective individual off the field, while remaining a leader on it. Charlton went on to win 106 England caps and won both the Football Association and European Player of the Year awards.

A more recent example of crisis leadership occurs with the story of Mitt Romney, now governor of Massachusetts, who in 1999 took over the running of the Salt Lake City Winter Olympic Games organizing committee. Debased by scandal, on the brink of financial collapse, and with federal investigators, bankers, and the press at its door, paralysis faced the Games. In his book *Turnaround: Crisis, Leadership, & the Olympic Games,*[18] Romney writes of the difficulties faced by the Games and how, with his committee's backing, he eliminated the financial problems and delivered a profitable Olympic Games, built a culture of excellence among employees, and won the support of government, corporate sponsors, local residents, athletes and the international Olympic movement. With 9/11 so close to the Games, achieving success and reinstilling nationalism and pride, as well as reaffirming a belief in the ideals of the Olympics, were essential. Romney's achievements were evidenced by the huge success of the Games.

We might ask what crucial attributes crisis leaders display that is not so easily observable in other leaders. One attribute is the ability to understand that a crisis is taking place and that without immediate leadership the crisis will get worse, probably very quickly. Foolish though it may appear, many "leaders" never really understand when crisis envelops them. Instead, they continue as normal, or worse, act not to end the crisis but rather to hide its existence. This was the case, for example, with Enron in the United States. Crisis leaders instinctively appear to recognize that a continuation of the status quo will rarely provide a resolution to a crisis situation. They also realize that actions taken during a crisis will frequently appear unpopular. The slimming down of airlines during the SARS epidemic, the closure of plants by cash-strapped Mitsubishi, or the sale of star players by an almost bankrupt Leeds United are examples.

Fortuitously, the role of leader often changes during different phases of organizational life, in particular those periods that are intense and dynamic, and such occasions provide a path for organizations to cultivate leaders ready for crisis situations. The role of leader during the start-up of a company or an expansion phase requires a different mindset to that required during day-to-day activities. And many organizations, for example during periods of minor crises, require leaders to rethink strategy. Such periods might be instigated by financial difficulties, changing patterns of consumer behavior, the loss of key personnel, or acts of nature like fire or flood. During these times, leaders must continue to display the traditional characteristics of leadership while combining them with moments of inspiration.

Genuine crisis leadership, however, requires a paradigm shift in the thinking of individuals. Vision, mission and long-term strategy must give way to immediacy of action. Leading during a crisis necessitates developing new ways of operating and behaving based on the demands and reality of a frequently changing situation. Rather than reacting in a knee-jerk fashion to the crisis, a leader must be dispassionate, even ice when others are fire. While never losing sight of the ultimate goal, focus must be on short-term objectives. In the case of Manchester United after Munich, while the ultimate goal was rebuilding the team, focus was always on the next match. Crisis leaders must instill optimism and self-belief in those who follow them, yet must remain grounded in reality. And perhaps, above all else, a crisis leader must display a sense of integrity and a strong set of values.

In the similar, but clearly different category to crisis leaders are what might be termed "accidental" leaders. Often they are the same individual. Bobby Charlton was such a leader. They are individuals who are thrust into positions of leadership which they infrequently seek. Other times, however, the accidental leader emerges, not as a result of a crisis, but simply because of fate. Although a cliché, accidental leaders become leaders through accident. Recent press coverage on the death of Pat Tillman is indicative of such a leader.

Pat Tillman was a linebacker at Arizona State University where he was acknowledged as a great athlete and named as the Pacific 10 Conference's defensive player of the year in 1997. He graduated summa cum laude in three and a half academic years, earning a degree in marketing. Despite being a college star, it was not until the 226th pick of the 1998 draft that he was selected to play professional football by the Arizona Cardinals, an NFL team. Only five months later, he was Arizona's starting strong safety. When he set a club record for tackles in 2000, he attracted the interest of another team, the Super Bowl champions, the St. Louis Rams, who offered him a five-year $US9 million contract. Tillman declined the offer out of loyalty to the Cardinals. Tillman then turned down a three-year, $US3.6 million contract with the Arizona Cardinals to enlist with his brother Kevin, also an athlete, in the army in May 2002 in the wake of the September 11 terrorist attacks, which killed about 3000 people in New York, Washington and Pennsylvania. "My great grandfather was at Pearl Harbor, and a lot of my family has ... gone and fought in wars, and I really haven't done a damn thing as far as laying myself on the line like that," Tillman told NBC News in an interview. Despite his high profile, Tillman denied requests for further media coverage during basic training, saying he wanted no special treatment or attention but wanted only to be considered a soldier doing his duty.

Together with his brother, Pat Tillman completed basic, individual, parachute and ranger indoctrination training and was quickly assigned to the Second Battalion of the 75th Ranger Regiment, the US army's premier light infantry unit, in Fort Lewis, Washington. In March 2003, he was deployed to Iraq and later to Afghanistan, where he served with his brother. On 22 April 2004, Specialist Patrick D. Tillman was confirmed by the army as having been killed in a fire fight during Operation Mountain Storm – the search in the mountains bordering Pakistan for top al-Qaeda and Taliban leaders, including Osama bin Laden and Mullah Omar. There is some controversy as to how Pat Tillman died. The initial reports indicated that Tillman's platoon was ambushed and Tillman, a team leader, directed his team into firing positions against the enemy and personally provided suppressive fire with an M-249 squad automatic weapon machine gun before leading his team out of the ambush position. For this, Tillman was awarded the Silver Star, the US's third highest award for gallantry on the battlefield. Although subsequent commentary suggests that Tillman died as a result of friendly fire, it does little to diminish the story of a football superstar who left glory and money behind because of his belief that a person should fight – and even die – for freedom, and in so doing, provided unsought leadership for millions of like-minded people.

Citizenship and Leadership

It's absolutely imperative to Earvin ["Magic" Johnson] that more players become more involved in their communities. *(Ken Lombard, president of Johnson Development Corp. and Johnson's key business partner)*

Earvin "Magic" Johnson is one of the greatest players in the history of basketball. Now he is spreading his charisma and his ability into the business world and inspiring other athletes to do the same. According to Eric Fisher of the *Washington Times*,[19] former Los Angeles Lakers center Shaquille O'Neal, Dallas Cowboys wide receiver Keyshawn Johnson, Toronto Raptors guard Jalen Rose, and Terrell Brandon, recently retired from the National Basketball Association after 11 seasons, are among those influenced by Johnson, each of them having invested six- or seven-figure sums in housing projects, restaurants and shopping centers in poor, urban areas – investments that require far more emotion, time and energy than simply purchasing stocks and bonds and watching the returns accumulate. Johnson himself has an estimated portfolio of over US$700 million, much of it invested in primarily African-American or underdeveloped urban areas. Fisher suggests that Johnson's motivation is simple: to provide an economic spark to the often-downtrodden neighborhoods in which he and other African-American players grew up.

There are a number of individual athletes who are already embracing social responsibility. Many, such as Australian swimmer Ian Thorpe, have set up charities. Others, like Johann Olav Koss, a gifted athlete in his time, winning four gold speed skating medals, three of which were at his "home" Olympics in Lillehammer, has put his ambition towards making a better world through sport for disadvantaged children. Koss is the president and CEO of Right to Play (formerly known as Olympic Aid), an IOC-endorsed organization that funds and delivers sport-based development programs around the world.

As we pointed out in our last book, *The Sport Business Future,*[20] the positive attributes of sport will be increasingly used by sports organizations to address both local and national social issues; not only because they are expected to, but because their membership depends upon it. A number of football clubs in Britain, for example, have recently implemented anti-racism campaigns within their regions. Corporations undertaking citizenship programs are likely to seek similar alliances with sport organizations in order to leverage positive community perceptions about the benefits of sport. In this way, sport will be the recipient of corporate citizenship programs, bolstering the ongoing viability of grass-roots participation and regional events.

Citizenship in the future has to be global to be relevant. James Post suggests that global corporate citizenship is "a company's response to their social, political, and economic responsibilities as defined through law and public policy, stakeholder expectations, and voluntary acts flowing from corporate values and business strategies".[21] Corporate citizenship goes beyond the legal, ethical and philanthropic responsibilities of companies. It requires companies to rely not simply on their legal responsibilities but on their wider responsibilities as world citizens.

The evidence is accumulating that being good corporate citizens does lead to higher performance in many different areas. According to social commentators John Weiser and Simon Zadek,[22] companies that are "stakeholder-balanced," who excel in managing the relationships with investors, customers, employees, suppliers and communities best, outperform their "shareholder-focused" counterparts four times in terms of company growth, and eight times when it comes to employment growth. There is also strong evidence that publicity about unethical corporate behavior has a direct correlation with stock prices. Evidence from Weiser and Zadek suggests that the shareholder return of "stakeholder superstars" over the past 15 years was 43 percent, whereas companies with a sole focus on financial shareholders returned only 19 percent.

> There are two kinds of people, those who do the work and those who take the credit. Try to be in the first group, there is less competition there. *(Indira Ghandi, former Indian prime minister)*

Increasing numbers of Americans believe that companies must seek social success as well as achieving business success. Surveys indicate that they believe that business has a growing responsibility for tackling issues related to crime, education and health. The statistics are even more overwhelming in Europe, where, according to Fleishman Hillard, some 87 percent of employees say that they are more loyal to socially engaged employers.[23] The logic is simple. Increases in social responsibility lead to higher levels of shareholder satisfaction, improved company profits, and higher employee retention.

So what of leaders or corporations who refuse to accept social responsibility? They will no doubt continue to function. But how foolish not to understand how the world is changing. Leaders can increase their profile by being involved in promoting social responsibility. Call it enlightened self-interest if you will. Investors will pick up on leaders who promote the positive role and potential of business around the world. Why would they do otherwise? There is now much evidence available indicating that social responsibility is becoming a standard against which companies in the future will be judged. Indeed, in 2001, US companies devoted US$9 billion to social causes as well as endless talent.

Post Game

> Leadership is more than just leading. It's a commitment
> to many other things. *(Unknown)*

At the close of this chapter let us once more turn our attention to Magic Johnson. As a leader on the sporting field of play, he contributed to a great team focus on winning basketball games as being the core business of the Los Angeles Lakers. Later in life he refocused on what was his "core business" and now leads towards social betterment, a bigger picture perspective than "only" winning a few basketball matches.

Leaders in general, therefore, are always in charge of the continuous change towards better achieving the core of the organization's business. Sport like no other industry shows us how to benchmark and measure performance towards achieving our objectives. The late Pat Tillman has shown that when the going gets tough, the tough get going; leaders will emerge during moments of crisis, simply because it is their duty to do so.

We can only look forward to Michael Schumacher retiring from Formula One racing to see where he chooses to further his tremendous leadership potential. Some may argue that it is easy to put money where your mouth is when you make as much as he does, but in the terrible aftermath of the Asian tsunami disaster, it was Michael Schumacher who donated US$10 million to the relief fund – responsible for results on the racing track and responsive to the needs of global society.

Notes

1   C. Zook and J. Allen (2001), *Growth Strategy in an Era of Turbulence*, Harvard Business School Press, Boston, MA.
2   C.K. Prahalad and G. Hamel (1990), "The Core Competence of the Corporation", *Harvard Business Review*, **90**(3), pp. 79–91.
3   *Expansion*, 19 July 2004.
4   L. Gettler, "Buzz Words, like Buzz Saws, Go Around and Around", *The Age*, 21 July 2004.
5   J.W. Weese (1995), "Leadership and Organizational Culture: An Investigation of the Big Ten and Mid-American Conference Campus Recreation Administrations", *Journal of Sport Management*, **9**(1): 119–34.
6   J.W. Weese (1996), "Do Leadership and Organizational Culture Really Matter?" *Journal of Sport Management*, **10**(2): 197–206.
7   J.P. Kotter (1999), *On What Leaders Really Do*, Harvard Business School Press, Boston, MA.
8   R.B. Denhardt (2002), *The Pursuit of Significance: Strategies for Managerial Success in Public Organizations*, Waveland Press, Prospect Heights, Il.

9 R.B. Denhardt and J.V. Denhardt (1999), "Leadership for Change: Case Studies in American Local Government", *The Pricewaterhouse Coopers Endowment for The Business of Government*, September, PricewaterhouseCoopers, Arizona.

10 http://www.chelseafc.com/article.asp?id=206540 accessed 2 June 2004.

11 Marcus A. Caton (1998), *Using Performance Indicators within Australian National and State Sporting Organisations*, A Paper presented to Sports Coach 98, Melbourne, 28 November.

12 "Performance Measurement for the Development of Sport – A Good Practice Guide for Local Authorities", *Sport England*, 2001, London, pp. 3–4.

13 www.audit-commission.gov.uk, accessed 28 July 2004.

14 W. Bennis and R. Thomas (2002), "Crucibles of Leadership", *Harvard Business Review*, **80**(9): 39–45.

15 J.W. Greenberg (2002), "September 11, 2001: A CEO's Story", *Harvard Business Review*, **80**(10): 58–64.

16 W. Bennis and R. Thomas, op. cit.

17 http://www.le.ac.uk/footballresearch/resources/factsheets/fs6.html, accessed 9 June 2004.

18 M. Romney (2004), *Turnaround: Crisis, Leadership and the Olympic Games*, Regnery Publishing, Washington DC.

19 E. Fisher (2004), "Life after Sports", *The Washington Times*, 4 April 2004.

20 A. Smith and H. Westerbeek (2004), *The Sport Business Future*, Palgrave Macmillan, Basingstoke.

21 J.E. Post (2000), "Moving from Geographic to Virtual Communities: Global Corporate Citizenship in a Dot.com World", *Business and Society Review*, **105**(1): 28.

22 J. Weiser and S. Zadek (2001), "Persuading Business to Address Social Challenges", *Conversations with disbelievers*, From www.conversations-with-disbelievers.net.

23 H. Fleishman (1999), *Consumers Demand Companies with a Conscience*, Hillard Fleishman, London.

CHAPTER 3

Fair Game: Leaders and Followers

Lead, follow, or get out of the way.
(PLAQUE ON TED TURNER'S DESK)

From the loyal supporter and cheer squad to the club chairman and team captain, this chapter reveals why sport followers' commitment is absolute throughout all levels of the organization. It builds upon this knowledge to demonstrate how followership can be engendered in all members of an organization through the right approach to leadership that emphasizes identity, ownership, and involvement. The chapter also provides the background for business leaders to understand the role of personality, charisma, tribal identity and other factors that contribute to organized followership.

It is probably worthwhile at this juncture to recall that although leadership is generally seen as heroic, the reality is that there are many poor and a few dreadful leaders. The almost blind belief of followers in the inherent goodness of leaders is often matched by the almost blind belief of leaders in the inherent foolishness of followers. The truth is that there are flawed leaders and followers everywhere and there are few leaders who do not display both good and bad leadership characteristics. Even bad leaders often obtain good results and we can learn from bad leaders as we can from good ones. Equally, we can learn from poor followers. We simply need to look for what each does right.

> Everybody wants to follow the leader; but, nobody wants to lead the followers. *(Unknown)*

We might also take the opportunity to remind readers that while the literature constantly suggests the adoption of business lessons drawn from other disciplines, many leaders and followers undertake the adoption process badly. There is no doubt that while many similarities exist between business and other fields, some similarities remain naive, inappropriate and, in some instances, nonsensical. Consequently, in our sport analogy, we should be seeking not only parallels with business but also differences. Despite what we might suggest, business is not sport, although the reverse is often true. Nonetheless, there are frequent instructive similarities.

The Concept of Leadership

> Leadership rests not only upon ability, but upon commitment and upon loyalty and upon pride and upon followers. *(Vince Lombardi, Green Bay Packers coach)*

As has been pointed out, there are literally thousands of books on leadership, many espousing specific requirements or attributes of successful leaders. The majority of these books are useful and some display detailed insight into various leadership styles and characteristics. By and large, however, as Gary Walton has reminded us, if leadership formulas do exist, they are at best vague and untidy.[1] As a consequence, we must understand leadership by studying what it is that leaders do and adopt those characteristics that we feel comfortable with, we believe will function in our organization, and are suitable for our individualistic style of leadership.

One similarity between sport and business lies in the way in which leaders understand and deal with subordinates. A great example here can be seen from the story of Vince Lombardi, the legendary Green Bay Packers coach. In the ten years prior to Lombardi's arrival, the Green Bay Packers constantly lost more games each season than they won despite changing coaches three times. By 1958, the year they really hit rock bottom, they were suffering near financial ruin. The story goes that the team was so unpopular with its fans that the only safe place they could socialize with their families was in the Packers' locker room.

When Lombardi arrived in 1959, his priority was in deciding which players to retain and which players he could let go. His experience had taught him that the fault often lay with the leadership and not the players. By talking to his players and his coaching staff and constantly reviewing old films of the Packers playing, he eventually made his choice. With the addition of a few new, capable players, Lombardi prepared his team. Lombardi knew that subordinates liked stability and feared change. To overcome this fear, he differentiated between individual change and organizational change. To allay players' individual fears he confirmed them in one playing position. They were assured of a position in the starting lineup, at least until they had a reasonable opportunity to demonstrate their ability. Prior to his arrival, for example, Paul Hornung, the all-American "Golden Boy from Notre Dame" had been played at quarterback and fullback. Lombardi told him that he would play in one position only – that of left halfback. Hornung, the "Golden Boy" was reborn and went on to win the NFL scoring title three year's running.

Lombardi also realized that subordinates required the requisite skills, training and self-confidence if they were to perform at the height of their ability. As a consequence, he placed tremendous emphasis both on mind and body. He interviewed each player and sought to understand their view of the organization and their own role within it. He gave praise and warning with passion, but also with sensitivity and fairness. He was, as all good leaders are, a capable psychologist. He so inspired third string quarterback, Bart Starr, that he was soon elevated to the starting role and subsequently went on to become a fine on-field general.

Rules were clearly signposted and were applicable to everyone including Lombardi. Training was so hard that Dave "Hog" Hanner, who reported to camp weighing some 273 pounds, lost so much weight in the first few days that he had to be hospitalized for dizzy spells.

Lombardi understood one of the first rules of leadership. The team was more important than any individual. All were treated equally. One of the famous stories about Lombardi concerned an interview with a newspaper reporter in which he was asked how many black players he had on his team. He replied to the effect that he could tell the reporter how many players he had on the team, which ones were lazy and were in danger of being dropped and which new players he had his eyes on, but he couldn't tell the reporter how many white or how many black players he had. He had just never noticed, he said. Lombardi's view suggests one area in which sport often differs to business. In sport, particularly team sport, ability is the primary criterion upon which a person is judged. Age, sex, religion, ethnicity, and schooling are minor issues.

> The strength of the group is the strength of the leader.
> (Vince Lombardi, Green Bay Packers coach)

Lombardi's success was not based on a consultant's report or a high-tech solution. He simply understood that the Green Bay Packers had a serious problem with leadership. The management situation Lombardi inherited was an organizational mess. Statewide, there were some 43 directors involved in various aspects of the game. Lombardi changed the structure so that he had total responsibility for all activities. Once he had total control, he was then in a position to dictate what and to whom to delegate. He understood the vital link between responsibility and authority. In his view delegating one without the other was nonsensical. The players had to be assured that whoever was responsible had the requisite authority to discharge that responsibility.

Lombardi's understanding of leadership, together with his ability and drive, underpinned his success. By the start of the Packers' first season under Lombardi, they were the best conditioned side in NFL history. They completed 1959 with a 7–5 record. In 1961 and 1962 they were NFL champions, and in 1965, 1966 and 1967 they became the first team to win three championships in succession. They also won the first two Super Bowl games (1966 and 1967). When Lombardi, at the age of 55, retired from coaching the Packers in 1968, the team had an astonishing win–loss–tie record of 99–29–4.

Born or Made?

> Leaders are made, they are not born; and they are made just like anything else has been made in this country – by hard effort. And that's the price that we all have to pay to achieve that goal, or any goal.
> *(Vince Lombardi, Green Bay Packers coach)*

The question of whether a leader is born or made is often posed by leadership theorists. The question is important because it often affects the way in which we view followers. The traditional theory of leadership was that people were leaders because of natural leadership traits with which they were born. The difficulty here is that a review of all leaders does not show common traits. Certainly there are some traits that are more common in leaders than in followers. But are there specific leadership traits? That depends on which book is read. Kotter suggests intelligence, drive, mental health, and integrity.[2] Others suggest judgment, decisiveness, ambition, honesty, and communication skills, or even physical characteristics such as height and strength.

Trait theory was followed by behavioral theory which suggested that leadership could be taught. The theory distinguished between whether leaders were task- or person-oriented or whether they were autocratic or democratic. A third type of behavioral theory suggested that the behavior of the leader depended on the situation in which they found themselves. More recently, contingency theory, which focuses on the organizational context which makes some leadership behaviors more effective than others, has appeared. Contingency theorists seek to isolate the situational conditions which determine the sort of leadership style that would be most effective.

To us, it is the contingency theory of leadership which has the most appeal. This view is echoed by Rakesh Khurana, who suggests that a leader is made and can only really demonstrate learned leadership qualities in the right organizational and cultural milieus.[3] This view has equal standing in the world of sport. Managers and coaches who change clubs and enter into different cultural arenas and subsequently fail to live up to expectations after being hired are plentiful. Certainly a leader can be born with certain characteristics that aid in leadership, or become more important when performing a leadership role. An individual can be mentored early, by parents or school. But very few are ever born leaders. Similarly, many can demonstrate leadership qualities in all they undertake, but to be recognized, the right opportunity has to be available. It is all a matter of context. A leader can emerge, given learned leadership ability and the right situation. In this respect, Lombardi was similar to most successful business leaders. He didn't just arrive on the scene, but was guided, nurtured and educated in leadership theory and wisdom over a period of time and was ultimately provided with the setting in which his leadership qualities could be explored and demonstrated.

Lombardi's mentor was a relatively unsung individual named Colonel Earl "Red" Blaik. Lombardi came to Blaik via stints as teacher and football coach at St Cecilia and director of physical education at Fordham College. He even worked in the construction industry as a foreman for the Brewster Construction Company. Blaik was the Army football coach at West Point and mentored Lombardi in the two years prior to his taking over as assistant coach of the New York Giants and then coach of the Packers. All leaders learn their job at the feet of others and Lombardi was no different. We pick up this point again in more detail in Chapter 5, which deals with coaching and mentoring.

There is an equivalent to Colonel Blaik in most organizations. The individual who can spot talent, nurture and guide it, and prepare it for a wider audience. It's the top sergeant to a new lieutenant, the academic supervisor to a Fulbright scholar. D. Wayne Lukas, America's top thoroughbred horse trainer, says that despite holding just about every record in racing, the thing he is most proud of is turning out top assistants. In a recent *Harvard Business Review* article, Lucas indicated that 11 former assistants were now highly successful trainers in their own right.[4] One mark of a future leader is the ability to identify, woo, win and accept the wisdom of the mentors who will guide their life. Lombardi learned both his trade and much of his leadership knowledge under Blaik. After leaving West Point, Lombardi would often state that he could not "conceive of a greater coach than Blaik." Nineteen of Blaik's former assistants later became head coaches in colleges or professional football.[5]

Followership

> The best executive is the one who has sense enough to pick good men to do what he wants done, and self-restraint enough to keep from meddling with them while they do it. *(Theodore Roosevelt, 26th president of the United States)*

Based to some extent on both Freudian and Jungian theory, many leadership models suggest that leaders are more effective when they understand and accept both their own psychological makeup and that of their subordinates. Under this theory, personality characteristics are considered as being strongly ingrained and are difficult to eliminate or change. Accordingly, working with those characteristics rather than seeking to oppose or change them is important for both leader and follower. This is a reasonable beginning for understanding why the relationship between leader and followers sometimes works, while at other times, it fails. The difficulty is that both leadership and followership constantly change depending on the type of organization involved, the individual leader and follower characteristics, differing points in the life cycle of the organization, the culture of the organization, the economy in which the organization is operating and a plethora of other factors. To suggest one style of leadership, or one style of followership, as being more appropriate than others is, therefore, nonsense. Nonetheless, a good leader or follower accepts that the relationship between leader and follower is not constant and that understanding your own personality characteristics as well as those of senior and junior colleagues is, at least, a good beginning.

As James Weese has pointed out, the provision of leadership should not simply be viewed as a panacea for organizational success. There is a role for followers also in determining organizational effectiveness.[6] To understand leadership, the role of followers needs to be studied. Indeed, the fundamental characteristic of leadership is the tie between the leader and the led. The relationship is truly symbiotic. In sport, the problem of whether good leadership causes players to perform better or whether good player performance enhances the role of the leader has never been adequately answered. It seems reasonable to accept, however, whether in sport or business, that the individual characteristics and personalities of followers all impact on the effectiveness of the leader and that the personality of the leader, as well as his or her actions, impacts on the followers. Equally, it seems reasonable to accept that the relationship between leader and followers combines with the leadership situation to determine the effectiveness of the leadership.

> A general is just as good as the troops under his command.
> *(General Douglas MacArthur)*

It needs to be remembered, however, that followers, like leaders, are not a monolithic block of people with similar needs and expectations. They are a diverse group. While followership may be, perhaps incorrectly, regarded as a set state, it does not automatically imply that followers blindly accept what they are told by their leader. Followership should not be a passive activity. Good followers, while loyal and competent, must constantly guard against simply telling the boss what he or she wants to hear.

Followers may be strongly influenced by the personality, activities and attitude of the leader and the culture of the organization. To be a good follower, identification with the organization is a must and such identification often becomes almost tribal. It is why the military give recruits similar haircuts, clothe them in the same uniform, have them live in the same barracks, and practice the same drill. They seek to deidentify them as civilians and reidentify them as soldiers. Organizations do the same but usually to a much lesser extent, putting newcomers through basic, and other, indoctrination courses. Individual professions frequently use their own distinctive "language" to differentiate them from other professions. Sporting teams achieve identification through wearing similar colors and having a club or country anthem.

Tribal identity can be so strong as to live with a person throughout their life. One of the most poignant scenes in all soccer history occurred in 1974 at a match between Manchester United and its close rival Manchester City. It was a time when the fortunes of United were at their lowest ebb. City had signed Dennis Law, a long-term United player and lifetime supporter of the club. Law, then in the twilight of his career, scored a magnificent goal for City, a goal that defeated United and saw them relegated to a lower division. When Law realized what he had done, that his goal had consigned his beloved United to relegation, he dropped his head and inconsolably shrugged off the congratulations of his teammates.[7]

> The appropriate form of leadership depends on issues such as the nature of the task at hand, the skills and attitudes of the followers, and the attributes of the leader. *(Dr Pete Mazany,* Team Think: Team New Zealand)[8]

Many leadership theorists suggest that the role of the leader is simply to provide the vision while the role of the follower is to execute that vision. Such a leader is often termed either "transformational" or "charismatic." Transformational leadership has been defined as "the process of influencing major changes in attitudes and assumptions of organizational members and building commitment for the organization's missions and objectives.[9] What this really means is that leaders energize followers to commit to their leader's vision. Transformational leaders, being, by definition, role models, are expected to maximize the collective performance of talented subordinates by encouraging them to emulate their leader. Charismatic leadership is essentially a subset of transformational leadership. Bass uses the term "charisma" to describe leaders who have a profound and extraordinary effect on their followers.[10]

It has been suggested that these leaders provide followers with focus, support, involvement, and appreciation, designed to encourage the follower to adopt the leader's vision as their own and be committed to making it a reality.[11] Unfortunately, reality is rarely so simple, and history suggests that there is little relationship between such leadership and organizational effectiveness. Theorists have written countless papers describing the various requirements of charisma, many of which, no doubt, have some validity. In practical terms, however, any leader who can effectively articulate a vision, communicate its validity to the organization, demonstrate the methods and behaviors required to achieve that vision and can convincingly sell that vision to subordinates and shareholders may be said to be charismatic.

While we do not dismiss visionary leadership – there is after all sufficient evidence to show that people work harder and have greater belief when they are on a mission – we do believe that good leadership requires far more than just a vision. There are but a handful of truly charismatic leaders who succeed by relying on charisma alone. Most charismatic leaders are also hard, realistic individuals who use a vision in place of, or as a supplement to, a strategic plan. The reality is also that the better and more practical leaders use the vision and insights of followers as a foundation for better vision and greater insights. Few leaders possess all the available knowledge and experience and good leaders understand this.

An organization led by a visionary leader, with followers who put that vision into practice, may well be fine while that leader remains at the helm, although vision has a habit of becoming a mirage. The nature of vision, after all, is not always rational. When that leader moves on, for whatever reason, the vision often collapses unless it has become, quite definitively, the vision of the followers. Many examples of this exist in sport. When Lombardi, a hard, pragmatic visionary, left the Packers as coach, he remained on the management board and so his overall influence did not disappear entirely. Nonetheless, no longer coach, he was unable to impart his own vision to the players. From 1968 to 1992 the Packers appeared in the play-offs only twice, in 1972 and 1982. Sir Matt Busby, Manchester United's great manager, was another visionary leader who saw his vision fade as soon as he retired as Manchester's manager. In Manchester's case, the vision did not return until another visionary leader, Alex Ferguson, took over many years later. Even then, the vision was different.

John Kotter suggests that it is managers, rather than leaders, who are dependent on others in the organization to perform their jobs effectively.[12] Perhaps so, but few leaders can really be effective unless they have the support of talented subordinates. Even someone like Lombardi, who wanted all the power in his own hands, had to rely on capable and dedicated coaching and support staff to ensure success.

In his book, *The Courageous Follower, Standing Up To and For Our Leaders*,[13] Ira Chaleff points out that the traditional model of the leader/follower is based on power, with the leader being able to control benefits, bonuses and promotions, and so on. Followers avoid jeopardizing their chances of obtaining these rewards by giving the leader what the leader wants. For the most part, good leaders hate this model. Sometimes, however, leaders, often great and highly successful leaders, forget the reality of interdependency between leader and follower. A challenge to their leadership or status causes an unexpected change in leadership behavior. Upset the manager in any sport and no matter how important you may be to the team, your chance of being in the starting lineup is limited. Even David Beckham, one of the world's greatest soccer players, was sidelined by his manager Sir Alex Ferguson when he challenged the manager's comments. Despite reducing the effectiveness of the team,

Beckham was kept on the bench as punishment. In the end, he was sold to another team. In sport, and often in business, this type of relationship, as Chaleff indicates, does not serve the organization, the leader or the follower because it shuts down the open flow of communication and sincerity that leaders need to do their job effectively.

The role of followers or subordinates often varies with the size of the organization. The closer they are to the leader, the greater will usually be their effectiveness. By the same token, the smaller the organization, generally the greater the need for positive leadership traits to be visible. The closer the leader is to subordinates, the more easily can they be influenced and the more readily can followers, in turn, influence the leader. Leaders exert power over followers, but followers also display power over leaders. Being a successful follower, with the opportunity and ability to influence upward, is an essential part of leadership.

In similar manner, followership can be strengthened by making followers part of the leadership plan or vision; essentially by giving them ownership of that plan or vision. Many organizations endeavor to do this by having middle and coal face leaders heavily involved in the production of the organization's strategic plan. Followers will more willingly follow a leader when they perceive that they will benefit from the interchange.

When leader and followers differ, the results can be wholesale change. Take, for instance, the recent situation with Chelsea FC. Despite coming second in the English Premiership and getting to the semi-finals of the prestigious Champions League, disagreement arose between Roman Abramovitch, the owner of Chelsea, and Claudio Ranieri, the Chelsea manager, which resulted in Ranieri's sacking. Chelsea's new boss, José Mourinho indicated before even formally taking over that Chelsea's backroom staff would have two weeks to prove themselves.[14] Within a matter of days, Mourinho had brought in four backroom staff from Porto, his previous club, to make up his management team at Chelsea.[15]

Underlying the business team is another group of followers – the customers. In sport, it is the supporters. Customer or supporter, both groups play a similar role. The sport supporter is the customer of the business. Provide a good product at a reasonable price, advertise it well, and it will sell. Provide a product that lacks interest, say ice hockey in the Sahara, and business will die or dissolve. The key to success is to provide what the customer wants. A good supporter, like a good customer, will sell the product by word of mouth. Use the New York Giants as a search criterion via Google and almost two million sites will be shown. Of these, almost half will relate to sites sponsored for, or on behalf of, supporters of the Giants.

Why are supporters so fixated on their team and on their sport? The reality is that they were probably indoctrinated from birth via one or other of their parents. As a result, they give allegiance willingly and tend to ignore or overlook the team failures. It is no different in business. If a father has always owned a Ford car and has continually sung its praises, chances are that the son will also become a Ford man when he reaches maturity. In giving guidance and passion to their offspring, parents are providing leadership. So too is the role of the passionate supporter.

Customers and supporters are part of the team and most companies operate better when all work as a team. Teams, whether business or sport, need to have the right mix of players – leaders, middle managers, workers and supporters. In practice, a good cross-functional team may be made up of several subteams, each requiring a different kind of leadership. One, or several, such subteams in an organization work at what is generally termed, "the coal face," or where we actually produce the products of the organization.

Leadership at the Coal Face and in Teams

> Assuming no luck is involved in winning, the crew comes first, the sails next and the boat comes third and last. *(Philip Rhodes, America's Cup defender in 1958)*

The coal face is a strange place to be. It implies that the person there is at the cutting edge, literally providing the essence of the business. It does not appear to be a place where leadership is regularly undertaken. Yet, our understanding of leadership within an organization is changing. In the past, the leader was the person who asked the questions and presented the answers. Today, to have a successful company, it needs to be recognized that questions arise in many places, outside and within the organization, and that no single leader can possibly have all the answers. The leader may have a vision or have laid down a strategic direction. The leader may even have designated solutions. But, in practical terms, the most effective solutions about how best to meet the challenges of the moment should be made by the people closest to the problems – the people at the coal face.

Most organizations need, and provide for, leadership at two levels, strategic and operational. In smaller organizations the same person may carry out both functions, while in larger organizations they are frequently two distinct roles. This does not deny a hierarchy of leadership; rather it acknowledges the reality that functions of leadership can be delegated. Often, the strategic leadership is provided by a board of directors. Operational leadership, although nominally placed in one person, is usually delegated down to operational units. In soccer, for example, there is a separate coach responsible for a club's first team, reserve team and academy sides. Senior leaders can authorize resources and more importantly can act as corporate champions. If leadership is successfully delegated, the loss of leadership at senior levels will have a lesser impact on organizations.

Change the definition of leadership and you change how a company is run. In the past few years, working practices have changed significantly and there is now far greater emphasis on team skills, with many of these teams working at the coal face. Of course, teams still require defined tasks and objectives given to them by senior leaders, but such teams also require their own, inherent leadership. Good coal face teams are diverse in experience and personality and numerous studies suggest that such diversity improves performance in terms of decision quality.[16] A team is not composed of one individual; neither is an organization. In business, there are several levels of management and workers and all, to varying degrees, display aspects of leadership, and so it is in sport.

To be successful as "coal face leaders," individuals need to be part of the planning process and are required to be empowered by the senior leadership, provided with whatever resources are required and then held accountable. In this way they identify with the organizational needs and become invested with both the problem and the solution. Their familiarity with the business processes (the coal face) provides them with the required knowledge to undertake and lead tasks. In this process, the role of the leader changes from that of director to that of coach, mentor and teacher.

An example of this in sport occurred with Manchester United in the latter part of the 1940s. At that time, Manchester was managed by the legendary Matt Busby. Manchester's home ground, Old Trafford, had been demolished during the Blitz and the club was forced to play its home games at Maine Road, home of its rivals Manchester City. United was also heavily in debt, a debt which was compounded by attempts to rebuild its home ground, and this forced Busby to learn the lesson of leadership called "innovation." One of Busby's ideas was to recruit young, talented junior players and mature them quickly, thus providing him with an increasing number of individuals from whom he could choose his team. The results are history. By the late 1940s, players like Danny Blanchflower, Eddie Colman, Duncan Edwards, and David Pegg began to appear.

The first "Busby Babes," as they later became known, did not simply appear. Once the task of recruiting youth was made clear, Busby delegated responsibility and accountability for the task to two of his coal face leaders. In this he was most fortunate. The first of these subordinates was Joe Armstrong, the chief scout responsible for traveling Britain in search of soccer-mad schoolboys and promising amateurs. Armstrong was a refined, cultured, retired civil servant, whose honesty and sincerity persuaded many parents to trust their sons to Manchester's care. Once identified by Armstrong, the junior players were placed in the hands of Bert Whalley, a former Manchester center half who was appointed trainer after an eye injury forced him to retire from the game. Whalley, later to die in the Munich air crash of 6 February 1958, was a proficient trainer who responded well to teaching youngsters and mentored many of them. Under his careful guidance, youthful talent was matured. One of those youngsters under Whalley's guidance was Bobby Charlton, who had spurned family tradition by not following his uncle Jackie Milburn to Newcastle United. Regretfully, the Munich air crash deprived Manchester United of many of their finest youngsters and required the building of a new generation of Busby Babes.

> Players are made in the off season, teams are made during the season.
> *(Unknown)*

Leadership at the coal face is not always undertaken by middle range staff. At Manchester United, one of the hardest working teams is the property services group which is responsible for everything from the upkeep of all United's property, including the ground and the stadium, through to finding and furnishing homes for incoming foreign players. Leadership of this group is provided by a relatively junior employee. Despite this, it is an indispensable coal face position.

Organizations in general invest considerably more time, money and energy into hiring and retraining senior leaders than they do in hiring leaders at the coal face. This is understandable. Recruiting leaders who appear to have the potential for leading organizations into the future is an essential requirement if a company is to survive in the long term. But good leaders ensure that the organization is well led at all levels. Good leaders understand that the organization is strengthened as the team is strengthened. They believe that a team working together can achieve much more than an individual working on his or her own. Good leaders trust, invest in and empower team leaders. So why is it then that those ostensibly good leaders frequently fail to reward team leadership at the coal face?

Again the reality differs from the theory. In theory, organizations identify talent at all levels and systematically encourage and train that talent via leadership, management and other courses. This was, and is, how some organizations operate, and it is indeed successful. But many organizations, who claim to operate in a similar manner, in practice do not. They subconsciously place their staff into four separate categories.

Their first team players are the stars. When a new leader comes in, some are promoted, many continue as they are, and a few are released. It can be seen every time a new coach takes over any sporting team. Given too many stars, each displaying their own variation of leadership, an organization can suffer. Chelsea FC, under manager Claudio Ranieri, with some 30 plus international players available for selection in a team of 11, had to rotate players in starting positions so frequently that it was unable to determine a single playing style. The team of stars was unable to perform as a star team. This is a core theme of the following chapter which tackles team leadership specifically.

A further example of this was shown during the recent European Championship, when Luiz Felipe "Big Phil" Scolari, Brazil's coach during their 2002 World Cup win and currently Portugal's coach, pulled Luis Figo, a national hero in Portugal, off the field in the quarter final game against England, a game Portugal went on to win. Scolari disliked Figo's approach to the game. For Scolari, a coach who submits to the "star system" is in trouble. "You cannot have stars in winning teams – only great players" is Scolari's mantra.[17]

Second team players are often coal face or middle ranking leaders. Frequently, they are as capable as the first team players, but either because they call less attention to themselves, are specialists, or are such accomplished and steady but invisible performers, their efforts are commonly overlooked. These second team people are often the backbone of an organization, providing leadership both at the coal face and in various teams. A change of senior leadership sees them continuing to perform as before. The third team players create the noise in an organization and frequently receive the recognition that should have gone to the second team players. With leadership change, they retreat into their shells until everything is back to normal when once again they start making noise. The lowest team comprises those individuals who simply seek to undertake their daily task and then go home. They rarely display leadership and, unlike the team above them, are, at least, honest in their endeavors.

Is it necessary for leaders at the coal face to make noise or display overt ambition for them to be noticed? Not in well-led organizations like international companies BHP-Billiton or Toyota, where coal face leaders are regularly plucked from minor stardom to senior leadership positions. But, in many lesser organizations, coal face leaders should, at least, consider the option. Coal face leaders are frequently specialist by nature. As such, it is usually more difficult for them to rise in the organization than middle managers, who are generally seen as "leaders in waiting."

The Middle Manager

> Middle management provides a vital link between senior management and operational functions. At its best it ensures that strategy is turned into appropriate action and that the contribution of operational staff is maximised.
> *(Nick Raynsford, United Kingdom local government minister, 17 June 2004)*

Over the past 50 years, the role of the middle manager has changed substantially. From dominating organizational structure in the post-war industrial days of the 1950s, their decline has been slow and, perhaps, inevitable. As increasing emphasis has been given to the profit motive in business, organizations have seen the middle management role as being largely unnecessary, costing rather than making money, and simply an up-and-down information conduit creating bottlenecks between leader and worker. With the massive restructuring of organizations which character-ized the 1990s, many middle managers found their positions disappearing and with them their job opportunities. Entire layers of middle management were simply cut away. With the demise of many middle ranking positions, organizations made significant financial savings convincing senior leader-ship that such action was both valid and good for the organization.

Helping the downfall of middle management was the emergence of management concepts such as change management and re-engineering, and with them the belief that one of the sticking points to successful change or re-engineering was the middle manager. Management gurus like Mike Hammer, co-author of *Re-engineering the Corporation,* who, in referring to the middle-level managerial hierarchy as the "death zone" of re-engineering,[18] a reference to their supposed investment in the status quo and their dislike of change, helped to fuel this belief.

There's probably little doubt that middle management as a group had grown too bulky, too content and too fixed in their views. But, like many things, the movement to eliminate middle management went too far. As they disappeared, they left behind them their work and responsibilities as well as gaping holes in the leadership structure. Leadership development went into serious decline. With the emergence of the information tech-nology age, senior leaders became bogged down in work previously handled by their junior colleagues and, instead of focusing on major organizational issues, were required to spend large amounts of time on day-to-day concerns.

In the past few years, however, organizations have again understood the need for good middle management. There is an increasing awareness that organizations need capable leaders at all levels, and especially in middle management. Their role, however, has changed and is now somewhat of a leadership paradox. Being able to see the big picture, they are required to demonstrate leadership to junior staff, often without having the authority to change decisions. They are required to become both leader and follower. If effective, middle managers can demonstrate both leadership and followership skills and behaviors, depending on the circumstances. As such, good middle managers are essential to the organizational structure.

Effective middle managers tend to react more authoritatively than other followers. They are often more comfortable disagreeing with superiors and less inclined to be intimidated by status. Where authority is dubious they tend to work on the old military maxim of it being better to seek forgiveness later than to ask permission first. They are rarely afraid of taking authority when such authority is not clear cut. They understand that leadership is about influence and that authority gives them influence. Effective leaders seek the support of those at the middle levels, knowing that plans and ideas are far more likely to be successful if middle managers take them on board. The most capable of middle managers have informal communications networks that reach across the organization. They are a source of ideas for senior management and can understand the needs and requirements of junior staff. They work at the junction of stability and change.

One of the essential tasks of middle management is to serve as a bridge or conduit between the higher goals of senior management and the daily practicalities of the workforce. Having a perspective on both sides of the divide between management and workers, middle managers are in an ideal position to initiate and demonstrate innovation. They are also ideally placed to translate the vision or ideas of top management into concepts that can be understood and implemented by the workforce. In taking on this task, some middle managers become frontline managers on their own.

Take, for example, women's hockey in Australia under coach Ric Charlesworth. Charlesworth is often considered as the most effective coach in Australian sporting history. John Lyons, in the *Australian Financial Review* referred to him as "the greatest Australian legend the rest of the world hasn't heard of".[19] Charlesworth played 227 interna-

tionals for Australia between 1972 and 1988 and then, from 1993 to
2001, he coached the Australian women's team, the Hockeyroos. This
team became number one in the world, winning Olympic gold medals in
1996 and 2000, World Cup gold medals in 1994 and 1998, Champion's
Trophy titles in 1993, 1995, 1997, and a Commonwealth Games gold
medal in 1998.

But no matter how good Ric Charlesworth was, it is doubtful he would
have succeeded to the same extent without the help of leaders within the
Australian women's hockey organization. Consider, for instance, the role
of Meg Wilson, who took over the presidency of the World Hockey Association (WHA) in 1986 and who, during her 10-year presidency, became
an enormous influence in Australian women's hockey. In many ways she
prepared the path for Charlesworth to succeed. Wilson, a former member
of the Australian team, exhibited a people-focused leadership style. After
winning the presidency of the WHA, Wilson became the first Australian
woman ever to represent Australia in the Federation of International
Hockey (FIH). In this position, she used her international connections to
encourage national teams from other countries to visit and play in
Australia, thus giving Australia the opportunity to play against world-class
international opposition.

Meg Wilson wanted to win the right to host the 1990 World Cup in
Sydney. To achieve this, she needed both money and a capable administrator. She found her administrator in Pam Tye, a Sydney council member
of the WHA, elected president of the organization in 1996 and later
Australian representative in the FIH. Tye, a school principal, was the
perfect administrator and leader for such a task. When the Hockeyroos won
the Olympic gold medal at the 1988 Games in Seoul, Wilson was able to
obtain the major sponsorship of Telstra, the predominant Australian
telecommunications company. Wilson and Tye were never seen by the
public as the face or the leadership of women's hockey. That position was
reserved for Charlesworth. Yet, Meg Wilson, Pam Tye, and other dedicated
hockey leaders turned women's hockey in Australia from a largely amateur
run sport to being a totally professional and world recognized organization.

The underlying organization for women's hockey in Australia that
Wilson, Tye and others set up targeted talent at all levels. Systematically,
capable administrators and leaders at the state levels were identified,
given resources, charged with responsibilities, and then promoted to
positions of responsibility. Career progression became the norm, with
future middle management leaders being constantly identified and
promoted.[20] Charlesworth inherited the setup that leaders like Meg
Wilson provided.

From the Bottom Up

> Being a victim of prejudice is particularly traumatic. *(Arthur Ashe, tennis player)*

It is an often accepted wisdom that a leader emerges in a situation where one is necessary but has not been formally appointed. Individuals may take leadership by providing certainty and direction during times of ambiguity or crisis or may be thrust into the leadership because of their known capability and strength of conviction. That leader, once identified, may be officially approved by senior leaders or group members, or simply by "the system." Equally, the individual may be accepted as leader without any formal ratification. Formal or informal, such leaders are usually effective, particularly in the short term. Emergent leadership is not always permanent. Leadership may move around depending on the situation and the individuals concerned.

Emergent leadership may arise when an organization is in crisis and can come from any stratum of the organization or from outside it – Lee Iaccoca at the Chrysler Corporation is an example. Or it may occur when an organization, or part of that organization, decides that its concerns require a wider audience. Martin Luther King Jr. with the US civil rights movement springs to mind. What is apparent, however, is that the arrival of emerging leaders is not always signaled in advance. Generally, emergent leaders are either task-focused, like Iaccoca or socio-emotionally focused, like King.

Many emergent leaders do not actively seek the role of leader. Instead, they are thrust into that position because of circumstances and because their individual personality characteristics make them ideal for the position. Once placed in the role of leader, many of the individuals rise to the occasion and gather large numbers of followers. Take, for example, Arthur Ashe, the first African-American man to win a US tennis championship and to win Wimbledon. In his early days as a professional tennis player, Ashe was, on occasions, forced to use an alternative changing room to white players. He was a man of enormous character and courage and although never seeking leadership of the African-American cause in sport, he accepted leadership with such grace, conviction and pride that he endeared himself to millions of tennis fans throughout the world. He became the first US tennis player to earn US$100,000 in a single season. What Ashe did for African-American players in tennis, others like Chris Evert did for women's tennis. She became a leader of the feminist cause as the first tennis player to win 1000 singles matches as well as 150 tournaments, and the first woman to earn US$1 million in prize money.

When emergent leaders actively seek leadership roles, it is often as a result of other group members demanding a greater say for specific groups in the organization. In 2000, the US Olympic Committee, often criticized as the last bastion of "good old boys," elected Sandra Baldwin the first women president to lead the organization in its 106-year history. Baldwin, an administrator and leader of the highest repute, had so gained the respect of both male and female delegates that she was elected without great opposition.

When an emergent leader takes a leadership role, are their roles and behaviors different from formal leaders? Studies have shown that emergent leaders significantly and positively affect group performance and generally produce more favorable outcomes.[21] De Souza and Klein have also demonstrated that emergent leader groups tend to be more productive and effective compared to appointed leader groups.[22] Having chosen a leader, rather than having a leader designated, may well make groups more accepting of change and may make the followers more accepting of the leadership.

Post Game

> Leadership is action, not position. *(Davy Crockett, US senator and frontiersman)*

This chapter has looked at leadership and at followers and has considered some of the attributes shown by each. The symbiotic relationship that exists between leader and follower leads to the realization that both are integral parts of a whole. The 1995 championship team Carlton FC in the Australian Football League was coached by the legendary David Parkin. The secret to the success of this championship team, as reported by coach, players and the media, was that the positional orientation of who is a leader and who is a follower had limited validity. Performance requirements determined when an individual should follow or should lead. In that regard, Parkin regularly stepped away from even coaching the team, leaving key tactical decisions to a group of naturally emerging on-field leaders under the guidance of his senior playing general, captain Stephen Kernahan.

Leadership is not the sole prerogative of the person at the apex of the organizational chart. Rather, leaders can be found at the coal face and in the ranks of middle management. Leaders, at all levels, can do much to encourage effective followership by understanding their own behavior and that of their followers. Picking up on one of the threads from this chapter, that of teams, Chapter 4 explores further the importance of mobilizing, leveraging and coordinating the efforts of groups of individuals toward common goals.

Notes

1　G.M. Walton (1992), *Beyond Winning – The Timeless Wisdom of Great Philosopher Coaches*, Leisure Press, Chicago, Il.

2　J.P. Kotter (1990), *A Force for Change*, Free Press, New York.

3　R. Khurana (2002), "The Curse of the Superstar CEO", *Harvard Business Review*, September, pp. 60–6.

4　J. Kirby (2004), "A Conversation with Thoroughbred Trainer D. Wayne Lukas", *Harvard Business Review*, May **82**(5): 49–54.

5　M. O'Brien (1987), *Vince – A Personal Biography of Vince Lombardi*, William Morrow, New York, p. 88, p. 104.

6　J.W. Weese (1996), "Do Leadership and Organizational Culture Really Matter?" *Journal of Sport Management*, **10**(2): 197–206.

7　http//www.interstudent.co.uk/displayarticles616.html, 25 June 2004.

8　P. Mazany (1995), *Team Think: Team New Zealand*, Vision Plus Developments, Auckland, NZ.

9　G.A. Yukl (1989), *Leadership in Organizations*, (2nd edn), Prentice Hall, Englewood Cliffs, NJ.

10　B. Bass (1985), *Leadership and Performance beyond Expectations*, Free Press, New York.

11　A. Bryman (1992), *Charisma and Leadership in Organizations*, Sage, London.

12　J.P. Kotter (1999), *On What Leaders Really Do*, Harvard Business School Press, Boston, MA.

13　I. Chaleff (2002), *The Courageous Follower, Standing Up To and For Our Leaders*, (2nd edn), Berrett-Koehler, San Francisco.

14　http://www.chelseafc.com/article.asp?id=206540 2 June 2004.

15　http://www.chelseafc.com/article.asp?id=210270 23 June 2004.

16　S.E. Jackson, K.E. May and K. Whitney (1995), "Understanding the Dynamics of Diversity in Decision Making Teams", in R. Guzzo and E. Salas (eds), *Team Effectiveness and Decision Making in Organizations*, Jossey-Bass, San Francisco, pp. 204–61.

17　J. Lawton, "Big Phil's Big Lesson – Don't Pander to the Star System", *Independent*, 27 June 2004.

18　M. Hammer and J. Champy (1993), *Re-enginering the Corporation – A Manifesto for Business Revolution*, Harper Business, New York.

19　J. Lyons, "A Leaf out of an Olympic Coach's Manual on Tackling Challenges", *Australian Financial Review*, 3 September 2002, p. 50.

20　C. Gilson, M. Pratt, K. Roberts and E. Weymes, (eds) (2001), *Peak Performance – Business Lessons from the World's Top Sports Organizations*, Profile Books, London.

21　E.P. Hollander (1985), "Leadership and Power" in G. Lindzey and E. Aronson (eds), *Handbook of Social Psychology* (3rd edn), Random House, New York.

22　G. De Souza and H.J. Klein (1995), "Emergent Leadership in the Group Goal-setting Process", *Small Groups Research*, **26**: 475–86.

CHAPTER 4

Team of Champions or a Champion Team? Leading Teams

One man can be a crucial ingredient on a team, but one man cannot make a team. (KAREEM ABDUL-JABBAR, FORMER NBA PLAYER)

The imperatives associated with leading sport teams have often been considered a metaphor for leading any team to success. Teams are commonplace in most organizations, precisely because the ability to leverage and mobilize the collective knowledge of employees has long been accepted as prudent management and sound leadership. The use of well-organized teams has been linked to improvements in business innovation, productivity and levels of customer service. This chapter therefore seeks to demonstrate the value and importance of effective team leadership, as illustrated by the plethora of sporting metaphors used to describe the process. It will also observe that while collective identification lies at the heart of team development, a critical fault of many team leadership approaches is their intentional or implicit advice to completely suppress individuality in favor of the collective. While the team is naturally more important than any individual, we shall point out the critical nature of the individual contribution in sport teams and the subtle but dynamic tension that exists between variables within the continuum spanning from the individual to the "groupthink" cult.

As organizations flatten their structures and abolish the hierarchies that are inherent in bureaucratic designs, the leadership of comparatively small and responsive groups or teams, rather than large unwieldy departments, has become something of a fashionable new imperative for organizational success. As both profit-seeking corporations and not-for-profit organizations, such as government bodies, introduce hybrid structures such as networks in place of product- or function-based departments, the importance of teamwork for focused tasks and projects has gained acceptance. It is in this context that sport offers a useful metaphor, because the business environment is becoming more like that in the world of competitive sport. It is fast-changing and uncertain, where a simple change can stimulate a cascade that finishes in chaos, but can equally manifest a sublime moment of spontaneous delight.

Perhaps the most relevant dimension of the metaphor can be found in our own experiences and fantasies. Most of us have at some point engaged in sport, and we have seen and felt for ourselves the impact that teamwork and leadership can have on success. There is no need to labour the point when it comes to sport. Even though it is sometimes in the faintest (sometimes sublimated) shadows of our memories, we can still remember that goal, that feeling, that day. Whether of glory or humiliation, the memories are powerful because they embody the team leadership lesson: Good or bad, it did not have to be like that, but for the role of the leader. Teams are universal characteristics of human civilization. We are not solitary animals; we need social interaction and a sense of worth and value.

Meaning is the currency of team success, and meaning comes from identity and belonging, the benchmark for which can be found in great sport teams. Teams are tribal in nature. The most powerful clans are family based, bound in blood and the recognition of a common destiny. From this platform the team can yield more than the sum of its parts. Great sporting teams exhibit emergence; they show spontaneous innovation that brings competitive advantage and sustainable success. In other words, a champion team is superior to a team of champions. But, as we will discuss, this does not mean that individuals are not important.

> Gentlemen, it is better to have died as a small boy than to fumble this football. (John Heisman, American football coach)

From sport we appropriate four characteristics that we use to tackle team leadership in this chapter:

1. Its approach to membership. We consider the importance of team construction and composition, including its key positions and members.
2. Its unparalleled ability to generate a sense of membership and belonging. We discuss the critical nature of cultivating this powerful force.

3. Sport's precisely determined structures, systems and boundaries. We use these as a foundation for highlighting the structural dimensions that frame the team and its leader's intentions.
4. Sport's uncommon degree of ritualization. We examine the need for institutionalization and enculturation while maintaining a critical balance between the needs of the individual and those of the team.

The chapter concludes by illustrating how these elements can collectively foster a culture of success, productivity, innovation, and responsiveness.

When representative teams are brought together as the best of the best, they often disappoint. The problem is not a lack of skill or even hunger to win; it is, of course, a matter of teamwork. And so, champion teams can defeat the best teams of champions. Arguably the most awesome team of champions in the modern times of professional sport was formed to participate in the Barcelona Olympic Games. The question was never whether it was going to win – it always was – but by how much, and that was a function of their ability to put aside ego and personal glory and play as a team.

For once the marketing rhetoric was accurate. It was, in fact, the "dream team". The first and probably only genuine US basketball dream team effortlessly won the gold medal at the 1992 Olympics in Barcelona and acquired more press off the court than any other Olympic competitors. Coach Chuck Daly described it like Elvis and the Beatles put together; like traveling with 12 rock stars. The team represented the who's who of basketball in the era: Michael Jordan, Larry Bird, and Magic Johnson. Add in the uncompromising Charles Barkley, centers David Robinson and Patrick Ewing, power forward Karl Malone, playmakers Scottie Pippen, Chris Mullin and Clyde Drexler, with on-court general John Stockton as point guard.

But in the end, the legacy of the dream team was more than basketball prowess. Although its domination, which resulted in the defeat of its eight opponents by an average of 44 points, was breathtaking, it was the teamwork which was sublime. Coach Chuck Daly had infused the star group with a work ethic and sense of equality that had a strong cohesive effect. He insisted that the team rotate its starting five, avoiding the stigma of being relegated to the bench for any of the stars. Not known for aggression or flashy tactics, Daly emphasized the importance of a collective vision and the need to put individual glory aside for national honor.

The team met Daly's challenge, sharing around the ball and points. In the first game against Angola, Barkley shot 24 points in a 116–48 stroll down the court. Jordan came to the party in the next game with 21 points against the skilled Croatians, leading the team to a 33-point victory. As if team leadership had been rotated again, Larry Bird took control in game three against Germany, contributing 19 points, with Karl Malone kicking in 18. Game four against Brazil was indicative of the way the team was playing. Charles Barkley set an Olympic record with 30 points, while six other players racked up double digits in the 127–83 win. Rounding out the pool games, the dream team crushed Spain 122–81. In the quarter finals, a different player again, this time Chris Mullin, led from the front. His 21 points allowed the Americans to easily account for Puerto Rico 115–77. Comprising several of the best players from the 1988 gold medal winning Soviet team, the dream team took the next match against the Lithuanians seriously. So seriously, in fact, that nine of the US players scored in double figures, helping to record a 127–76 birth into the finals. Once again the on-court leadership rotated, Michael Jordan shooting 22 points with Barkley 17 and Ewing 15, in the gold medal winning 117–85 game.

Spare a thought in all of this for star-struck Christian Laettner, the sole college player the rules specified had to be included in the otherwise all-professional side. It is perhaps indicative of the team's leadership both from Chuck Daly and the superstars themselves, that Laettner was given court time at all. In fact, he scored a total of 38 points at an average of 4.8 per game for the tournament, with some solid rebounding as well. The nature and boundaries of the team had been set effectively by Daly, who had brought the group of basketball rock stars together and, recognizing their status and experience, threw the responsibility for on-court leadership back to them. And they responded in a way that showed that they were not made of ego alone. Perhaps they had done it all before and had nothing left to prove other than the ability to play together? Perhaps they were each leaders who knew that success depended on the team rather than any one player?

Chuck Daly commented presciently that while there would be future professional teams competing, there would never be another team like this one. And he was right. One recent incarnation of the dream team skulked off the court after finishing sixth in the 2002 World Basketball Championship, by most commentators' assessments, a B squad, and hampered by only two weeks of practice together. The Athens 2004 dream team took the bronze and looked as though they had no idea how to work together as a team, given that individually they were the best players in the tournament.

Building Teams: Key Positions and Players

It has taken a long time for businesses to realize the usefulness of team structures for productivity and morale. Up until the end of World War II, few organizations employed groups or teams to undertake complex tasks, instead focusing their efforts on the "scientific" management approach, which emphasized specialization. The ideas of teams and teamwork, although commonplace in sport, were not to be found in business literature until the late 1970s. In this sense it is surprising that sport teamwork has not stimulated direct parallels with business until more recently.

The essence of the first team leadership lesson contained in this section is easy to distil. Successful sport teams have worked out the best ways of building teams. Because professional sport teams are so used to changing their lists regularly, they have been quick to recognize the need to identify key roles. There are key position players, stars, support roles, specialists and rookies. All of these play a role and it is unwise to expect that they all contribute equally. Unlike their business counterparts, team leaders in sport are prepared to structure and build a team around their needs and the key skills of members.

What are teams? And what is team leadership? Teams are small in size, typically between five and fifteen people, are composed of members with complementary skills, have a purpose, a set of performance goals, a common approach, and hold assumptions of mutual accountability.[1] However, of all its characteristics, a team's leader communicates more about the team than any other. Aside from the fact that the leader determines many of the key features of the team's activities and boundaries, they also distinguish a team from a group. A leader transforms uncoordinated effort into cooperative action. Team leadership therefore, encompasses the behavioral management of a group brought together for a purpose. This can be achieved through any number of different styles. Take, for example, the approach of Alf Ramsay, who led England to World Cup victory. His reported army sergeant style was uncompromising in the best British tradition. Alternatively, consider the gentlemanly confidence of English cricket legend W.G. Grace, whose charisma was a rallying cry for his team. Both leaders succeeded within the same cultural context, but with totally different approaches.

At the same time, team leadership goes well beyond mere style or approach. In the first instance, it involves constructing the team itself, and as we discuss in the following sections, cultivating a collective identity, determining the structural characteristics, and reinforcing the patterns of thinking and behavior that are desired. However, in this section, we begin with the simple questions: What are the driving motivations of leaders of teams and their members, and why are team leaders so important?

> The world has but three sports: Bullfighting, Mountain Climbing, and Motor Racing. All the rest are merely games. *(Ernest Hemingway, author)*

Power and Status

Success and failure in our lives are inextricably linked to the state of life around us. Often, we interpret the decisive forces to be those operating around and outside our direct influence. For the successful, this means that the world (of both business and sport) is essentially structured appropriately, while for those still hungry for success, it represents a world requiring change. But discontent, as Eric Hoffer once pointed out, invariably creates a desire for change.[2] Other factors have to play a role as well, before discontent turns to action. Of these, the most important is a sense of power. It is to acquire this sense of power that people are attracted to join teams, notwithstanding the fact that in the business environment sometimes people are forced to join.

The acquisition of personal power (and success) is the driving motivation and hope of all team recruits. This is why the leader is so important. Leaders represent that compelling taste of power, which when tied up in some new and irresistible concept, doctrine, method, technique or approach, and allied to a sense of discontent about previous or alternative possibilities, promises a changing of the guard and great prospects for the future. In the end, this is why a team of champions cannot succeed in the longer term. They will be unable to sublimate their leadership drive for an extended period, as they acquire some of their power through a followership. Leaders play the failsafe director of this new motion picture. Like Douglas Jardine who offered a way of stopping the batting domination of the greatest cricketer ever, Donald Bradman, through the bodyline series of 1932–3, the leader represents the future, the opportunities, and the acquisition of power. To counter the batting supremacy of Bradman, Jardine devised a tactic later to become known as "bodyline," which involved the use of dangerous, short-pitched bowling that aimed directly for the body or head. Had it been employed in baseball, the bench would have cleared for an all-in brawl in the first innings.

Leaders therefore have to show recognition to their team, while yearning for legitimacy in return. If leaders cannot offer this symbolism, they will be unable to galvanize the group into a cohesive team. In the struggling cricket teams of England and the West Indies, the team captaincy has been passed around waiting for the person who can deliver this allegory. Unfortunately, sport teams sometimes go wrong in this area, assuming that a leader can achieve cohesion and on the field performance overnight.

> As a manager, you always have a gun to your head. It's a question of whether there is a bullet in the barrel. *(Kevin Keegan, football player and former England manager)*

Looking at successful sport teams is useful in helping to identify the kinds of members and the respective contributions that are needed. Successful sport teams are not made up exclusively of superstars, and when national sides are put together it often takes considerable time for the team to work well together. It is not necessarily the team that looks best on paper that performs the best. Chelsea, in the English Barclays Premiership, has been a good example of this for years. A paper-based assessment of the skills and experiences of Chelsea's players indicate that it should have finished many seasons far in advance of other teams which have worked more favorably together. Their current success is overdue.

A Sporting Perspective

Based on sport, we can specify a number of characteristics that are attractive in prospective team members. Naturally, few individuals possess all these elements, but the more the better.

1. Experience is advantageous, particularly from playing in important games. It is important to find the business equivalent of "big-game" veterans, but not too many. Sometimes experience can be a handicap when team members bring with them a vivid appreciation of the pain and sacrifice associated with success. There is sometimes value in youthful naivety.
2. The ability to solve problems rapidly and spontaneously make something happen from "nothing" should be sought. Good team players can stimulate a significant opportunity from a mundane beginning.
3. Ideal team members are pressure-oriented. In other words, they perform best when placed in difficult circumstances, with stringent demands on time and quality.
4. They are action-focused, willing to experiment and innovate. Veterans in both sport and business can become conservative. While one or two members of this kind can be advantageous for risk management, a cohesive team will be motivated by a renewed sense of adventure, often partly through the promise of doing "things" differently.
5. "Thinkers" are essential, capable of seeing activity several moves ahead, rather than just reacting to present circumstances. These are the playmakers of any team.
6. On the field of play, practice and training does not substitute for communication; it is best to limit the number of strong, silent types.

As Meredith Belbin, one of the original gurus of team building, showed, teams based purely on the sharpest or smartest people do not perform as well as those selected with particular roles in mind. The 1980 US Olympic ice hockey team exemplifies this fact. They were essentially a group of anonymous amateurs who defeated a high-profile and seemingly unbeatable Russian team in the final.

The first thing that you will notice when you begin looking at the vast literature on team leadership is the different perspectives on the role of the leader. From various books and articles we can declare that leaders should be visionaries, strategists, boundary setters, advisors, change agents, commanders, inspirers, confiders, judges, supporters, champions, rulers, coaches, builders, mentors, guards, facilitators, partners, rewarders or punishers, reflectors, and analysers. There are also endless typologies of leadership roles. Bolman and Deal's typology has caught on and is as good as any.[3] They differentiate leaders on the basis of the degree to which they emphasize any of the following four roles:

1. *Structural*, focusing on structure, strategy and the environment.
2. *Human resources*, focusing on people and communication, empowerment, supporting, sharing and developing relationships.
3. *Political*, focusing on the distribution of power, monitoring stakeholders, persuading, negotiating and coercing, in order to achieve goals.
4. *Symbolic*, focusing on the theatrical presentation of vision.

There is nothing wrong with approaches of this sort to help to distinguish the varying roles of leaders. The only danger is that they imply that leadership roles are like leadership styles, in that it is something inherent to the individual and that a focus on one approach is not unreasonable. A leader's style can be selective, but roles are not. Roles should be seen like the contents of a job description. It is not a smorgasbord to choose from. Taking on the position of leader demands the discharge of a range of roles, including all those listed in the previous paragraph. The best coaches and captains invest time in understanding how each of their players tick in order to determine how they are best managed. Mike Brearley, a former English cricket captain, spent hours getting to know his players, including their motivations, ambitions, and, most importantly, what they needed from him. The winning Ashes team in 1981 was at least partly a reflection of his investment and a preparedness to play whatever leadership role each of his players required in order to perform at their best.

Team members' roles are more ambiguous. But again we can find some guidance from the nature of sport teams. For instance, specialization is a central feature of sport team membership. Few sports illustrate this better than American football, where each team member plays an important but extremely narrow role toward the achievement of the broader objective, that of scoring or defending a touchdown. The 1985 Chicago Bears are a good example of this premise, where each section of the team delivered. Quarterback Jim McMahon passed effectively, the running attack was powerful, and the defensive team was rock solid.

It is important to recognize that performance on the field of play precludes an individual from seeing the big picture. That is why it is so important that coaches and managers can observe from outside in order to make judgments about tactics, players, and positioning. This is an important structure for the business team to embrace, as its leader is typically part of the action. Where sport has an advantage is that it utilizes a leader on the field of play and off. This is one of the reasons why military metaphors have been so useful for leadership. The off-field leader – the coach or manager – is the archetypal "general", giving strategic directions and receiving tactical advice from supporting assistant coaches and observers (other officers), while the team captain, the "sergeant", busy on the field of play, is charged with the operational implementation of tactics. Business teams have been slow to appreciate the advantages of leaders both inside and outside the action. Most importantly, it allows team members to pursue their specialties while also maintaining an awareness of their broader contribution.

> If a team is to reach its potential, each player must be willing to subordinate his personal goals to the good of the team.
> (Bud Wilkinson, American football coach)

Using sport as a metaphor allows for one further insight that the military perspective cannot deliver. The sport fan or supporter and the army of volunteers that work within sport illustrate another level of followership of which leaders must be cognizant. In the business environment, these potential fans or other organizational members are not part of the team, but may be aware of its activities. They play a support role, and jump on the bandwagon when the team is successful, but do not directly intervene on the field of play. Most business teams do not make use of these potential supporters, instead going about their business somewhat anonymously. These people, however, can make a huge supporter base, which can encourage and elevate successful teams.

Setting Team Direction: A Common Identity

> All winning teams are goal-oriented. Teams like these win consistently because everyone connected with them concentrates on specific objectives. They go about their business with blinders on; nothing will distract them from achieving their aims. *(Lou Holtz, former Notre Dame football coach)*

The study of leadership tends to focus on the post hoc identification of key dimensions or elements of successful leadership performance. There is nothing wrong with this from an academic viewpoint, but it does not reflect the key component of team leadership. The actual practice of leadership is concerned with the issue of identity. From this perspective, the critical questions revolve around members' answers to identity-related questions such as: Who am I? What do I really want? Who do I want to be? Members therefore must grapple with belonging to a team within the boundaries of their personal questions, while the leader is charged with the challenge of forging a set of collective answers. Sports organizations have used this axiom to attract consumers. Nike, for example, has set the benchmark for marketing through sport because it recognizes that it is not selling apparel, but rather a marker of identity. The Nike logo or "swoosh" is a vehicle that conveys a set of mental programming.

Team sports exemplify the notion of collective identity. In Brazil, for example, soccer fans can purchase condoms with their team's logo printed on them. Both Flamengo Club in Rio de Janeiro and Sao Paulo's Corinthians are approaching one million sales each. Sport is the great integrator, where a sense of collective identity represents the base of the team leadership pyramid. Upon this are built common values and beliefs, which underpin the importance of achieving a predetermined goal. These are, in turn, used to build a supportive, self-motivated environment wherein pride and satisfaction come from team membership and, ultimately, team success. Leaders facilitate the evolution of this hierarchy, allowing for a balance with the team's collective consensus. These relationships are illustrated in Figure 4.1.

Underpinning the pyramid is the development of a sense of collective identity, the benchmark for which comes from sport. The key to this is the leader's ability to create a new and shared *paradigm*. A paradigm is a mental model to create the context in which the team operates. In facing Australian fast bowler Brett Lee or Detroit Tigers pitcher Matt Anderson, we would likely possess a different paradigm concerning the ball than a professional player. We would view it as a dangerous missile, while they

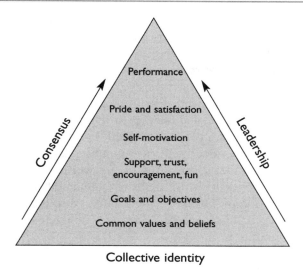

Figure 4.1   The team leadership pyramid

would see it as something to be hit. Paradigms can be remarkably robust and offer the platform from which a team can face a hostile world without coming unstuck. If sport is any guide, leaders should take responsibility for instilling new mental programming into the team. For example, when English Premiership club Arsenal brought out Frenchman Arsene Wenger from Japan to manage the side, he immediately installed a new system of thinking about training. Regimes were restructured to emphasize flexibility and education, particularly on matters such as eating and drinking. In doing so, he replaced the drinking culture with a new set of programming that yielded one of the fittest sides in the league.

> The fewer rules a coach has, the fewer rules there are for players to break.
> *(John Madden, NFL coach and commentator)*

This may sound a little like brainwashing, and so it is, in the same way that our parents condition us from an early age to believe in a whole range of things, from the importance of wearing clean underwear to the significance of particular sports teams. But as adults this is not so easy. Team members arrive with a generally engrained set of values and ideas. Their mental programming has been written, and changing it is a difficult and lengthy task. This is why the most effective sport leaders recognize the importance of understanding what it is that their team members think, before they act.

A universal truth of sport leadership is that new paradigms and programming cannot be quickly forced or encouraged into unwilling minds. Completely new ways of thinking take many years to instill, if ever, and in the same way that marketing messages can fall upon deaf ears, no amount of persuasion will convince those who have already defected. The key to changing the mindset of team members – to encourage their sense of collective association and focus their minds on the team goals – is to accept that open minds are the easiest to fill. In other words, rather than instilling opinion and doctrine into the team, rather than telling them what to believe, the skilled leader articulates the deep wellspring of passion and drive that already resides within the minds of team members. This requires the supple use of many forms of motivation and behavior, always attempting to use the beliefs that already exist inside members, fuelling the flame instead of igniting it.

> If you're a champion, you have to have it in your heart.
> *(Chris Evert, tennis player)*

This can be seen in effective sport leaders, although their approaches are often distorted by the media. For example, the impression most observers would obtain from listening to many coaches, managers, and captains would be that of a frenzied warrior prior to battle. However, this approach is only a small and overt aspect of the leader's programming methods. The coach or manager can place themselves outside the group and promise performance rewards or punishments. At the other end of the scale, captains can build relationships that encourage members to evaluate their contribution through more personal and subjective feelings of fulfillment and personal power. It is a matter of circumstance as to which is the most appropriate at any given time.

Big or Little Picture?

Most leadership focuses on the big picture – vision and strategy. Of course, this is a sensible perspective, but it tends to overlook the fact that human lives are lived in the minutiae, in the everyday and the mundane. Team leadership is as much of the everyday as it is of the crisis; as much Prozac as it is Viagra. This is especially true for teams, which have contact with a leader constantly. Team leaders cannot discharge clichés about vision all day, every day. The stories of humankind can be summarized to a few trite words, if they are sufficiently objective. We each come and go from organizational life, few of us making a substantial difference, and none of us, however important, are irreplaceable. But the leadership of teams cannot be objective because it deals with the lives of a close group of people. Team leadership is personal. On the field of play and during practice, the team captain is as immersed in personal experience as the rest of the team. The fact that a coach or manager can sit above much of this is one of the reasons why sport has an advantage over other forms of teams.

> I am one who dreamed of being *Ferrari. (Enzo Ferrari)*

Team leadership resides in the stories, narratives, and personal journeys of every team member. Teams are built on the collective meaning that comes from being characters in the same story, unfolding together with a common fate. Thus, one of the greatest errors of vision that sport illuminates about the practice of team leadership is that it is about suppressing individuality in order to achieve collective goals. In fact, unleashing individuality is part of developing a sense of belonging. All team members need to feel as though they are accepted for who they are, yet are also part of something bigger than themselves. Fairness is not equality; the more complex the activities to be undertaken – as exemplified on the field of play – the more important individual freedom becomes. It is counterproductive to assume that all team members should be treated alike. Sport reminds us that this approach is doomed to failure. Coaches and captains put their "form" players forward for key roles. Indeed, the greatest sporting teams have always had a few critical leaders, stars or characters that help to define the team. William "the Refrigerator" Perry of the Super Bowl winning Bears comes to mind, along with the *Super Bowl Shuffle*, a video the team recorded before actually winning the game. Other examples are as easy as picking a great team from history: Pele, Jordan, Bradman, Schumacher, Van Basten, Lomu, Wilkinson, Gretzky, McGwire and so on.

Naturally, individuals must make decisions that are best for the team, but if these contradict their own best interests, the team will not last. This stands as a fundamental axiom: All humans join teams to leverage their own best interests. All human actions are motivated by the desire for self-advancement or the fear of losing current benefits. It is the ability of the team leader to harness these desires toward the team objective that defines the level of collective identity that will be formed. For some team members this means using the promise of the carrot, and for others the fear of the stick.

I play with a fear of letting people down. That's what motivates me.
(Johnny Wilkinson, England rugby union player)

Teams achieve goals through leaders. All teams have agreed objectives. These objectives may dictate when a team is needed, and how team members are to work together. Mostly these objectives are hands on and developed by leaders on the job. Distributing the leadership role throughout the team can help to create long-term effectiveness, and a feeling of being needed to make important decisions. This factor also creates member satisfaction and team cohesiveness. In order for a leader to create a cohesive team, the team must be united behind a task, as well as united in a social sense. However, working in an enjoyable social situation might not be sufficient to get the job done. A leader can provide vision and purpose on an organizational level, but it is clear that articulating these is equally as important on a small team project level. This of course, must be underpinned by their expertise in their industry – knowledge vital to crafting strategy and vision.

Cohesion is reflected in the harmony or concordance of a group. It has been examined in many different settings and has been shown to be associated with adherence or conformance behavior, low absenteeism, satisfaction, and effort.[4] However, as sport has demonstrated, a completely cohesive team is nothing more than groupthink. It is not only important, it is essential that the team has conflicting ideas. Debate is indicative of passion, and from this comes creativity. Detachment means contentment and boredom. Discontent is the mother of action. Cohesion, therefore, must be considered from both a task and a social perspective.

Cohesion helps to explain why teams perform sporadically despite improvements to the playing list that should be advantageous. There is a circular relationship between cohesiveness, success, and satisfaction. Studies on sporting teams show that coaches increase task cohesion with training and instruction, democratic behavior, and positive feedback rather than autocratic strategies.[5] The role of motivating support is critical here, and is exemplified by the role that coaches play in stimulating player performance.

A Forged Identity

The sport–business metaphor has led to some compelling evidence that identifies essential elements of team leadership. If a model of team leadership were to be developed from studies, it would be centred on facilitating the empowerment and development of self-managed teams and ensuring quality social interaction in a nurturing environment. Coaches tend to point to skills such as communication, counselling, empowering others, and group facilitation as vital for developing effective teams.[6] But in the end, it is the power of a forged identity that forms the basis of the leadership pyramid, enhanced by the galvanizing force of a common enemy. This factor is exemplified in the greatest teams of all time, such as the current Australian cricket side.

Was the Australian cricket team from 1999–2004 the best cricket side of all time? Under the leadership of Stephen Waugh, the Australian team set a new record with 16 straight Test wins from October 1999 to March 2001. How many sporting teams can claim to have remained unbeaten for three years? During its reign, it also managed to secure 16 Test series out of a possible 19, and two World Cup victories, with Waugh the most successful captain of all time, with a winning percentage of 72 percent (41/57). What was it that made Waugh and his team so successful?

According to the present captain, Ricky Ponting, who took over in 2004, the secret to the team's performance under Waugh was bonding. He commented in an interview that the players were

> doing it not only for themselves, not only for the country but for all of us in the dressing room as well. After every boundary, they would look towards the dressing room, and there was grit and determination in their eyes.[7]

Perhaps another of Waugh's enduring legacies has been in nurturing the players in the team toward individual distinction as well as team glory. This is evident in the fact that every single player in the team has at some point been a match winner. Ponting also recognized that the strength of the team has been its capacity to stimulate someone to lift during a poor performance when hope for victory seems to be lost. In that sense, the defining feature of a great team is its ability to see opportunity when things are not going well. It is the performance during the bad times that counts, rather than the successes.

Ponting described Steve Waugh's leadership style as collaborative but uncompromising:

> He is very easy to approach, and each and every member of the side is asked for suggestions at team meetings. Every one contributes, and that's the way it should be. Stephen is extremely demanding as well, and he is very clear in what he wants from the team. The team looks up to him, respects him a lot

because he is a sort of guy who leads from the front. His own performance has been top class. He is never satisfied, and has instilled a habit of winning in this Aussie side.[8]

> Winning is not a sometime thing. It's an all time thing. You don't win once in a while. You don't do things right once in a while. You do them right all the time. Winning is a habit. Unfortunately, so is losing. *(Vince Lombardi)*

Making Teams Work: Managing the Dimensions of Team Structure

It is the leader's responsibility to create an environment that fosters teamwork, collaboration, cooperation, and cohesion.[9] Leaders can achieve this by providing resources from an organizational or policy level, as well as on a more personal level. However, seldom is it discussed exactly which areas a leader should focus upon. As we have already considered the "who" dimension of leadership in terms of building teams, as well as the "why" in the form of identity, we now turn our attention to the "what" aspect of the leadership equation. In other words, what are the dimensions of organizational life and the environment that a leader should manage with a view of cultivating the collective "soul" of their charges? We use some of the lessons of sport to help frame our thinking.

Specifically, sport teams help us to identify seven areas in which leaders can systematically manipulate the properties of organizational life. We have named these the seven dimensions of team structure, including tasks, time, boundaries, goals, environment, members, and roles. This is illustrated in Figure 4.2.

As the figure shows, there is a relationship between these dimensions. At the heart of the seven dimensions are goals. This represents the core of a leader's actions, and influences all other dimensions, as implied by its centrality in the model and the way it sits on the borders of all dimensions. A leader needs to be aware of these relationships in forming the structures that will bolster their attempts to generate collective identity and build the team leadership pyramid. However, the first step is for a leader to recognize that they can have an influence on each of the seven dimensions and that a lack of policy is a vacuum that is going to be filled one way or another, irrespective of the leader's intentions. This is not to say that a leader has to be highly dogmatic and prescriptive about these dimensions, but it does mean that if they wish to sidestep or delegate a judgment on any issue, they do so advisedly, and with a deliberate intention to create a particular outcome or

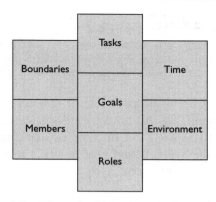

Figure 4.2 The seven dimensions of team structure

context as a result. We do not make judgments about the choices leaders should make, but we do comment on the implications of certain decisions.

Goals are the first dimension to manage. Naturally, this is the opportunity for leaders to set a direction for, or with, the team. These decisions lie at the heart of strategy and represent the marriage of opportunity and capability. A failure to set goals with performance standards will weaken the structure of all the dimensions, as they are all relative to the objectives that are being sought. The second dimension is roles and was discussed earlier in the chapter. The most important issue is that team members' roles are managed and modified in accordance with goals and the capabilities of members themselves, the third dimension. Team members must also be managed with an awareness of their boundaries. Boundaries are the imposed or empowered structures that control the power team members possess and the degree and scope to which they can employ it. Thus, the boundaries that members deal with will have a direct bearing on their freedom and sense of opportunity. The boundaries that are set will reflect the leader's philosophy about consensus, contribution, experimentation, and the nurturing of novel ideas.

Bringing people with different personalities and ways of thinking together into teams is challenging for leaders because it forces them to manage diversity without curtailing innovation or creativity. Teams are also social elements of the workplace. Some people thoroughly enjoy the camaraderie of working with others, especially when working on difficult projects, while others prefer a solitary style of work. It also reflects their views on discipline and conduct. As the business environment further matches the complex, competitive field of sporting play, contemporary leaders have also become moral agents, making decisions about right and wrong well beyond the dictates of law, and making black or white areas of gray.

> The main idea in golf as in life, I suppose, is to learn to accept what cannot
> be altered, and to keep on doing one's own reasoned and resolute best
> whether the prospect be bleak or rosy. *(Bobby Jones, golfer)*

The environment is the fifth dimension of structure that a leader must manage. As sport reminds us, this must include an awareness of the nature of adversaries as well as the field of play, or marketplace. In practical terms, this includes the systems and procedures a team leader puts into place to deal with the environment, such as regular scanning, reconnaissance, and competitor analysis.

Environment is impacted by the sixth dimension, time. After all, environmental circumstances are relative to the time in which events occur, whether it is over a season or a product's life cycle. Current trends suggest that there are many different ways to organize teams in the workplace, including cross-functional teams, committees, project teams or task forces, employee involvement teams, virtual teams, and self-managed teams, all of which can be appropriate depending on environment and time. The last dimension, tasks, is also relative to the time available to complete them. These tasks may vary in complexity, and include the training and preparation that the leader considers relevant.

Excellent team leadership can be found in the McLaren Formula One racing team, formed by Bruce McLaren in 1963. It was immediately successful on the CanAm North American racing circuit and in the Tasman series in Australia and New Zealand. But it wasn't until 1966 that the team produced a Grand Prix car to be raced in Monaco. Two years later the team won its first Grand Prix in Belgium, but was struck by tragedy in 1970 when Bruce McLaren was killed when his car crashed during testing. Teddy Mayer took over the role as team principal, but a merger with the Project Four racing team eventually saw its leader Ron Dennis emerge as the driving force behind McLaren International. The 1980s, with Dennis in charge, proved to be McLaren's time. Driver Alain Prost took the driver's championship in 1986 and the team's success culminated in a season that has yet to be bettered. In 1988, with a Honda engine, the team won 15 of 16 races, split between the two drivers Ayrton Senna (8 wins) and Alain Prost (7 wins), who finished first and second respectively in the driver's championship. Much of the success of this astonishing year was attributed to the management of Dennis, whose leadership style revolved around quality and preparation. His was, and remains, a team of tactics and attention to detail.

What does sport tell us about the best application of these seven dimensions? A sports approach would suggest the selection of structures that maximize flexibility, self-organization, and innovation, with preparedness for empowerment and few boundaries for members. In sport teams, leaders tend to accept chaos and uncertainty as a normal part of the environment; the sport environment is inherently unstable, which fosters a culture of risk taking, support for innovation, and new ways of thinking and operating. It is important to recognize that the management of dimensions should be consistent. It is no use imposing stringent rules in one area, while offering self-guidance and empowerment in others. Team members can be quite cynical about empowerment because they recognize the essential truth about humans: power and hierarchy are forever. There will always be forces that determine the destinies of members. They mistrust empowerment because to do otherwise is naive. As the cliché suggests, nature abhors a vacuum, and a power vacuum is the fastest to fill.

> Leadership is doing what is right when no one is watching.
> *(George Van Valkenburg, political commentator)*

Enculturing the Team: Rites and Rituals

To summarize so far, we have observed several characteristics that are common in the development and composition of successful sport teams. These have included the role of selecting the right people to "play" in the right positions, the importance of cultivating a sense of collective identity, the modification of team structures to facilitate this sense, and now, we call on the final dimension of sport that illustrates the usefulness of the metaphor: the process of institutionalization or culture building. Put simply, this section is concerned with how team leaders can use rituals and symbols as ways of nurturing collective identity and those common beliefs and values that they would like to reinforce. There are two main ways this is done to great effect in sport teams.

The first method involves the management of those readily apparent and observable qualities of a team, such as the physical environment, the public statements of the leader, the way individuals interactively communicate, the form of language used, what clothes are worn, and even the memorabilia that fills the offices or meeting areas. For example, the Los Angeles Lakers NBA team has a unique playbook, complete with signals and patterns that new players have to learn before they are allowed on court. The team is therefore bound into a common fate where their collective ability to adhere to the agreed patterns of play is pivotal to their success. Sport is, of course, the ultimate example of this form of environment management.

One of the most important observable qualities involves the place of past and present heroes within the team. They are culturally rich and are highly visible indicators of the culture that is sought. Moreover, heroes indicate those qualities in individuals which are respected and admired by a wider audience. By understanding the orientation of hero figures, both past and present, it is possible for a leader to map dominant values which may or may not be advantageous for the team's future. Heroes can be both reactionary and progressive. Heroes that reinforce the dominant culture of a team will not change the values and attitudes that it collectively holds. On the other hand, a hero that transcends and transforms the dominant culture will be a catalyst for change in the behaviors and values of the team. Often a hero is the most powerful medium for change to come about in a team, and as we shall discuss in Chapter 7, it is naturally desirable for that hero to be the present leader, which in itself can be a marketing feat.

The second method deals with team rites, those activities that are regularly performed and which tend to reflect shared values. For the leader this means that they have an opportunity to change forms of expression employed by the team, such as certain customary language or jargon, gestures, and artefacts. These rites, which are effectively shared understandings, are additionally conveyed through myths, sagas, legends, or other stories associated with an occasion, and in practical terms may take the form of celebrations of success or social events. Examples of sporting rites and rituals are commonplace but some are really quite odd. Basketball player Darrell Armstrong of the Orlando Magic consumes six cups of coffee packed with sugar before every game. John Thompson of college team Georgetown taped his ankles before every game he ever coached. Joe Louis reportedly drank cow's blood before every fight. But the most powerful rituals are the ones that involve the entire team, like the pre-game talk or chant.

Because meaning is the chief currency of team identity and therefore one of the most important factors for success, leaders need to be aware of the meanings that reside behind the history, tradition, legends, myths, and stories of a team. Where a team is newly formed, with no history to either hinder or reinforce it, the leader must be prepared to fill these gaps with new rites and rituals that underpin a collective vision for the future. If the leader does not actively shape these patterns of behavior, the team will inevitably fragment. Pele's 1970 Brazilian team is considered by many to be the best football (soccer) team ever assembled. Winning the World Cup, the team was certainly successful, its extraordinary forward line comprising Pele, Jairzinho and Tostao scoring three goals or more in every game but one in the tournament (a 1–0 defeat of England). Supported by the pinpoint accuracy of playmaker Gerson and the sublime Rivelino, the team personified attacking strategy. According to Pele, the team had remained fairly consistent for the five previous years, and had become accustomed to playing and working together. Pele's leadership secret was that he was able to keep the group unified for an extended period, his players given the time to mold together to become a group of individual champions who had learned to play as a team.

Psychologists recognize the power of manipulating team behavior through the processes we have outlined in this chapter, and they would rightly counsel that leaders should be aware of the need for a dynamic tension between the power of team collectivity and an awareness of the outside world. In short, leaders that allow themselves to be seduced by their own publicity are in danger of creating cults rather than functional teams. From his review of cult behavior, Chris Robertson provides eight areas of group interaction and team training that must be balanced:[10]

1. Team collectivity cannot give way to *closed systems*. Teams cannot afford to hide from the outside world, and sacrifice competitive reconnaissance and possibilities for new ways of working. The use of twin leaders in sport teams, the captain and coach or manager, has proven effective to combat this.
2. *Group conformity* can go too far, and preclude the sort of individuality that inspires new approaches.
3. *Idealization of the leader* to the point where they can do no wrong is counterproductive to the learning and development of a team.
4. *Scapegoating*, where nonconformists are removed from the team, is also harmful as it can suppress debate and discussion about innovation; some vigorous disagreement is beneficial to a team as it ignites passion and critical thinking.
5. A *charismatic mission* can be pursued to unhealthy extremes, such as the use of drugs in sport, or in working unsustainable hours in a business team.
6. The *denial of shadow* suggests that team members can avoid discussing and confronting the negative aspects of team life, which if unresolved can simmer beneath the surface, creating concealed unrest and discontent.
7. *Group narcissism* reflects a fear of testing the team in an outside environment, and can lead to a group that is exclusively self-referential and absorbed.
8. All teams have *secrets*, which can give power to members in the way they exclude outsiders, but can also turn inward in dangerous ways if the secrets are only held by certain people in the hierarchy.

> If you wait, all that happens is that you get older. *(Mario Andretti, driver)*

Perhaps the true mark of the best teams comes in the form of sustainable performance. With this criterion in mind, it is difficult to go past the Chicago Bulls basketball team in the 1990s. The triumvirate of Michael Jordan, Scottie Pippen, and Dennis Rodman were the most effective offence in the league, with coach Phil Jackson at the helm. The team's performance has become legendary, winning five championships during the decade (although interestingly, the record is held by the Boston Celtics of the 1960s, which won nine NBA championships). In the 1995–96 regular season they won an astonishing 72 games with only 10 defeats. Despite contract disputes, such as when the team owner Jerry Reinsdorf proclaimed publicly that Jackson was expendable, the key players stuck together, Jordan insisting that he would go if Jackson was not reappointed. It was Jackson's leadership approach that was unusual for a sport dominated by egos and superstars. He referred to his philosophy as "mindful basketball", a sort of attempt to lead the players toward self-awareness. In his book, *Sacred Hoops: Spiritual Lessons of a Hardwood Warrior*,[11] Jackson reveals his leadership genius to be less about strategy and more about the ability to construct a team that finds its meaning in the game itself.

> Great teamwork is the only way we create the breakthroughs that define our careers. *(Pat Riley, former coach Los Angeles Lakers, Miami Heat)*

Post Game

Examining sport teams can yield important lessons for business leaders. Specifically, we have noted four major characteristics of the way sport teams are developed and managed by leaders. Initially, we observed that sport teams pay careful attention to the composition of their members. Next, we emphasized that the currency of teams is meaning, which in turn leads to a sense of collective identity. Identity and the power to foster it, we have argued, is one of the critical lessons to be observed in sport team leadership. But this identity and meaning requires structure as well. We specified seven dimensions of structure that leaders should manage. Finally, we indicated that once the leader has made decisions with the team about structure, their collaborative view of the world should be reinforced through rites and rituals.

> The best teams have chemistry. They communicate with each other
> and they sacrifice personal glory for the common goal.
> *(Dave DeBusschere, NBA player and coach)*

The at times chaotic turbulence of sport team activity gives rise to patterns of self-organization, the sort that produce new ways of thinking and acting. In practical terms, change is encouraged when team design is there only to gently direct informal behavior toward goals. Leaders should not seek to control teams that comprise independent professionals. This chapter therefore has emphasized that flexibility is critical to the organization of teams and their ability to develop a structure and working relationship that matches the demands of the game or business environment. In addition, the utility of the notion of the coach who encourages spontaneous innovation has been implicit, rather than the dogmatic and authoritarian supervisor. In the end, while talented individuals can produce their own moments of glory, it is the leader who opens the door to that effortless perfection that characterizes a group of ordinary people who have come together in extraordinary ways. The ability to create the relationships from which groups can be brought together is the subject of Chapter 5 which examines coaching and mentoring.

Notes

1 J.R. Katzenbach (1998), *Teams at the Top: Unleashing the Potential of both Teams and Individual Leaders*, Harvard Business School Press, Boston.

2 E. Hoffer (1951), *The True Believer*, Harper Perennial, New York.

3 L. Bolman and T. Deal (1991), *Reframing Organizations*, Jossey-Bass, San Francisco.

4 A.V. Carron and H. Hausenblas (1998), *Group Dynamics in Sport* (2nd edn), Fitness Information Technology; Morgantown, WV; A.A. Cota, C.R. Evans, K.L. Dion, L. Kilik and R.S. Longman (1995), "The Structure of Group Cohesion", *Personality and Social Psychology Bulletin*, **21**: 572–80.

5 P. Turman (2003), "Coaches and Cohesion: The Impact of Coaching Techniques on Team Cohesion in the Small Group Sport Setting", *Journal of Sport Behavior*, **26**(1): 86–104.

6 P. Kellett (1999), "Organisational Leadership: Lessons from Professional Coaches", *Sport Management Review*, **2**: 150–71.

7 R. Ponting (interviewed by Tapan Joshi), "The bonding in Australian team is amazing: Ponting", http://www.cricketnext.com/interviews1/interviews035.htm.

8 R. Ponting, ibid.

9 J.R. Hackman (2002), *Leading Teams: Setting the Stage for Great Performances*, Harvard Business School Press, Boston.

10 C. Robertson (1993), "Dysfunction in Training Organisations – Power Issues within the Training Context", Association of Humanistic Psychology Practitioners Conference.

11 P. Jackson (1995), *Sacred Hoops: Spiritual Lessons of a Hardwood Warrior*, Hyperion, New York.

CHAPTER 5

From the Sidelines: Coaching and Mentoring

> *Coaching is nothing more than eliminating mistakes before you get fired.* (LOU HOLTZ, UNIVERSITY OF SOUTH CAROLINA FOOTBALL COACH)

There are millions of coaches around the world, thousands of them in sports most of us have never heard of. The fact is that the majority of them are probably not particularly good. As in business, outstanding leadership in coaching is rare. Also as in business, examining the practices of some of the best coaches in the world can elicit some useful leadership lessons. As we have argued throughout this book, the high-performance sport metaphor can add another dimension to the way businesspeople think about leadership. In this chapter, we examine the coaching and mentoring aspects of sport. We suspect that business leaders can benefit from a better appreciation of the coaching and mentoring function inherent in sport because it throws new light on one of the most important aspects of leadership, the cultivation of relationships with followers and colleagues. Sport provides a twist to business leadership that neither exclusively prescribes a command nor consensus approach. Instead, it is all about the relationships.

Our chief premise is that the best sport coaches in the world have developed and managed the relationships with their players and athletes as a priority in their leadership methods. Allied to this notion are three business leadership lessons that emanate from sport.

1. The leader is a personal mentor for athletes and players.
2. The leader is a coach (rather than commander) of a team or group.

3. The leader is in a unique position sandwiched between the performers and the organizational decision makers.

A successful approach therefore needs to align with the capabilities of the players and support staff as well as the ambitions of the owners or governors of the organization. As seen in professional sport regularly, balancing these twin imperatives is indeed difficult, but when done well provides a useful model for aspiring middle managers in business. Leadership lessons can be seen in the ground between operational success (short-term winning) and strategic vision (future development). These three leadership metaphors are the themes of this chapter, and reflect its structure. The chapter is also best considered in conjunction with the previous chapter on teams, although we maintain our objective of allowing any chapter to be read independently. For this reason, the previous chapter and this chapter have some overlap.

> The lads ran their socks into the ground. *(Alex Ferguson, Manchester United manager)*

The Sport Coach Approach

David Conway's research looked at the ways in which project managers can learn from sport coaches.[1] He summarized his findings under seven headings: Roles; skills; performance; motivation; planning; change; and team building. The lessons for sport he uncovered are summarized in Table 5.1, and make for a useful introduction to some of the principles contained in this chapter. We have made some adaptations for leaders in general.

Dan Gable, US amateur wrestling athlete and coach, epitomized many of the leadership lessons highlighted here. Preparation and tenacity were his hallmarks. Dedicated to the level of obsession, Gable was one of the most focused wrestlers ever to compete. During high school and college he remained undefeated with the exception of a single match. He won the National Collegiate Athletic Association (NCAA) title in two weight categories and went on to win a gold medal at the 1972 Olympics. Injury forced him into retirement, but he returned to wrestling to embark upon an even more celebrated career as a coach. By 1977 Gable was the wrestling coach at the University of Iowa, a position he held for 21 years. During this time, Gable secured the most impressive win–loss record of any wrestling coach ever. His teams had a 355–21–5 record including 15

Table 5.1 Lessons from sport coaches for business leaders		
Area	**Coaches' activities**	**Lessons for leaders**
Roles	Play a variety of roles depending on the level of coaching and circumstances.	Need to be aware of the high variety of roles that they need to play. These roles will be determined by the level and composition of the team to be managed.
Skills	Use interpersonal, managerial, and planning skills. Great scope of activity in planning.	Require a variety of skill sets both in planning and implementation. Important to plan to the correct level of detail.
Performance	Use of wide variety of techniques to improve performance. Always innovating and developing new methods. Coaches' performance significantly affects the team performance.	Need to identify and prioritize the factors that lead to performance. Performance needs to be monitored.
Motivation	Players are naturally motivated, but coaches need to channel their energy.	Need to identify what motivates the team and determine effective rewards and compensation.
Planning	Tactical down to the smallest detail.	Awareness of the planning level needed to achieve goals.
Change	Sport by its nature encourages coaches to be comfortable with change. Team members tend to embrace change.	Work hard to get buy-in for change early in the process of leadership.
Team building	Nature of sport allows opportunities for team building to occur.	Need to structure working activities to make best use of team-building situations.

Source: Adapted from David Conway. See Note 1.

NCAA championships; nine were successive. The success was not limited to team performance. Gable's wrestlers produced an astonishing 78 individual national champions, 152 all-Americans and four Olympic gold medals. He even coached the US wrestling team in three Olympic Games.

Although Gable's technical expertise is unchallenged, given his successful personal career as a wrestler, the fact remains that few of the best athletes go on to become the best coaches as well. What is it about Dan Gable that allowed him to shift into a leadership role so readily? Above all, Gable's life is a study in focus and discipline. His parents were strict disciplinarians and yet Gable's father drank excessively. Most traumatic, however, was the rape and murder of Gable's older sister. The event shocked Gable into a focus on wrestling that was uncommon for anyone of his age. It became a work ethic that never left him, practicing seven hours a day for the three years prior to the 1972 Olympics.

After more than a dozen knee and back operations, Gable retired at the end of 1997, no longer able to get down on the mat to demonstrate moves. Recorded in Nolan Zavoral's biographical account of Gable's final year coaching, *A Season on the Mat: Dan Gable and the Pursuit of Perfection*, Gable said: "[Wrestling] is the only sport I've ever competed in that puts you totally in a situation of constant [motion] without breaks".[2]

Gable's focus, technical savvy and rigid discipline were matched by an intensity of character, which added to his legend. He used this intensity to bond with his athletes, mentoring them through the trials and pressures of elite sporting performance. As the following anecdote by Iowan politician James Leach reveals, Dan Gable's leadership style emphasized focus, but also character:

His coaching challenges have not always been easy. I remember, for instance, his first year as head coach at Iowa he had a wide-eyed 118 pounder named Johnny Timid who was more eager than capable. One evening Johnny was pitted against Oklahoma State's defending national champ, Jim Star. Star had a legendary pinning record, utilizing a unique move called the pretzel, which is a kind of double guillotine. Just before the match Gable grabbed Johnny Timid, looked him in the eye, and with his fierce motivational capacity, told him it was important for the team to avoid fall points and that in fact he had a chance to win if he just stayed out of the pretzel. Timid ran out to meet his destiny, which didn't look too promising. Within a few seconds Star took him down, and then started stretching Timid's arms one way, his legs the other in the pretzel clamp. But all of a sudden as the Iowa crowd began to groan and the ref started to raise his hand to pound the mat for a fall, the old Hawkeye gym was filled with an extraordinary "argh" sound. With a flutter of winged arms and legs Johnny reversed positions and splayed Star's shoulder blades to the mat. Near pandemonium broke out as the ref signaled an Iowa fall and Johnny limped off the mat. Gable quickly collared him with the query: "Johnny, how'd you break the pretzel?" Explained Johnny: "Coach, all I know is I looked up and there hanging above me – here, as I'm in public life I'll have to be elliptic – there was this delicate part of the male anatomy and instinctively my teeth chomped." Incredulous, Gable responded: "Johnny, winning is important, but you know it's against the rules to bite your opponent. It's not the Iowa way." "But coach," Johnny responded, "it wasn't Star I bit ..." What, a non-Iowan might ask, is the Iowa way? The wrestling room is a microcosm of the Iowa way – of competition, of discipline, of the dilemma of good choice making.[3]

> When you finally decide how successful you really want to be, you've got to set priorities. Then, each and every day, you've got to take care of the top ones. The lower ones may fall behind, but you can't let the top ones slip. You don't forget about the lower ones though because they can add up to hurt you. Just take care of the top ones first. In 25 years as a head coach and assistant, I think I might have missed one practice. Why? Because practice is my top priority. A day doesn't go by when I don't accomplish something in my family life or my profession because those two things are my top priorities. *(Dan Gable)*

The Leader as a Mentor

It may first be sensible to differentiate between the terms "mentor" and "coach," which tend to be used interchangeably in some contexts. In broad terms, we view coaching as a specific job or profession associated with the preparation of an individual or team for a performance of some sort. In our case, we draw from the obvious source, that of sport, for examples. When we talk about the business leader as a coach, we mean that the business leader plays a role like that of a sport coach in the way that they perform their duties as a leader. It is the duty of the sport coach to build and guide an athlete or team towards winning; the business leader in similar ways is coaching others towards business performance. In the following section, we will discuss what this behavior involves. In addition, we are using the term mentor to describe a *component* of the coaching role; that of developing a personal relationship between a leader and any one of his or her subordinates, or between any experienced individual and a less experienced individual. This relationship has as its aim the improvement of the subordinate's performance and can be achieved in a myriad of ways, as we shall consider next. Again, the purpose is to consider the advantages for business leaders in acting like sport coaches as they mentor individual athletes and players.

Mentoring is therefore an additional tool that leaders may choose to employ in order to deepen the relationships they form during coaching. We are also arguing that while mentoring is an optional extension of the essential coaching relationship, acting as a mentor from time to time can be advantageous as well. Table 5.2 highlights some differences between the coaching and mentoring relationships.

When asked for their secret to success, some of the best professional sport coaches in the world have referred to the importance of creating relationships with their players. Mike Krzyzewski, Duke men's basketball

Table 5.2 Differences between coaching and mentoring	
Coaching	Mentoring
A component of all leadership roles	An option for leaders to develop close relationships with specific, usually high potential, individuals
Usually within line-management authority or team	Can occur outside direct line-management authority
Tends to be exclusively focused on the performance of individuals within their designated jobs	Can be career and life-style focused as much as performance
Recipients of coaching get feedback whether they really want it or not	Interest from the leader is driven by a personal desire to help
Driven by the leader or coach	Relationship needs to be voluntary on both sides and driven by the recipient.
Relationship is contained within job focus, and ends or changes with the assumption of a new position	Can cross job boundaries, and may even continue in a diminished capacity throughout the recipient's career

coach, led the team to three national titles, earning him a status of one the greatest ever US sport coaches. Referring to the ubiquitous chalk boards of sport coaches, Krzyzewski once commented: "We aren't coaching X's and O's, we are coaching people." He believes that the more time spent learning about players the better, as relationships are the cornerstone of success. Krzyzewski argues that this means that coaches have to listen to their players, right down to knowing about their family life, personal relationships, and birthday. This, in turn, builds trust and confidence, allowing players to reveal their fears and performance anxieties without feeling vulnerable.

When a sport coach acts as a mentor, he or she draws on their superior experiences to help the player to navigate difficulty as well as success. For the leader, there are several assessments and decisions that need to be made before acting as a mentor. In the first instance, a leader comes to terms with his or her strengths and weaknesses before engaging in any mentoring. Pat Summit, six-times national championship winning coach of Tennessee women's basketball, believes that example is important. She argues that if she wants her players to be on time, she has to be on time first. Similarly, coaches and leaders have different skills and abilities, some of which might be too underdeveloped to employ in a mentoring role. Despite popular opinion, successful leaders are not more extroverted than the average person. In fact, some leaders are quite shy and find the

people-centered activities associated with their work difficult. An awareness of these tendencies is important to how mentoring takes place.
Leaders also do not always realize that they can be intimidating to some
people. Feedback from a trusted source helps to make a reasonable assessment of these personal strengths and weaknesses.

A second necessity is that it is important to make a conscious decision
that mentoring is appropriate and practical. For example, professional
sport head coaches sometimes restrict their mentoring relationships to key
players, while specialist coaches mentor specialist players. The same
holds in business. A senior organizational leader can only practically
mentor a few individuals, so must make a decision as to who will be the
best beneficiary. Alternatively, the leader may need to request that others
of his or her senior managers will take on a mentoring role. However, an
organizational leader need not take on any protégés in order to benefit
from acting as a mentor on an occasional basis in order to enhance the
strength of their relationships.

In professional sport, players seldom lack the motivation or desire to
talk about how their performances can be improved; athletes are used to
receiving constant feedback about their activities, but in business,
employees may not be so eager to talk about themselves and their performances. As a result, leaders need to assess carefully whether a candidate is
interested and open-minded. When a new trainer was asked what it was
like to apprentice with legendary horse trainer and 11-times winner of the
Melbourne Cup, Bart Cummings, he told the media that it was like
spending two years at university. Cummings did not just train horses to run
3200 meters, he said, Cummings made them *want* to run 3200 meters.
Later when asked what his secret of success was, Cummings shrugged and
replied that he couldn't think of anything.

A third requirement before beginning involves devising a set of guidelines that can be agreed on by both parties. Expectations on both sides
need to be voiced and ground rules established so that each knows where
he or she stands. In professional sport the relationships between coaches
and players can run deep, with virtually nothing taboo, from relationships
to financial planning. In addition, this is an opportunity for both sides to
identify some common goals and standards. This becomes the springboard
for evaluating the success of mentoring activities for both parties involved.

> Managing is like holding a dove in your hand. Squeeze too hard and you
> kill it, not hard enough and it flies away. (Tommy Lasorda, former
> New York Yankees manager)

Mentoring Stages and Roles

As in the formation of teams, many psychologists have recognized that there are different stages of mentoring, depending on the circumstances that have brought the two parties together. It is generally accepted that a mentor needs to play a different kind of role in the early stages of the relationship in contrast to the later stages, especially if the protégé is inexperienced. This rule of thumb can be seen in the sport environment. For example, when a "rookie" joins the team, the head coach, or even an assistant coach, tends to play a more prescriptive role. A new team member with no experience at that level of competition needs more support and direction. As a result, the coach is reasonably forthright in offering advice and suggestions.

Over the first season, the rookie player receives feedback on their performances, which when framed by the coach, emphasizes praise and reassurance. As time advances, and the relationship is bolstered by a firm foundation, the coach becomes more persuasive. At this second stage, the player is encouraged to stretch themselves and take some risks. This requires the coach to be quite persuasive in their communications in order to ensure that the player is prepared to sacrifice some security for the opportunity that accompanies trying out new tactics. This can be the most confronting stage of the relationship, as players can resist asking questions about their own limitations.

As the mentoring relationship sees through the persuasive stage, it means that the player has successfully made a transition toward independence where they are prepared to challenge advice that they might receive. It is at this point that the coach becomes more of a collaborator than advisor or mentor. Together the coach and player consider performance issues, each playing a part in determining resolutions. In a good relationship between a well-established player and his or her coach, this means debate and conjecture. Finally, the collaboration stage gives way to one of confirmation. When Phil Jackson coached the Chicago Bulls, he spoke of his relationship with the senior players in these terms. Jackson did not so much direct his starting five as affirm them, acting as a sounding board for their ideas and coordinating their efforts. He attributes much of the team's collaborative success to the relationships he formed with the senior players, and especially Michael Jordan. Indeed, according to Jordan, Phil Jackson is a master listener who was able to provide confirmation to the world's finest player when he needed it. Clearly, Jackson understands the importance of establishing the right kind of relationship with his charges; skills evidenced by his ability to take the Los

Angeles Lakers to the NBA title, despite the reputations of his two star players, Kobe Bryant and Shaquille O'Neal.

> If you meet the Buddha in the lane, feed him the ball.
> (Phil Jackson, Chicago Bulls, Los Angeles Lakers)

It is not enough that when leaders act as mentors they understand the dynamics of the evolving relationship from the prescriptive to confirmative. In addition, they must be prepared to play different roles – be different kinds of people – depending on the circumstances. Perhaps it is the greatest challenge of good coaches and leaders to be able to switch between different behaviors simply on the basis of an intellectual decision as to what is needed. This is exemplified in great coaches. Bear Bryant, legendary former American football coach of the University of Alabama, was well known for his ability to pace his players and provide them with the emotional and technical impetus for success. Indeed, Bryant became one of the most successful college football coaches of all time without needing to recruit superstars. Instead he developed relationships with players and learnt to read their psychological states. He was the sort of leader who always passed on the credit for success and shouldered the blame for failure. Although deadly serious about his football, Bryant, in a famous (possibly apocryphal) comment when asked to contribute US$10 toward a sportswriter's funeral, replied: "Here's a twenty, bury two."

> You must learn how to hold a team together. You lift some men up, calm others down, until finally they've got one heartbeat. Then, you've got yourself a team.
>
> Football changes and so do people. The successful coach is the one who sets the trend, not the one who follows it. (Bear Bryant, former University of Alabama football coach)

Outstanding coaches like Bryant and Jackson have developed the ability to play the right role at the right time. These roles range from being an educator to a role model. Some of the most common roles that a coach or leader has to play as mentors are summarized in Table 5.3.

	Table 5.3 Roles of mentors
Role	**Description of leaders' tasks**
1. Educator	To provide information about "how things work", including the roles of other team members. Leaders may share anecdotes and experiences from their past to illustrate.
2. Guide	To decipher and interpret situations and events that require inside knowledge or experience, but which are essential to know in order to stay out of trouble.
3. Counselor	To offer a trusting and confidential environment in which someone can share information they consider personal.
4. Motivator	To encourage an individual's inner drive and ambition toward success or toward achieving a particular goal that they may not be sufficiently prepared for psychologically.
5. Role Model	To behave as an example of the values, beliefs and practices that would be advantageous for the protégé to duplicate.
6. Champion	To create opportunities for the protégé that they may otherwise have missed by promoting their skills and value to others.
7. Technician	To give technical feedback about how to develop performance in the future.
8. Assessor	To highlight the shortcomings and strengths of an individual's performances.
9. Advisor	To make suggestions about decisions and foreshadow the implications of each based on experience.
10. Partner	To act in concert with the protégé as an equal on a project toward a common goal.

Developing Relationships

This chapter would be incomplete without mention of the essential pre-requisites of a successful relationship between mentor and protégé. Although often mired in cliché, issues such as trust, respect, esteem, loyalty, and commitment are worthy of mention. Undoubtedly, these characteristics are commonplace in successful elite sport, and there are plenty of examples offered in other books about lessons from sport, without going into much detail here. To choose one great coach who made the characteristics mean more than just a cliché, it is difficult to go past John Wooden, Basketball Hall of Fame member as both player and coach. After a successful career at Purdue University where he gained recognition as an all-American, Wooden became a successful high school coach achieving a record of 218–42. Despite the interruption of World War II, Wooden coached at Indiana State University then took over as head coach at

UCLA. Here he reset the record books, winning 665 games including ten NCAA titles, of which seven were consecutive. Wooden claimed that he recruited based on character and emphasized trust and respect. Noteworthy is John Wooden's seven point creed, passed onto him by his father Joshua on graduation from grammar school:

1. Be true to yourself
2. Make each day your masterpiece
3. Help others
4. Drink deeply from good books
5. Make friendship a fine art
6. Build a shelter against a rainy day
7. Pray for guidance and give thanks for your blessings every day.

A famous quotation from Wooden encapsulates his approach to coaching and leadership: "It's what you learn after you know it all that counts."

There is no shortage of these character-driven assessments of great coaches and their philosophies, the majority of which are written by the coaches themselves. They are undoubtedly inspiring, if difficult to emulate. For readers seeking a coaching "classic", we recommend *Sacred Hoops* by Phil Jackson, *Wooden* by John Wooden, *The 12 Leadership Principles of Dean Smith* by David Chadwick and *Joe Torre's Ground Rules for Winners* by Joe Torre.[4] Dean Smith was the coach of the North Carolina men's basketball team and remains the "winningest" college sport coach ever. Joe Torre is the manager of the New York Yankees. Each of these books is filled with "war" stories and to the point advice for leaders.

The implications of a lack of trust and respect go without saying. In the words of Allen Iverson after the not so dream team – the Athens Olympic Games US basketball team – returned with a bronze instead of the anticipated gold: "You can't just show up at a basketball game because you have U.S.A. across your chest and feel like you're going to win the basketball game."

> A coach is someone who can give correction without causing resentment.
> *(John Wooden, former UCLA men's basketball coach)*

The Leader as a Coach

There is a perception from outside sport that the most important role of the coach is to be a great motivator and a never-ending source of inspiration. This generally translates into an assumption that brilliant coaches are all charismatic speakers, blessed with energy and an engaging turn of phrase. While there are certainly many charismatic coaches in professional sport, few of them attribute their success to how they yell at their players prior to performance. Instead, most coaches who have enjoyed sustained success are more circumspect about their roles. Many, as we noted in the previous section, counsel that relationships with players are paramount, but they also tend to observe that they have a responsibility to create an environment where winning is a habit. Screaming at players has its place, but it does not replace infrastructure, planning, and training. In any case, as English football great turned coach Sir Bobby Robson once remarked: How do you motivate 11 millionaires? The fact is coaches cannot motivate players continuously; they have to find their own inner drive.

> The first ninety minutes of a football match are the most important. *(Bobby Robson, former Newcastle United coach and former England manager)*

High-performance sport coaches, whether for teams or individuals, hold four key responsibilities that are relevant to business leaders when it comes to building the foundations of success. They have first, to envision strategy; second, offer support; third, develop skills; and fourth, provide structure. Each of these is worthy of further comment.

Coaches have to provide direction. This has to occur at the strategic level so that all members of the team understand the bigger picture, as well as at the tactical level where the coach must match the capabilities of the team against their opponents and the conditions under which the game is played. Since we have discussed the importance of vision making in the previous chapter, we shall not go further here other than to reinforce the importance of an overarching vision, performance measures, timelines and markers, and appropriate rewards, as prerequisite infrastructure.

> All winning teams are goal-oriented. Teams like these win consistently because everyone connected with them concentrates on specific objectives. They go about their business with blinders on; nothing will distract them from achieving their aims. *(Lou Holtz, former Notre Dame football coach)*

The second aspect of infrastructure a coach needs to provide is emotional support. Whether it is from the coach (potentially in the form of mentoring), an assistant coach or a sports psychologist, elite athletes need an outlet for the psychological and emotional pressure they experience as a result of demanding training and performing to the expectations of fans. In the business context this translates to the opportunity for team members to debrief after periods of heavy effort or after major projects. Sometimes in the business setting this can largely be achieved by giving team members a sense of closure when a project reaches a conclusion. This includes an assessment of performance through predetermined performance measures. Unless an emotional and psychological debriefing can occur regularly, performance stresses find their way into the personal lives of team members. It is the leader's responsibility to ensure that this does not occur. Business leaders can benefit from a reminder of the effort to which coaches go to look after their players. While from the outside it looks as though coaches pander to the whims of a bunch of overpaid babies, the pressure of professional sport is immense, and managing this stress through support is essential. Business has been slow to recognize that stress significantly diminishes the value of organizations' most valuable assets.

> You have to listen to develop meaningful relationships with people ... You can't do that by talking. You do that by listening. What I have learned is, coaching is not all about me going into a locker room and telling them everything I know about basketball. It's a matter of knowing how they think and feel and what they want and what's important in their lives. Listening has allowed me to be a better coach.
> *(Pat Summitt, Tennessee women's basketball coach)*[5]

The third responsibility of coach-leaders is the skill development of their players. However, by the time they are coaching professional athletes, the skill development side of the job has diminished. This is probably also the case in business. As a result, coach-leaders must manage the strengths and weaknesses of their team. Perhaps the most useful lesson from sport here is the importance of capitalizing on strengths, without spending too much time on weaknesses. No team wins by focusing mainly on their weaknesses. Instead, great coaches win by turning strengths into major competitive advantages.

> A particular shot or way of moving the ball can be a player's personal signature, but efficiency of performance is what wins the game for the team.
>
> Being a part of success is more important than being personally indispensable.
>
> Being ready isn't enough; you have to be prepared for a promotion or any other significant change. *(Pat Riley, former coach Los Angeles Lakers, Miami Heat)*

The final responsibility of a coach-leader is to provide the structures with which to ensure that the team can systematize the habits that will develop their championship qualities. This includes the provision of necessary equipment and facilities, systems to support strategic and tactical innovation, emotional support, and skill development. In the end, structural responsibilities boil down to systematic preparation. UCLA Bruins men's basketball coach John Wooden was the master of preparation. He even admits that he did not do a lot of coaching during the game. His players were so well schooled that they always knew what to do. Bobby Knight, another extraordinarily successful US college basketball coach and 1984 Olympic gold medal team coach, was renowned for his discipline in preparing his players.

> The will to succeed is important, but what's more important is the will to prepare. *(Bobby Knight, former Indiana University and US Olympic team coach)*

Embracing these four responsibilities tends to imply that good coaching and leadership are universal in application. This does not necessarily mean that coaches can shift between different sports without the technical expertise that goes with it, but it does suggest that there is some "universal" infrastructure that coaches need to supply. It is interesting to note that moving between sports is considered highly unusual for coaches, but moving between different forms of business is viewed as quite normal for business leaders. As we noted earlier in this book, the change of context might not be as easy to manage as business leaders assume. Either this is because the technical complexities of different businesses are smaller than between different sports, or good sport coaches would tend to be good irrespective of the sport they worked in. While we cannot resolve this issue, we do believe there is enough evidence to suggest that the four dimensions of infrastructure mentioned previously are necessary but not sufficient for coaching or leadership success.

Leadership Transferability

Sir Clive Woodward, former England rugby union coach and leader of the 2003 World Cup winning squad, takes the view that both good leadership and coaching are completely transferable. For example, Woodward argues that he ran the England team as a professional business. His sole aim when he assumed the position of head coach was to make England the best team in the world, a declaration that was ridiculed by the press at the time.

According to Woodward, his coaching leadership was characterized by five rules:

1. *Enjoyment:* Fun and pleasure are essential aspects of high performance.
2. *Critical non-essentials:* The thousands of minor details that can make coaching laborious and boring, but if handled well can make the difference between success and failure.
3. *Think differently:* There are no rules to innovation and success necessitates thinking laterally in order to find sources of competitive advantage.
4. *Understand your customer:* Without a basic understanding of who you serve and why, success is impossible.
5. *Understand your team:* In order to understand the team, a leader has to be part of it and work with it to achieve results.[6]

Certainly, Woodward's activities as a coach were always embellished with innovative approaches. When tired of the uninspiring rooms at Twickenham, he invited the television program *Changing Rooms* to give it an upgrade. Similarly, as a part of the psychological process of changing the team's poor performances at the outset of the second half of games, he had the team put on a fresh set of gear to give them the feeling of starting a new game in the second half. Woodward also introduced the use of ice baths to speed recovery and eye exercises to enhance peripheral vision and reaction times. Not all the innovations were Woodward's idea, however. He practiced what he preached in terms of being part of the team, rather than just its director. On his first day as coach, Woodward reported that there was chaos, with player's phones constantly going off. Instead of ordering the players to turn them off, he simply asked the team to talk over the problem amongst themselves and return to him with a solution. The team resolved that phones must not enter the changing rooms and had to be kept in the hotel or car. The rule was so successful it stood for the entire period of Woodward's reign as coach. On occasions when the rule was broken, the players considered it their responsibility to issue a reprimand.

Perhaps the most interesting aspect of Woodward's coaching leadership approach is his philosophy that excellent leadership is completely transferable. This perspective is perhaps behind his recent resignation as England coach, and suggestions that he would like to transfer to football (soccer), his true sporting passion. Although at the time of writing, Woodward has only been linked to a possible but unconfirmed position with Southampton FC, he has hinted that the job he really wants is with the England side, presently occupied by Sven Goran Eriksson. This is consistent with his preference to be seen as a "manager" rather than just a "coach." As journalist Gerard DeGroot observed, though, coaching success can often be short-lived.[7] Consider the fortunes of Detroit Pistons coach Larry Brown. He had shown how a cohesive team of solid players could beat the team of individual champions, when the Pistons gave the Los Angeles Lakers a basketball lesson in the 2004 NBA finals, only to find himself with the other side of the equation with the latest and not so greatest dream team in Athens. The twist is also ironic in that Los Angeles Laker's coach Phil Jackson is renowned for his ability to deal with egos, and has succeeded with the Lakers and well as the Chicago Bulls before. Fortunes change quickly in sport, and indeed, business.

Woodward's book *Winning,*[8] is part autobiography and part management handbook, but the reader does get a sense that he is a master of preparation and planning, with an intense dislike of distraction and buzzwords. In a recent interview with Dean Freeman, Woodward spoke of motivation:

> Motivation is an over-used word. You can get into management talk, and a lot of it is bullshit. If you ask how I motivate the team, the answer is: I don't. I don't believe in motivating the team. If you get the right people working with you and for you, you don't have to talk about motivation.[9]

Whether Woodward can successively make the transfer to football, only time will tell, but it is clear that if he does jump into football management, he will employ the same principles that took him to the top in rugby union. Woodward's principal message is unambiguous: there can be no shortcuts to success.

Whereas Woodward employs lessons from business in his coaching, Karren Brady has used the lessons of her own sport in the management of Birmingham City FC. In 1993, Karren Brady became the first woman to run a football club in England when she took the reins at Birmingham City. Although in her early twenties when she began, Brady has transformed the club from the brink of closure to a Premiership team and a publicly listed company with a £30 million turnover. When asked whether there were any management lessons taken from the playing field, Brady commented that she remained opinionated about putting her staff first. From what she described as the most competitive team game in the world, she had learnt that the ability to build a team, nurture, and reward it are the most critical lessons. Brady practices her team-building mentality in player recruiting as well. The club has tended to go for younger, hungrier players who have been given the chance of a lifetime.[10]

> Respect is essential to building group cohesion ... You don't have to like each other. But you do have to respect your colleagues' opinions and decisions, because your personal success depends on commitment to the overall plan and doing your part to make it work. *(Pat Summitt, Tennessee women's basketball coach)*

The Leader as Tactician

One of the little discussed consequences of middle-level management is the problem of being "stuck in the middle." Here, as for coaches, there is a constant tension between strategy and operations. There are imperatives placed on coaches by owners and governors of sport, usually demanding immediate success. On the other hand, there are the imperatives required by players who demand attention, security, and assurance for their development in the future. Moreover, good coaches know full well that in their first few seasons they are the beneficiaries or victims of their predecessor's foresight. In English football in 2001, for example, 8 Premiership managers left their jobs, 15 from the Championship, 13 from League One, and 21 from the 24 clubs in League Two. Of course, some of these managers were promoted rather than dismissed, but in all there were 57 departures from 92 positions. In that year, 45 of the league managers who started the previous season still held their jobs by the end; their average tenure was under two years. It was not a particularly unusual year.

Coaches, like middle managers, must strike the balance between delivering success now and developing more sustained success for the future. Sport in general, and sport coaches in particular, provide us with some excellent examples of failure. In elite sport, coaches can be nice people, technically the best available (former players), but still not leaders who can strike this troublesome balance. Of course, adopting the principles and practices of top sport coaches is not easy for business leaders. In the words

of former English football manager Terry Venables: "If you can't stand the
heat in the dressing room, get out of the kitchen."

> I'm not a believer in luck but I do believe you need it.
> *(Arsene Wenger, Arsenal manager)*

Dan Lyons, Olympic rower and now management trainer, believes there
are lessons to be learnt from sport for the business leader. He refers to a
practice known as race seating, where members of the team are substituted
one at a time. Accordingly, the best teams are not a combination of the best
individuals on paper, and some rowers, Lyons observes, although weaker
than others, inexplicably make the boat go faster. The leader in a boat is
called the "stroke," who is responsible for setting rhythm and pace. In
Lyon's view, the business leader is like a stroke attempting to sense the
timing of the boat in the context of the race and the performance of the
crew. This can all go wrong at any time, however, if just one of the crew
falls out of synch.

During the Athens Olympics the Australian women's eight crew turned
against each other when one rower lay back and dropped her oar 100
meters from the finish line, relegating the crew from bronze medal
contention to being out of the race. Sally Robbins, the rower in question,
said after the race that she had given it her all and could not continue. She
was confident, however, that her teammates would understand if she was
given a chance to explain. They didn't, and the media fight that ensued
was only curtailed when Australian Olympic Committee President John
Coates stepped in. The reality was that the rowing coach Harald Jarhling
was stuck between the pressure of a powerbroker who was justifiably
angry that the sport was being brought into disrepute, and a team that
needed to air its grievances before it would be able to move on and work
together in the future.

> We can't win at home. We can't win on the road. As general manager, I just
> can't figure out where else to play. *(Pat Williams, Orlando Magic general
> manager, on his team's 7–27 record)*

Although it may be a little unconventional in a chapter that has dealt
with reasonably contemporary coaches, the principle that we are trying
to convey has been known to great sportspeople and performers for some
time, so to conclude we will introduce a different kind of coach. The

legendary Japanese swordsman Miyamoto Musashi, although perhaps an unlikely example, wrote extensively about the need to understand the context in which one has to perform, as well as the masters a leader must serve.

Born in 1584, Musashi has become a cult figure of sorts, his approach to self-discipline and pursuit of skill perfection immortalized in a short book, ostensibly on swordsmanship, the *Gorin no sho* or *A Book of Five Rings*, but often reinterpreted as a doctrine on self-realization, philosophy, excellence, and strategy in areas as diverse as art and business. The reason Musashi's book is so extraordinary is that it cuts to the heart of success with an authority and penetration that is unexpected in a volume 400 years old. In many ways, Musashi, by Western standards of morality, is cold-hearted and shameless; unaffected by the needless violence of his era and the deadly imperatives of combat or honor duels to the death. However, it is this absolute focus which gives Musashi's sometimes simple words a ring of unusual clarity. Heavily influenced by Zen Buddhism, Shinto, and Confucianism, Musashi wrote about his manuscript that it was not a rulebook of battle strategy, but "a guide for men who want to learn strategy."[11] He penned the work in but a few weeks before his death while living secluded in the mountains of Kyushu.

> Winning can be defined as the science of being totally prepared.
> *(George Allen, NFL Hall of Fame coach)*

Each of Musashi's five rings is a chapter with particular themes and lessons. In the first chapter, "Ground," he proposes what might today be considered an admirable mantra for sport practitioners and this book in general:

1. Do not think dishonestly
2. The Way is in training
3. Become acquainted with every art
4. Know the Ways of all professions
5. Distinguish between gain and loss in worldly matters
6. Develop intuitive judgment and understanding for everything
7. Perceive those things which cannot be seen
8. Pay attention even to trifles
9. Do nothing which is of no use.[12]

It is easy to fall into the trap of assuming that we live in times of unprecedented change. Actually, most generations in recorded history have proclaimed that they have endured more change than any generation before them.[13] Understanding the importance of contextual forces is critical to managing the relationships that coaches have to forge with their players "below" them and their bosses "above." Musashi lived during one of the most tumultuous periods in Japanese history. It is easy to imagine that the changes he experienced in his life gave rise to many of his philosophies. In times of change, many great leaders have adopted rules like Musashi's nine, designed to help navigate through uncertainty. As in his sixth and eighth rules, though, judgment, and attention to detail are important in a changing world.

Following around four centuries of unceasing war amongst feudal lords in Japan, a series of leaders emerged triumphant, having reunited the land by conquest and sheer power. Nobunaga made significant ground to begin the process, but was cut down by a traitorous aide before he could complete the task in 1582. Nobunaga's most powerful general, Hideyoshi, took up the reigns and successfully reunified the country, but died before his infant son could take over. In turn, Hideyoshi's strongest supporter Ieyasu gained ascendancy, and ruled Japan from his fortress in Edo (Tokyo) with an iron fist. In 1600, Ieyasu's forces crushed a coalition of enemies, solidifying his dominance over the nation. He took the mantle of shogun (emperor) and, shortly afterwards, passed it onto his son. The Ieyasu legacy maintained order until the Imperial Restoration of 1868, but it was achieved with strict regulation of government, education, law, and, most particularly, class.

Ieyasu realized that the only real threat to his power and that of his heirs was from the lords, or landowners. To prevent the lords from organizing, Ieyasu devised various schemes that rigidly controlled their activities and movements. For example, each lord had to live in Edo on alternate years. Ieyasu gave land to extended family and created a network of spies, secret police, and assassins. More important, however, were the social changes. Bureaucracy was inflexibly determined through four classes: samurai, farmers, artisans, and merchants. Samurai held the most status, made up of lords, government officials, warriors, and soldiers.

Despite their honor status, the newfound era of peace left many samurai jobless. Musashi was one such wandering samurai, or "ronin"; esteemed but poor, and caught between the necessities of serving a master in order to sustain a meager living, and the strict sense of honor, discipline, and chivalry that was demanded by following the code of Bushido. Like the coaches in examples earlier in this chapter, Musashi came to appreciate the burdens of two masters. He, like his comrades, upheld the highest values of honor and integrity, but lived in a society that was increasingly bureaucratic and where the weight of gold held in one's purse was becoming the more important mark of position and authority. It is not hard to imagine that samurai like Musashi felt marginalized and bitter about the corruption of their art.

As a ronin, Musashi regularly tested his swordsmanship in duels, typically ending in death. He won his first duel at 13. At 16, he defeated an accomplished swordsman. By 30, Musashi was undefeated after 60 duels. Musashi's dedication to his art was absolute. There are scores of stories recorded by dozens of historians of the time concerning his bouts, the majority of which ended in the merciless slaughter of his opponents. Despite the fact that it is accepted that Musashi abandoned the use of real swords in favor of wooden ones, he still tended to cripple his adversaries. Musashi was known for his slovenly appearance and was interested in nothing but his study. If we consider Dan Gable's 25 years with only one or two missed training sessions to be a remarkable commitment, consider Musashi's refusal to enter a bathtub for fear he might be caught unawares without a weapon.

> Management works in the system. Leadership works on the system.
> *(Stephen R. Covey, self-help author)*

The periods of solitary wandering in Musashi's life were, however, punctuated by periods of war and gainful employment as a teacher of swordsmanship (kendo). For example, he took up against Ieyasu's forces and survived the ensuing massacre where 70,000 men were hunted down and killed. He also became the teacher of several highly important lords, whereupon he demonstrated a keen sense of politics, as both their teacher and servant. For the samurai, like the coach, success meant harmonizing a constituency of two: his lord and his Bushido code of honor.

It is interesting to conjecture whether the nucleus of Musashi's nine rules had already been shaped by this stage. Many successful contemporary coaches like Clive Woodward manage the competing pressures of employers and players by devising ground rules. This way, coaches like Musashi who are committed to certain values, can exercise flexibility in their political interactions. Musashi was prepared to ebb and flow with the machinations of his wealthy pupils' egos, but to break his code of honor was unthinkable, the consequence of which could mean only one thing – death by his own hand. Notwithstanding the contemporary impracticality of suicide for a professional coach (or business leader), the most successful have shown fierce discipline and loyalty in adhering to their principles.

It was around this time that Musashi refined his techniques of large- and small-scale strategy, combining the importance of physical skills with psychological preparation. His psychological tactics are worthy of a modern professional coach. Prior to one duel, sensing an ambush by his adversary's soldiers, Musashi arrived early and waited until it was assumed that he was not going to show up. As they were leaving he leapt out of hiding and struck down his opponent and cut his way through the guards to make his escape. On another occasion, Musashi deliberately arrived late to take advantage of his opponent's nerves. When he arrived, Musashi laid out his opponent with a savage attack, knocking him unconscious with a blow from his wooden sword.

Musashi believed that he had finally understood strategy by the time he was fifty. For us in understanding Musashi's work, it is striking how he balances seeming opposites in tension, from violence to art. He wrote: "When you have attained the Way of strategy there will be not one thing that you cannot understand"; You will see the Way in everything."[14] Accordingly, Musashi was an accomplished painter, his artistic output is today highly valuable.

> Do not wait for leaders. Do it alone, person to person. *(Mother Teresa, modern-day saint who worked with the poor in Calcutta)*

Post Game

While Musashi preferred to be alone, he clearly understood how to deal with people. Action was a theme in his life, but so too were preparation, thought, analysis and meaning. Indeed, we could easily be talking about the spiritual basketball of Phil Jackson. Musashi and Jackson's lives share an uncommon passion for perfecting their art. This kind of "spiritual" passion gives leaders an unshakeable focus and certitude, as we shall discuss in Chapter 6.

Notes

1   D. Conway, ETP The Structured Programme & Project Management Company. http://www.etpint. com/leadership.htm.
2   N. Zavoral (1998), *A Season on the Mat: Dan Gable and the Pursuit of Perfection*, Simon & Schuster, New York.

3 Representative James A. Leach, Bettendorf, Iowa, November 12, 1996.
4 P. Jackson (1995), *Sacred Hoops: Spiritual Lessons of a Hardwood Warrior*, Hyperion, New York; J. Wooden (1997), *Wooden: A Lifetime of Observations and Reflections On and Off the Court*, McGraw-Hill, New York; D. Chadwick (1999), *The 12 Leadership Principles of Dean Smith*, Total Sports, New York; J. Torre (1999), *Joe Torre's Ground Rules for Winners*, Hyperion, New York.
5 Quoted in J. Janssen (2001), *The Seven Secrets of Successful Coaches*, Janssen Peak Performance Inc, Cary, NC.
6 C. Woodward (2004), *Winning!: The Story of England's Rise to Rugby World Cup Glory*, Hodder & Stoughton, London.
7 G. DeGroot (2004), "It's a Different Ball Game", *Scotland on Sunday*, 5 September.
8 C. Woodward, ibid.
9 D. Freeman (2004), "One Word: Winning", *Business Life*, September, pp. 32–6.
10 See www.growingbusinessmag.co.uk for full interview.
11 M. Musashi (2000), *A Book of Five Rings*, translated by V. Harris, Overlook Press, New York, p. i.
12 M. Musashi, ibid., p. 49.
13 C. Grey (2003), "The Fetish of Change", Tamara: *Journal of Critical Postmodern Organization Science*, **2**(2): 1–19.
14 M. Musashi, op. cit., p. 22.

CHAPTER 6

The Flow State: Spiritual Leadership

We are all lying in the gutter but some of us are looking at the stars. (OSCAR WILDE, AUTHOR AND DRAMATIST)

This chapter explores the importance of personal development and readiness as a function of leadership development and performance. It provides a discussion on the psychological mechanisms necessary for individuals to develop spiritually and emotionally as a platform for a leadership contribution. Traditionally there have been few educational pathways for coaches, resulting in their need to develop some of their skills through self-development and reflection. Although the importance of professional management training for both coaches and business managers is undisputed, the advantage that coaches have acquired has included greater flexibility in their work environment to employ different approaches to developing players, particularly on an individual basis rather than one exclusively based on organizational standards and rules.

Sport has long been viewed as a character-building pursuit, but this assumption has been undermined more recently, particularly with the abundance of petulant sporting superstars. Nonetheless, it is impossible to argue with the fact that sports stars are attuned to perform under high pressure and have the ability to manage their emotions in critical situations on the field. This is a gift bestowed on them by top coaches. They learn how to employ the correct emotional perspective and how to cultivate the most effective transmission of leadership messages. Ultimately, this translates into a personal situation that in sport is also described as "the flow state" or "being in the zone." It is at those moments when successful leadership translates into peak performance; playing for the championship, going for gold, establishing that merger or successfully floating the organization on the stock exchange.

Self-awareness and Self-development

> I'm sure there is a champion mindset. I can perhaps describe it as a mindset that blocks out all else apart from the goal or task at hand. *(John Eales, former Australian rugby union captain)*

Although there is a constant flood of books and articles on the subject of leadership, few actively suggest experimentation in leadership. Certainly, they might suggest one style over another style, or these rules over those rules, but few authors imply that leadership may require for some a degree of experimentation. And yet the logic is quite clear. Almost every leadership situation contains elements that are different. All contain what we term "the 6 S differences", that is, in every leadership circumstance, there are differences in the situation, staff, style, surroundings, sacred rituals, and sensitivities within an organization. All must be dealt with in a different manner and a leadership approach that is successful in one arena may not be successful in the next. For some leaders, adaptability is not an issue – it's as automatic as walking. For others, the task is more difficult, yet the ability to change approach, to experiment, to challenge the orthodoxy is essential if they are to become, or remain, a good leader.

By and large, few successful leaders undertake their working life without changing style. For the majority, the leadership style adopted is the one most appropriate to cope with the "6 S" set of circumstances. To determine the correct approach, the one most effective to motivate people, drive performance and achieve success, a leader must be prepared to experiment.

Recall, for example, David Packard, co-founder of Hewlett-Packard, who experimented with, and then totally accepted, the radical concept of sharing profits with employees, John Tisch, CEO of Lowes Hotels who introduced a "down-the-ladder-day" for top executives every six months, or even wartime leaders like Churchill and Eisenhower, who both re-invented themselves as successful peace-time leaders.

In sport, perhaps far more so than in business, experimentation may be acceptable. This may well result from the difficulties in maintaining continuous success in sport. Sometimes, experimentation meanders towards disaster; a football coach trying out a new, but unsuccessful, play. Fortunately, a good leader recognizes this pathway and looks for an alternative route extremely quickly. Sometimes, experimentation is spectacularly successful and the perceptive leader picks up the pace and heads for home. For some, it is this journey of experimentation that leads to self-development and self-awareness.

Percy Cerutty is perhaps the most controversial athletics coach in Australian history. Yet, he was the epitome of experimentation. Although an athlete of some note as a youngster, his story really starts in the late 1930s when he suffered a complete physical, mental, and emotional break-down as a result of undiagnosed illness. What caused his illness is still uncertain, but the likelihood is that he suffered severe migraines and prob-able epilepsy. The end result was that his weight went down below 99 lbs and he began to believe in his own mortality. It was a religious epiphany, together with new medical insights that advised that the medicine for his cure was in his own mind, which eventually led him on a new path. It was a pathway he found littered with different perspectives about himself. He became motivated by continuous learning and self-development.

Cerutty read widely on nutrition and began to understand the new science of vitamins. He eliminated animal fats from his diet and concentrated on eating fruit, grains, and vegetables. He also found that when involved in physical activity, his migraine receded and he felt more capable of dealing with life. Conventional wisdom opposed Cerutty all the way, yet he persisted. When Cerutty decided to take up coaching, he read everything there was to know about conventional methods. He read, and understood, that coaching involved repetitive preparation. Training, he noted, involved undertaking a set training sequence day after day. Cerutty, however, had an inherent belief that there was a better way and, for him, a more successful way of motivating his charges and producing more successful athletes. He was unafraid to experiment and he followed the Franklin D. Roosevelt dictum: "It is common sense to take a method and try it. If it fails, admit it frankly and try another. But above all, try something."

Weight training, the concept of *fartlek* training which emphasized variety in training, resting in the Australian heat before a race rather than spending half an hour warming up, endurance work up and down sand hills, and longer training periods, all were to be tried and, to various degrees, accepted. Not content with simply coaching from a single posi-tion, Cerutty insisted on leading from the front. Cerutty argued that he had to be fit to teach fitness and had to lead to show leadership. He had his athletes working out several times a day, working on speed and endurance. "Run with intelligence, run hard and run often" was the Cerutty motto.[1]

Cerutty, as a professional coach, worked with some of the top athletes of their generation, athletes such as Herb Elliott and John Landy, both mile and 1500 meter world record holders. He instilled in them a belief that to be great, an individual had to be prepared to step out of the ordinary. He constantly used Jesus and St. Francis as examples. In business and in sport, he argued, it was those who sought success who generally competed and the best prepared who generally won. Cerutty's mantra, that if you sought success, were well prepared and unafraid to experiment, then all you had to do was to run by instinct, has become a lesson for the business world.

Preparation combined with a willingness to experiment had given Cerutty a new epiphany. He had become more aware of his own capabilities and with that knowledge came self-awareness and self-development.

Self-awareness includes recognition of strengths and weaknesses, capabilities and needs. To confront it requires honesty and courage. It is, however, often a prerequisite for effective communication and interpersonal relations, as well as for developing an understanding with others. It is absolutely essential in a leader. Cerutty was like many successful coaches and athletes. To achieve self-awareness he had to learn about his own inner resources, abilities, and limits.

> Concentration is the ability to think about absolutely nothing when it is absolutely necessary. *(Ray Knight, baseball player)*

This understanding of one's own capabilities, this awareness of self, is equally important for those few who do not seek or perhaps do not need experimentation. A number of athletes and coaches find one method of training that works for them and stick to it. David Hemery, Britain's Olympic 400 meter hurdle gold medal winner at the 1968 Mexico City Games, was a firm believer in working hard in training but he preferred to train to a routine. So too did Franz Stampf, a superb athlete of the 1930s and a great athletics coach of the 1950s and 60s. First ever to run the mile in under four minutes, Roger Bannister, by comparison, claimed he never needed a coach (although he did eventually team up with Stampf), preferring to develop his own training systems and work out on his own. And he trained for only a comparatively few hours per week.

This diversity in attitude can be seen equally in business. Some leaders prefer to operate by instinct, others will stick to set principles and constantly abide by them, while still others follow the Bannister method of seeking to lead virtually in isolation. The reality is that any and all methods can work. Most leaders, however, really do need to experiment with leadership style if they are to remain successful. The common factor with Cerutty, Hemery, Stampf, and Bannister is that all of them wanted success, all were exceedingly well prepared, and all fully understood their own capabilities. All were, in fact, self-aware.

Psychologists have long argued about how self-awareness occurs – how the self acquires knowledge about itself. Alain Morin suggests that individuals in a state of self-awareness often talk to themselves using words to describe their own personal characteristics, behaviors, emotions, sensations, motivations, and so on. He additionally suggests that individuals who achieve self-awareness also frequently examine themselves by using imagery.[2]

The Use of Mental Imagery

> The manager's job in those days was to assemble a good team. Once he had done that he just let them go out and play. There was none of this blackboard nonsense you hear about today. Team talk? Johnny [Cochrane, Sunderland team manager in the 1930s] used to stick his head around the dressing room door just before a match, smoking a cigar and smelling of whisky, and ask, "Who are we playing today?" We'd reply, "Arsenal, boss," and he'd just say, "Oh well, we'll piss that lot," before shutting the door and leaving us to it. *(Raich Carter, soccer player)*

Many athletics coaches have found that it is possible to change the psychological environment of the athletes under their charge in such a way as to enhance motivation. They use the basic tricks of leadership such as replacing negative responses and critical commentary with a more positive approach thus reinforcing appropriate behaviors rather than punishing inappropriate behavior. They improve teamwork among all the athletes, and they vary practice routines. In addition, they use what they term "mental imagery" or "visualization."

Imagery, in its most simple form, is the mental rehearsal of an activity before actually undertaking it. It might be purely visual, a series of images or pictures in the mind. It might also involve auditory experiences such as imagining the roar of the crowd or kinesthetic experiences involving how the body may feel. Watch an athlete before he or she starts to run or jump. They will often use the time leading up to a performance to mentally rehearse and imagine how the competition will unfold. You can see their eyes close, and their body begin to move. They effectively rehearse all that they expect to occur during the sporting event.

Footballer David Beckham has stated that he visualizes many aspects of a game while still in the dressing room. He mentally pictures every free kick or penalty he might be called upon to take during the course of the game. The majority of athletes in all sports, and at all levels, complete many runs and many jumps in their minds before major competitions. It might be considered as the development of a mental blueprint for the forthcoming event. Psychologists have demonstrated on many occasions that creating, or recreating an all-sensory experience can have significant effects, both on physical performance and psychological functioning.

Imagery can also be extended to include the mental practice of specific performance skills, performance review and analysis, and problem solving. Once learnt, imagery can be applied in many different ways to aid sports performers. The image scenario may be called up in the mind at any time, enhancing a particular skill through repetition or rehearsal. It can additionally be used to manage stress, set and review goals, practice interpersonal skills, and build confidence. To use imagery correctly demands self-awareness. That is, there must be an understanding of the emotions experienced and an ability to manage them. The path towards self-awareness is often difficult, yet it can be rewarding when the destination is reached.

According to Kay Porter and Judy Foster, the effectiveness of visual imagery comes from the ability to physiologically create neural patterns in the brain which are similar to small tracks engraved in the brain cells which can ultimately enable an athlete to perform physical feats by mentally rehearsing the activity to be undertaken. Porter and Foster suggest that mental imagery trains the mind and creates the neural patterns in the brain which teach the muscles the task required.[3]

The opposite of positive mental imagery is negative thought. A number of athletes, especially those less strong willed can fall into the temptation of having negative thoughts about themselves. Instead of positive imagery, they see themselves being beaten by more experienced or more well-known athletes. Rather than optimizing performance, they degrade it. The mind will believe what you tell it and, consequently, it is important to combine visualization exercises with positive affirmations.

Guided imagery can be particularly useful in sport where performance and success can be measured in one hundredths of a second or in centimeters. But the ability to rehearse an activity in the mind is not an action solely undertaken by sportspeople. It is an ability equally useful in business. In business, as in sport, the degree of preparation required to manage stress, set and review goals, practice interpersonal skills, and build confidence is equally high and the need to master a mental state is equally necessary. Indeed, many businesspeople undertake visual imagery without fully realizing what it is they are doing. They rehearse speeches in their mind, imagine difficult conversations with employees or colleagues, or imagine set activities. Studies have shown that mental preparation in business is as important to performance as basic skill and training.

Mental strength is vital for elite athletes. It is equally important for a business leader. Without that mental strength, stress and anxiety can reduce performance and, perhaps, even diminish it entirely. This is clearly understood by most athletes and accounts for their preoccupation with understanding, controlling, and developing their mental ability – their psychic energy. Mental strength, however, can arise from factors other than the formal use of mental imagery. It can arise from within a person, from character, upbringing, and belief. Take, for example, the case of Jesse Owens.

Spirit and Character

> It don't profit a man none if he gets the whole world but loses what's inside himself. *(Harry Owens, Jesse Owens' father)*

Back in 1936, in Berlin, Germany, the XI Olympiad was about to start. Representing the United States of America was a young African-American athlete named Jesse Owens. The Games, more political than any in the modern era, was already the subject of much debate as to whether it should be the focus of a boycott by Western nations. Germany, the host nation, led by the outspoken anti-Semitic leader of the Third Reich, Adolph Hitler, had already cooled its rhetoric towards Jews and African-Americans, but still retained an obvious hatred for those people.

The atmosphere surrounding the Games and the palpable enmity towards athletes like Owens made life more than uncomfortable and augured poorly for the successful performance of African-American athletes. Yet, once the Games started, the young Owens seemingly shrugged off the pressure and claimed four gold medals, in the 100 and 200 meter sprints, the long jump and the 400 meter relay, all with new Olympic records. How was this possible? The answer was in the mental strength of Owens, in his case instilled by hard work, discipline, and a strong belief in ethical values. There's a wonderful quote of Jesse Owens in one of Tony Gentry's books, *Jesse Owens, Champion Athlete*,[4] which says it all. When discussing his races, Owens commented: "It all goes so fast, and character makes the difference when it's close."

Owens was one of nine children. He grew up amid northern Alabama poverty. Never well as a child, he suffered from chronic bronchial congestion and frequent bouts of pneumonia. For Owens, like many other African-American children, religion provided a form of comfort and a stable base from which to face the world. Although that dependence on religion failed him during long periods of his later life, his belief in ethical values, hard work, and patriotism, instilled in him by his father, never left him.

It was, in particular, the combination of his ethical values and his patriotism which, in 1968, led Owens to oppose Harry Edwards, an African-American sociology instructor at San Jose State College in California. Edwards led a revolt of African-American athletes against discrimination both prior to, and at, the Mexico City Olympics. Owens opposed the move for African-American athletes to boycott the Games, believing that it was necessary for African-American athletes to be "everywhere it counts." For his opposition, Owens was ostracized by many African-Americans, but he stuck to his belief that a leader should see and work toward the larger goals, even at the expense of a temporary loss of popularity and stature in the community. The mental strength and fortitude that this stand required caused Owens much anguish and it was not until near his death that he again became a widely respected individual within the African-American community.

The strength that Jesse Owens exhibited is not uncommon in great leaders – names like Lech Walesa, David Ben-Gurion, Mohandas Gandhi, Nelson Mandela, Martin Luther King, and Mikhail Gorbachev spring readily to mind.

It is the larger goals that poor leaders often ignore, preferring instead to capture the "gold" at lower and easier levels. Sometimes, leaders join, follow or lead the pack, not out of a sense of personal gain but simply because they lack the moral fiber to stand up and be counted when the chips are down. Mental and inner strength are essential prerequisites for great leadership, but they often come at a price. Inner strength has an alternative – that of fear.

The emotion of fear originates in the brain as a result of hormonal and neurochemical responses to certain events. It is a primeval instinct. Once released, these responses trigger defensive mechanisms such as raising adrenaline and cortisol levels. They also increase the heart rate and respiration. The medical world refers to this action as the "fight or flight" response. In nature, such responses are meant to last for seconds only – long enough for the individual to fight off an attacker or run from one. The problem, however, arises when the fear is emotional or imaginary. In such circumstances, adrenaline may remain in the body for a much longer period of time and may, in turn, generate anxiety and stress which, in turn, can lead to burnout or emotional collapse.

During the Great Depression of the early 1930s, Franklin D. Roosevelt, the 32nd United States president, said: "There is nothing to fear but fear itself." Roosevelt was wrong. Given the right circumstances, we can all experience fear. It is a basic emotion that fulfills an important role, however unwelcome. Fears, real or imagined, consume many lives and frequently stop us from achieving our goal. Fear has a way of working into one's very soul and once established becomes difficult to remove. Fear is a factor common to many successful athletes and business leaders and needs to be confronted, preferably in a safe environment. For many, that safe environment is within the mind.

In athletes, like businesspeople, pre-activity nerves are a familiar experience. Few athletes have such absolute confidence in their own ability that they can compete without some self-doubt emerging, whether expressed openly or kept hidden. Few businesspeople can go into an important conference or discuss vital issues without some doubts. Occasionally, the misgivings begin long before the activity, possibly even days or weeks before. For most athletes and, we suspect, businesspeople, though, it is the minutes before the start of an activity that pre-event nerves begin to seep into confidence.

Successful athletes face their fears in many ways, by deliberately slowing down breathing, undertaking relaxation exercises, or simply mentally preparing for the forthcoming activity. They seek to gain confidence in their own ability to successfully perform. Many visualize how they will tackle the event, while others meditate or use mind tricks such as convincing themselves that the race is really a normal training run and the outcome is unimportant. Athletes often internally affirm their abilities, drawing on their success in similar situations. Once the race has started, however, it is a matter of focus and commitment.

In business, the fear of making a mistake, perhaps even ruining a company, or simply not doing well enough, is common to many leaders. Indeed, a total lack of nerves and complete self-confidence may even be a little unhealthy.

When faced with extreme stress or fear, many people pray, even those who do not normally follow a faith. This is not uncommon, odd, or incorrect. Fear, of anything, can be faced in many ways, but because fear is created internally, it must be controlled internally. For an athlete, knowing that he or she has worked hard and prepared well is a sound basis from which to fight fear, but it is often insufficient. Knowing also that fear will lie to us, understanding that lie is important. To overcome the fear it is necessary to recognize the symptoms, become aware of its presence and consciously control it in the mind. It is necessary to make fear work for us.

Despite the suspicion that many traditional mental health specialists hold about expressions of spirituality, some athletes confront fear with their personal faith. For many individuals, the positive impact that religious faith can have on their life and well-being is easily and well recognized. Vince Lombardi, for example, considered his own personal faith as the bedrock of his coaching career. Increasingly, research studies in medicine and social sciences, such as psychology, have shown the benefits that reliance on spirituality can have on mental and physical health.

Self-concept and Development

> No, no ... I was not very talented. My basic speed was low. Only with willpower was I able to reach the world-best standard in long-distance running. *(Emil Zatopek, 1952 Olympic champion, 5000 meters, 10,000 meters and marathon)*

Fear is but one expression of doubt within an individual. Doubt and self-concept are intrinsically linked and have been since René Descartes reasoned that doubt meant thought and thought meant existence – "I think, therefore I am." In 1947 Carl Rogers combined the concepts of "helping" and "self," maintaining that there was a basic human need for positive regard both from others and from oneself. Rogers also suggested that in every person there was a tendency towards self-actualization and development, providing this was both permitted and encouraged by an inviting environment.[5]

No one is born with a fully developed sense of fear or self-concept. It is a product of experiences, either gained from external sources or taught during upbringing, and personality. Because it is involved with the self, individuals can have a different concept of their own attributes and capabilities from that held by outsiders. In psychological terms, the idea of "self" relates to a mental attitude which can be accessed through introspection. This implies that individuals can have a much clearer understanding of themselves than can outsiders. As a result of this, it seems reasonable to assume that the most effective method of amending one's self-concept is through an individual's own mind.

With most people, self-concept has developed as a result of countless experiences and provided those experiences have been reasonably normal, the effect is a stable and rational being who has a sound idea of their own being. Often, self-concept determines the direction life can take.

With our target audience in mind, we might reasonably assume that for most people reading this book, self-concept is not a negative experience but an acceptable reality. Intrinsically, most athletes accept this and use their internal focus to strengthen their self-concept, accepting that a positive self-concept aids to the well-being and improvement of an individual. Interestingly, those in the business world often have a heightened sense of self-concept, a greater ego if you wish, yet they tend to rely on outside stimuli to feed and support that self-concept rather than seek self-improvement.

There are a few signs that things might be changing. We noted recently that one company in the United States had introduced a "put-up" box. This box was installed, effectively, to achieve the opposite of the traditional "put-down" comments. This was a box whereby individuals could put up messages of thanks or appreciation that workers had written to one another. It was a positive source of improvement in the self-concept.

There are few organizational behavior textbooks that provide a serious examination of self-concept in the workplace. The theoreticians amongst us would probably argue that the integration of self-concept and the workplace has been around since Maslow's seminal work on self-actualization. They may well be right, but we believe that the fundamental "need" to maintain or enhance the phenomenal self is based on self-image and self-esteem, rather than on the closely related constructs of existing self-perceptions of personal capabilities. At this stage we realize that we are opening a pedagogical can of worms and we hasten to close it as quickly as possible.

What we do know is that there is much evidence to suggest that a poor self-concept promotes poor performance. This is readily seen in athletes. A slight change in self-perception of personal capabilities may well turn a world beater of today into a runner-up of tomorrow. Anxiety, stress, and even anger or concern over performance can become the forerunners of depression. Athletes understand this. So, learning to cope with anxiety and stress is essential.

Athletes frequently use mind techniques when it comes to coping with anxiety and stress. It's probably a result of their constant usage of mind imagery and visualization techniques. They tend to emotionally work through the problem in their mind rather than pretending the problem does not exist. By this method they obtain some form of stress immunization. They employ relaxation and stimulus control procedures. This has the tendency to provide more positive and unconditional feedback which they then internalize to improve their self-concept.

Negative self-concept may be unpleasant but it is not entirely bad. Efforts to improve negative feelings sometimes compel individuals to work harder. Self-doubt, anxiety, and fear can become motivators. They use those doubts and fears to accentuate their strengths and capabilities. The corollary of this may occur with individuals who possess such an inflated self-concept that they believe that any action they undertake is fundamentally correct. These individuals can become totally unfazed by their actions, regardless of how damaging they might be.

Emotional Intelligence

Allied with the notion of self-concept is the idea of emotional intelligence. In this instance, business appears to be leading sport and may well be a positive example for it. Unlike the traditional concept of intellectual intelligence, emotional intelligence has more to do with knowing yourself and having the ability to perceive, use, understand, and manage emotions. Emotional intelligence requires the ability to intermix thought and emotions and in so doing, use those emotions as a form of information. In the language of Peter Salovey and John Mayer, emotional intelligence is "the ability to monitor one's own and other's feelings and emotions, to discriminate among them, and to use this information to guide one's thinking and action".[6]

Not that this is new, of course. Sun Tzu, a Chinese general of some 2400 years ago, commented:

> If you know the enemy and know yourself, you need not fear the result of a hundred battles. If you know yourself but not the enemy, for every victory gained you will also suffer a defeat. If you know neither the enemy nor yourself, you will succumb in every battle.[7]

In writing this, Sun Tzu was merely anticipating the results that were later to emerge from twentieth-century emotional intelligence studies.

The ability to manage emotions has been found in numerous studies to be a predictor for success. The studies have shown that where individuals are happy and enthusiastic, cooperation and group activity increases. Conversely, where there is unhappiness or annoyance, cooperation and group activity decreases. This has implications for team sport and team concepts in business.

> A man who is trained to his peak capacity will gain confidence. Confidence is contagious and so is lack of confidence and a customer will recognise both. *(Vince Lombardi)*

At its simplest, successful emotional intelligence requires individuals to understand their emotions and be able to discriminate between them, to be able to react appropriately to those emotions and use them for self-motivation, and to understand and recognize emotions in others and use this knowledge to handle interpersonal conflicts.

Daniel Goleman, the man most widely associated with emotional intelligence, has pulled the topic out of the scientific arena and has firmly established it in the popular press. Goleman puts the requirements for emotional intelligence more explicitly. He states that there are five competencies associated with emotional intelligence. They require that an individual has the ability to:

- identify and name one's emotional states and to understand the link between emotions, thought and action
- manage one's emotional states – to control emotions or to shift undesirable emotional states to more adequate ones
- enter into emotional states associated with a drive to achieve and be successful
- read, be sensitive to and influence other people's emotions
- enter and sustain satisfactory interpersonal relationships.

Each of these abilities, suggests Goleman, builds on the ones before it. Thus, for example, you need to identify emotions before they can be managed.[8]

Emotional intelligence has some useful contributions for both business and sport. For example, it allows an additional factor to be incorporated when analyzing and making decisions and it allows for negative emotions to be better understood in terms of self-concept. Once negative emotions can be recognized, the opportunity occurs for those negative emotions to be changed into more positive ones.

Arnold Palmer has suggested that the difference between great players and good ones is not so much ability as emotional equilibrium. In sport, an understanding of emotional intelligence may allow competitors to better maintain control, despite the pressures and expectations placed upon them. Athletes like Michael Jordan, Ian Thorpe, and David Beckham learnt at a young age to control the everyday pressures they face, in practice and in competition. Indeed, not only are they able to control the pressures on them, they use those pressures for added motivation. These individuals are highly capable of self-control, and they can, by understanding the emotional signals coming from competitors and teammates, affect the way in which the competition is conducted, slowing it down in one instance and speeding it up in another.

Clearly, emotional intelligence is an essential ingredient for both the business leader and the athlete. Controlling and understanding emotions, both our own and those of others, allows for the maintenance of focus particularly when under severe pressure. Interestingly, some individuals wear their emotions on their sleeves, but rather than hinder them, such emotion often allows them to better understand the emotions that are all around them.

Moral and Ethical Leadership

> Can honesty be honesty, without an ethical conception?
> (G. Koizumi, judo 7th dan)

In Chapter 3, we spoke about the leader–follower relationship. This relationship, we noted, is interrelated and works best when mutually supportive. Effectively, we stated, leader and follower, each possessing different aspects or degrees of power and motivation, work best when working together to achieve a common goal. In working together, the mutual support of a common cause often leads to what William Sparkes has referred to as "a moral relationship" by "raising the level of human conduct and ethical behavior of both the leader and those being led."[9] This, Sparkes suggests, transforms both the leaders and the followers behind a moral purpose, one of self-sacrifice and principled behavior.

According to J.M. Burns, effective leadership requires leaders and followers to engage in a mutual process "of raising one another to higher levels of morality and motivation."[10] To successfully achieve this, there needs to be in existence a culture of trust based on shared purposes, actions, and vision. Unfortunately, achieving such a culture is not as simple as it sounds.

In sport and in business there is frequently a lack of ethical and moral values. We have only to look at Enron or WorldCom to see how easily ethical and moral values are corrupted in business. But sport is no better. Charles Dubin, who authored the Report into the Use of Drugs in Sport,[11] commented that sport was at a crossroads and people must decide whether the values that once defined the very meaning of sport still had meaning in the context of modern sport. Although Justice Charles Dubin was specifically investigating the circumstances surrounding sprinter Ben Johnson's positive test for steroid use in Seoul in 1988, his comments still hold the same validity today. When he made the statement, his intent was to focus public opinion on ethical and moral problems facing high-level sport in Canada. He suggested that the term "moral crisis" was appropriate because the values that once motivated participation in sport such as the quest for personal growth and excellence, the enjoyment of sport, and the pursuit of sportsmanship had been usurped by other values such as those of winning, fame, and money.

In sport, there is a constant interpretation of what is ethical. It varies from nation to nation, sport to sport. For the Australian cricket team, sledging opponents, for example baiting the batsman in order to upset his concentration, has in the past been seen as totally acceptable. They believed it to be a legitimate form of psychological warfare. That it reduces the game, denies sportsmanship, and transfers the competition from the physical to the mental was unimportant. The aim is to win and the method of winning is immaterial. More recently, however, the team has announced the creation of a code of conduct in which sledging is considered improper. But why has sledging been considered a form of strategy and not a form of cheating in the past? Much of it has to do with the fact that in sport, and or business for that matter, society rewards winners with immense riches. Winning consumes all other considerations. As a consequence, athletes are given greater freedom, to cheat, take drugs, engage in violence, and generally behave offensively.

In sport we demand winners. Coaches are sacked if teams stop winning. In business we demand winners. Executives are sacked if profits are down. If winning is so important, then athletes and businesspeople will do anything to avoid losing. That it might mean the taking of drugs or the loss of ethics might be important, but less important than losing. Interestingly, different sports have different cultures. Few would expect to see drug taking in women's netball or hockey. Nor would we expect to see visible signs of cheating in tennis or golf. Yet, in cricket, doctoring a ground to suit either fast or spin bowlers or to favor batsmen is considered quite legitimate in some countries. The argument is that you play to your strength. What are known as "professional fouls" are common in football and many other sports. In heavyweight boxing title matches, rounds have been known to go on longer than the authorized three minutes and the ten-second knockout count has frequently taken more or less time than the rule book's ten seconds. All these examples are nothing more than acts to achieve an unfair advantage.

Personal integrity and reputation is slowly diminishing. In few places now, is a person's handshake sufficient to seal a deal. Trust has become almost meaningless. Yet organizational norms within a corporation's culture can determine thought and behavior in the workplace. And such culture almost invariably stems from the top of the organization. Leaders remain the most important and significant influence on the culture of an organization and are responsible for creating credibility and trust. Their example provides the guidelines for those beneath them. Without guidelines from leaders, followers often seek the lowest acceptable level.

Lest we be accused of portraying only one side of the ethical argument, let us clearly state that there are many examples of genuine morality and ethics in both sport and business. In basketball there are examples of players' deliberately missing free throws because they were aware that the foul that had been called was not legitimate. In business, what happened at Enron and WorldCom is not indicative of all corporations. Most corporations are led by ethical and highly moral individuals who try very hard to balance shareholder, employee, and customer concerns.

However, that we need to consider ethical behavior and morality as a subset of leadership, rather than as a normal aspect of leadership, is indicative of the problem. Nonetheless, as we indicated in the previous paragraph, there are many examples of ethical leadership. In sport, one can point to the Australian swimming trials for the 2004 Athens Olympics. During the trials, world record holder Ian Thorpe overbalanced at the starting blocks during the 400 meter freestyle heats and was disqualified. Thorpe accepted the decision calmly and insisted that he would not appeal, the judge was completely correct, and whoever competed in Athens in his place would receive his full support. Thorpe advised that it would be unethical to seek to change the rules to allow him to compete despite a virtually guaranteed gold medal.

The need for ethical and moral behavior needs to be constantly endorsed by leaders. Ron Clarke, one of Australia's finest ever athletes commented in his new book, *The Measure of Success* that

> cheating, in any of its many forms, is disdained as it detracts from the honesty of the test. Unethical behavior, propagating misinformation or plain lying is avoided as they falsely influence the validity of your progress towards your goals and targets. These are the tools of failures, of those afraid to test themselves fairly and squarely, who are frightened they cannot achieve without artificial aids and who have no conscience or self-respect.[12]

He is correct.

Peak Performance

> At the peak of tremendous and victorious effort, while the blood is pounding in your head, all suddenly becomes quiet within you. Everything seems clearer and whiter than ever before, as if great spotlights had been turned on. At that moment you have the conviction that you contain all the power in the world, that you are capable of everything, that you have wings. There is no more precious moment in life than this, the white moment, and you will work very hard for years just to taste it again. *(Yuri Vlasov, Russian weightlifter)*[13]

One of the most puzzling aspects of sport relates to the variation in performance that can occur almost on a daily basis. Sporting teams can perform brilliantly one day and poorly the next. So it is with the individual athlete. To help to counter such fluctuations, sports psychologists are frequently employed. They work with the athlete using techniques such as mental imagery, relaxation techniques, performance review and analysis, and positive reinforcement.

Psychologists have found that the most important factor determining performance capability is the mental thought process of the athlete. They have discovered that to achieve optimal results, athletes must achieve optimal mental functioning and total absorption in their task. If, and when, such total mental commitment to the task is achieved, athletes are said to have arrived at what is variously described as "peak or optimal experience," "peak performance," "flow" or simply "being in the zone." Once achieving that status, athletes believe they possess such capacity that they can anticipate things before they happen and performance simply flows without effort or thought.

While unsure of what causes athletes to enter the peak performance zone, there is growing awareness that such athletes prepare themselves mentally for any challenge they may encounter. Frequently they employ visualization techniques to such an extent that they have practiced a particular skill or event in their minds on countless occasions. Thus, when the activity actually occurs they perform flawlessly.

"Being in the zone" can actually refer to one of several stages of experience. Often, these stages are separate and often they are cumulative. They may start with an athlete competing in what may be called the *experience zone*. That is, the athlete competes in his or her sport on such a frequent basis that actions become instinctive and automatic. At this time, the athlete may almost switch off mental thought and operate on autopilot as it were. Athletes competing in endurance events or older athletes frequently enter such a zone.

A second place in the zone may be referred to as the *painless zone,* where pain can temporarily be put to one side but may have debilitating effects later. Again, this is a zone for endurance athletes. One athlete to compete in such a zone was Jim Peters whose marathon run in the 1954 Empire Games in Vancouver remains an enduring memory. Peters, some three miles ahead of his closest competitor, entered the gate to the arena to wild applause. Just inside the gate he collapsed. Over the next 15 minutes, he stumbled and collapsed several times, progressing just 200 meters in the process. He fell several more times before crossing what he thought was the finish line. It was indeed a finish line, but the one used for track events. As he crossed the line, the team masseur, acting on the instructions of the team manager, caught him as he fell yet again and led him off the track. Not having crossed the correct finish line, Peters was disqualified and promptly retired from the sport.

A third experience may be referred to as the *arousal zone*. This zone is slightly different, in that athletes can experience it many times or rarely. On those occasions in which an athlete outperforms on a one-off basis, the achievement may have occurred as a result of anger, a desire for revenge, or from competing in a one-time event such as the Olympics or a World Cup. Athletes who experience the arousal zone more frequently are able to effectively "psych themselves up" for an out of the ordinary event such as a play-off series. Sometimes, athletes who perceive the world as slowing down, a phenomenon known as *tachypsychia*, are in the arousal zone. Sir Donald Bradman, perhaps the world's greatest ever cricketer, commented on several occasions after a marathon innings that "the ball looked twice its normal size and came at me in slow, slow time." David Gould and his colleagues noted that the concept of an arousal zone dated back to Coleman Griffith, the father of North American sport psychology when he discussed the advisability of "keying up teams" and identifying strategies for dealing with athletes undergoing "anxiety and stress" states.[14]

The next state occurs when an athlete is in the zone known as the *flow zone*. In this stage, athletes may experience a state of almost total euphoria. The pioneering book on flow, Mihaly Csikszentmihalyi's *Beyond Boredom and Anxiety*[15] was built on Maslow's seminal work in the area of peak experience and self-actualization.[16] Maslow believed that achieving peak performance was a moment of highest happiness in one's life, which, in turn, led to the growth or the actualization of the individual. Csikszentmihalyi described the flow state as being in perfect physical, emotional, and intellectual harmony and performing in an effortless and successful way. He believed that in such a state, the individual was totally absorbed in the task at hand, with all their senses working together to help the individual stay in balance and function well. Interestingly, Csikszentmihalyi did not confine the flow state to athletes. He and others believe that such a state is equally applicable in certain instances in the business world, as his latest book suggests: *Good Business: Leadership, Flow, and the Making of Meaning*.[17]

When individuals are in the flow state, they will be totally at one with the experience; they will function without external distractions and ignore internal physiological activity. This does not translate automatically, however, to optimal performance. This is because the flow state reflects a person's mental performance rather than their physical performance.

The final state may be termed the zone of *optimal performance*. It is within this zone that an individual performs at the upper end of their capability. This is the arena in which world records are broken. Roger Bannister perfectly summed up the idea of operating in this zone in his 1955 biography, the *Four Minute Mile*. The following excerpt from his book is quoted in Hutchinson (2004).[18]

> There was complete silence on the ground ... a false start ... I felt angry that precious moments during the lull in the wind might be slipping by. The gun fired a second time ... Brasher [one of the two pace "rabbits"] went into the lead and I slipped in effortlessly behind him, feeling tremendously full of running. My legs seemed to meet no resistance at all, as if propelled by some unknown force. We seemed to be going so slowly! Impatiently I shouted, "Faster!" But Brasher kept his head and did not change the pace. I went on worrying until I heard the first lap time, 57.5 seconds ... At one and a half laps I was still worrying about the pace. A voice shouting "relax" penetrated to me above the noise of the crowd. I learnt afterwards it was Stampf's [Bannister's coach]. Unconsciously I obeyed. If the speed was wrong it was too late to do anything about it, so why worry? I was relaxing so much that my mind seemed almost detached from my body. There was no strain. I barely noticed the half-mile, passed in 1 minute 58 seconds, nor when, round the next bend, Chataway [the other "rabbit"] went into the lead. At three-quarters of a mile the effort was still barely perceptible; the time was 3 minutes 0.7 seconds and by now the crowd was roaring. Somehow I had to run that last lap in 59 seconds. Chataway led round the next bend and then I pounced past him at the beginning of the back straight, three hundred yards from the finish. I had a moment of mixed joy and anguish, when my mind took over. It raced well ahead of my body and drew my body compellingly forward. It felt that the moment of a lifetime had come. There was no pain, only a great unity of movement and aim. The world seemed to stand still or did not exist. The only reality was the next two hundred yards of track under my feet. The tape meant finality – extinction perhaps. I felt at that moment that it was my chance to do one thing supremely well. I drove on, impelled by a combination of fear and pride ...
>
> Bannister breasted the tape after 3 minutes, 59.4 seconds and collapsed, almost unconscious. The pain caught him like a bullet. He felt "like an exploded flashlight with no will to live".

Post Game

Preparation is essential in a leader. Part of that preparation reflects the ability to control the mind. It is equally important in business as in sport. Without some form of control, anxiety and stress can cause less than optimal performance. This chapter has looked at personal development and the way in which the mind and the emotions can affect performance.

At national and international level, the days of an athlete stopping smoking and drinking for a couple of weeks prior to a race, and then expecting to compete successfully, are long over. So it is in business. Leadership is a full-time occupation. It cannot be turned on and off at will. To be a successful leader means as much preparation, dedication, commitment, and hard work as it does to be a top athlete. That preparation is commonly as much mental as it is physical and, like other psychological skills, the ability to undertake mental preparation successfully can be developed and improved with practice. Spiritual leadership, in that regard, requires a flow state of performance where everything comes together in harmony; a balance between mind and soul that necessitates high levels of self-awareness, spirit and character, and emotional intelligence. This symphony of mind and body can then lead to individual and team peak performance – doing the best things for the right reasons.

Notes

1 G. Sims (2003), *Why Die? The Extraordinary Percy Cerutty – Maker of Champions*, C. Thomas Lothian, Melbourne.
2 A. Morin (1998), "Imagery and Self-awareness: A Theoretical Note", *Theory and Review in Psychology*, e-journal available on http://gemstate.net/susan/Imagry2.htm, accessed 20 November 2004.
3 K. Porter and J. Foster (1990), *Visual Athletics: Visualizations for Peak Sport Performance*, William C. Brown, Dubuque.
4 T. Gentry (1990), *Jesse Owens, Champion Athlete*, Melrose Square, LA.
5 C. Rogers (1947), "Some Observations on the Organization of Personality", *American Psychologist*, **2**: 358–68.
6 P. Salovey and J. Mayer (1990), "Emotional Intelligence", *Imagination, Cognition, and Personality*, **9**(3): 185–211.
7 L. Giles (1910), *Sun Tzu on the Art of War*, Samuel Griffith, London.
8 D. Goleman (1995), *Emotional Intelligence: Why it Matters More Than IQ*, Bantam, New York.
9 W. Sparkes (2001), "Leadership Visited: Integrity, Character, and Morality – More Than Perspiration or Inspiration?", *Quest*, **53**(4): 507–21.
10 J. M. Burns (1979), *Leadership*, Harper & Row, New York.
11 C. Dubin (1990), Report of the Commission of Inquiry into the Use of Drugs and Banned Practices Intended to Increase Athletic Performance, Sport Canada, Quebec.
12 R. Clarke (2004), *The Measure of Success: A Personal Perspective*, Thomas C. Lothian, Melbourne, p. 226.
13 Quoted in D. Ackerman (2000), *Deep Play*, Vintage, London, p. 132.
14 D. Gould, C. Greenleaf and V. Krane (2002), "Arousal – Anxiety and Sport Behaviour", in Horn, Thelma (ed.), *Advances in Sport Psychology* (2nd edn), Human Kinetics, Chicago, Il, pp. 207–41.
15 M. Csikszentmihalyi (1975), *Beyond Boredom and Anxiety*, Jossey-Bass, San Francisco.
16 A. Maslow (1964), *Religion, Values, and Peak Experience*, Viking Press, New York.
17 M. Csikszentmihalyi (2004), *Good Business: Leadership, Flow and the Making of Meaning*, Penguin, NJ.
18 Quote taken from G. Hutchinson (ed.) (2004), *The Best Australian Sports Writing 2004*, Black, Melbourne.

CHAPTER 7

Thinking Outside the Ball Park: Marketing Leaders

Leadership involves finding a parade and getting in front of it. (JOHN NAISBITT, TECHNOLOGY AND GLOBAL TRENDS COMMENTATOR AND AUTHOR)

Leading England to Victory ... Blair or Beckham?

Tony Blair has just experienced his worst week as Prime Minister ever. Unable to shake off the issue of Iraq for safer domestic topics, Mr Blair has been hamstrung over the continuing allegations of abuse of Iraqi prisoners by coalition troops.[1]

Meanwhile, in preparation for Euro 2004, England's other leader David Beckham had to deal with the aftermath of his own Iraq. Beckham denied that he had an affair with his former personal assistant Rebecca Loos. The scandal has not affected his approval ratings. As a matter of fact, a couple of months after allegations of his extramarital adventures became public, Beckham signed one of the biggest product endorsement deals ever with Gillette, to sell shavers to half of the world's population. A deal worth between 10 and 100 million US dollars, according to different sources, was going to be well worth the investment, given the fact that shavers are targeted at men. Marketing agencies argued that this is a consumer group that will not greatly hold adultery against the captain of England. In some cases, quite the opposite, in fact.

Meanwhile, irrespective of the youthful vibrancy, eloquence, and energetic style of presentation that helped his rise to stardom in 1997, Tony Blair is struggling to keep his head above water. According to the parliamentary sketch writer and former Tory MP, Matthew Parris:

> the undergrowth is tinder dry, and all it needs is the spark, I think, for a revolt against Tony Blair to spread. He has very, very little support now for his policies on Iraq amongst his own Members of Parliament. Trust in him has eroded away amongst his own Members of Parliament, and crucially, and this is absolutely critical, the belief that he is an election winner for them is beginning to ebb away as well. A lot of them have always disagreed with him, many of them have never supported his ideas, but what everyone has agreed with in the past, was that he was the best man to secure them the best majorities in their constituencies at the next election. People no longer believe that.[2]

In football it only takes a couple of wins, combined with a well-manufactured and cultivated image as a fashion trendsetter, to continue topping the popularity polls. In politics, style does not hide lack of substance for long.

Kirsten Aiken: "Now, when Tony Blair was first elected you told ABC that he was a reactionary with fluffy bits. How would you label him now?"
Matthew Parris: "The fluffy bits. I'd forgotten I'd said that. He's still a reactionary. The fluffy bits have all gone sort of bedraggled and sodden, I'm afraid; they're not fluffy any more. He is in urgent need of a blow drier."[3]

Or maybe this is better said in Blair's own words: "The art of leadership is saying no, not yes. It is very easy to say yes." As for Beckham's actions, this statement also applies to volunteering to take penalty kicks.

As both Tony Blair and David Beckham have shown in their own peculiar ways, great invisible leadership is a contradiction in terms. Greatness is a function of exposure and hence, to be recognized as great, it needs to be communicated to many. Research shows that the greatest celebrities on earth are athletes, actors, and entertainers, not politicians or businesspeople. More often than not, the greatest sporting celebrities are also the leaders in their sporting discipline and, when playing in a team environment, also the captains of their teams. They maximize their earning capacity by leveraging their celebrity status in order to sell their brand to the rest of the world. Equally, business leaders can do the same.

What we will argue in this chapter may well be considered controversial by some, as history has taught us that *marketing the leader* can easily turn into "marketing the ideology", or in other words, empty propaganda. This book, however, is not the place to discuss the inherent pitfalls of any celebrity marketing campaign; in this chapter we will merely apply the marketing knowledge available to us to maximize leadership effectiveness.

Of course, we cannot do that without at least acknowledging that in the case of marketing leaders, there are many ethical standards that need to be upheld and moral dilemmas that need to be considered. In order to market themselves in the organization and to external stakeholders as a role model and as a leadership exemplar, leaders need to have achieved (some) success and be recognized as potential heroes. Later in this chapter, we shall present an approach to using marketing in order to help supplement this perception.

Heroes in Sport and Business

Great leaders tend to be remembered as heroes. Heroes are essential players in society because they exemplify traits and behaviors that lead to desired outcomes such as winning battles or wars, achieving remarkable business success or winning in sport. In other words, it does not matter if one leads a nation, an organization or a football team, leaders become heroes when charisma is combined with success, or at least a genuine attempt to achieve success. In any type of culture, be it national, ethnic or organizational, heroes are part of the system in which groups of people define their identity and values.

Geert Hofstede,[4] a pioneering culture researcher, argued that culture is visually expressed in behavior much like the different rings of an onion. Culture becomes manifest from the more superficial indications of cultural belonging (the outside layer of the onion) through symbols like words, pictures, language or objects to the deeper, intangible and invisible sense of a cultural group (the value core of the onion) or what is valued as "right" or "wrong" behavior. In between these two extremes, Hofstede distinguishes between heroes, who are the dead or living, real or symbolic (non-existent) persons held in high regard in a culture, and the rituals that reinforce the collective perception of what is socially right. Rituals, for example, can be ways in which people pay respect to the deceased, how people greet each other, or how new members are initiated into an organization. This can range from the intense and intrusive initiation rituals of a student fraternity to an end of the week drinks session to welcome new colleagues to the workplace.

Mel Gibson in *Braveheart*, Evita Peron in troubled Argentina, Johnny Wilkinson in the English rugby team and Richard Branson representing the Virgin business empire, are all heroes, the boundaries between fact and fiction blurred. In order to become a hero, there must also be some adversary against whom a victory can be claimed. Heroism translates into a kind of celebrity status that in turn can be used to craft a personal brand and ultimately exert influence, whether it is in negotiating the next movie deal, international diplomacy, a more lucrative endorsement contract, or, on behalf of a company, increasing the value of company stock.

Selling Leadership

As we have discussed in earlier chapters, Vince Lombardi was a successful and respected American football coach. His success combined with his unique style and vision made him into a legend of the game. He is routinely used as an example of excellent leadership, although he died 35 years ago. Lombardi was a leadership legend who distinguished himself from the pack because he knew that "being different" by actively looking for new solutions to old problems would set his team apart from the others. Given the regimented, scripted, and potentially fragmented nature of American football, Lombardi realized that common team goals were imperative before empowerment could occur. Lombardi was an infamously regimented man.

> I've never known a man worth his salt who in the long run, deep down in his heart, didn't appreciate the grind, the discipline. There is something good in a man that really yearns for discipline. *(Vince Lombardi)*

Lombardi was also a master in playing to the emotions and egos of his stars, providing them with the necessary individual attention, whilst ensuring that their combined efforts would amount to more than the sum of the parts. No one is more important than the team, or in his own words: "Teamwork is what the Green Bay Packers were all about. They didn't do it for individual glory. They did it because they loved one another." Vince Lombardi practiced in the 1950s what has been suggested in the 1980s and 90s to be the foundations of excellent leadership.

The Leadership Marketing Blueprint

Leadership identity is at the core of successful leadership because it deals with that which is literally at the heart of the leader as a person. Identity, or the set of characteristics that somebody recognizes as belonging uniquely to himself or herself and constituting his or her individual personality for life, is all about "me." In other words, leadership identity is all about how

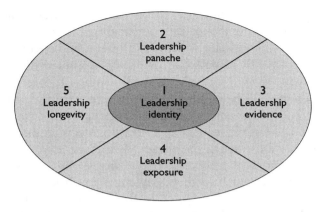

Figure 7.1   The leadership marketing blueprint

an individual perceives him or herself as a leader, an identity that may well be different from how they view themselves as a parent, spouse or hobbyist. From great sport leadership, we have appropriated five elements (see Figure 7.1) comprising the leadership marketing blueprint:

1. Leadership *identity* is at the heart of our leadership marketing blueprint because it impacts all other elements.
2. The unique aspects of leadership identity translate into a "leader-specific" style of operating, or leadership *panache*.
3. This in turn creates "leader-specific" *evidence* and outcomes.
4. How the leader communicates and is *exposed* to stakeholders is dependent on how marketing platforms and the use of the media best fit the leader's identity and image.
5. The way the leader will be remembered and referred to *(longevity)* after he or she has left the company will also be largely based on identity characteristics.

Leadership Identity: Transformational and Visionary

As we have discussed in Chapter 4, the importance of a common identity in setting team direction is unquestioned. From the team's perspective it is vital to be able to answer questions such as: Who are we? What do we really want? Who do we want to be? Great leadership facilitates the creation of a common identity, but from the individual leader's perspective, the leadership identity questions are: Who am I? What do I really want? Who do I want to be? As we said, leadership identity is all about the set of characteristics that somebody recognizes as belonging uniquely to the leader and constituting the leader's personality.

When we argued in Chapter 4 that sport offers the benchmark for the development of a sense of collective identity, we noted that collective identity is influenced by a leader's personal identity. If it is the leader's task to forge the mental model that affects the context in which the team operates, then it is the leader who has to believe in this paradigm and "live" it. At the heart of the leadership marketing blueprint therefore is the leader's statement to the rest of the world: "This is me as your role model, your innovator, your motivator, and your strongest supporter!" This attitude is exemplified by Dutch football player and coach Johan Cruyff.

Johan Cruyff is *the* legend of Dutch football. No other single person in the history of Dutch sport has had such an impact on football and the sport industry as a whole as Cruyff. Dozens of books have been written about Cruyff as the player, the coach, the leader, the analyst, and the human being. The most influential football magazine in Holland is called *Johan* and it is hard to imagine the Netherlands ever producing a better player, especially when we consider that other Dutch greats such as Ruud Gullit, Johan Neeskens, Abe Lenstra, and Marco van Basten were brilliant players, but, with the exception of van Basten, are generally not considered to be in the same league as Johan Cruyff. Cruyff was the European Player of the Year in 1971, 1973, and 1974 and in a poll conducted by the International Federation for Football History and Statistics in 1999, he was voted the European Player of the Century, ahead of German legend Franz Beckenbauer and Spain's Alfredo di Stefano. Cruyff has been credited with being instrumental in building the Ajax squad of the late 1960s when he was still a teenage player himself, which evolved into the invincible Ajax of the early 1970s, winning three European Club Championships (now Champions League Cup) in a row. He then led the Dutch team to the World Cup final of 1974, a final they should have won according to most experts, because they were playing a revolutionary style of football – total football – which is still described as a "typically Dutch" brand of play. Cruyff further set himself apart from fellow players by deciding, at the very last minute, that he would not join the Dutch team at the World Cup finals in 1978 in Argentina, where the Dutch again made the final.

Football as a game was transformed after the 1974 World Cup and Cruyff personified this transition. He continued to preach his football gospel as a coach, taking Ajax Amsterdam to a 1987 European Cup Winners Cup, a feat he repeated with FC Barcelona in 1989. The ultimate prize in club football, the Champions League Cup, was won with

Barcelona in 1992, the only time to date in the famous Catalonian club's history that they have taken the cup. Cruyff will always be treated as royalty in Barcelona as a consequence. Many armchair experts in the Netherlands believe that Cruyff is the only leader in Dutch football who can lead the flamboyant and sometimes arrogant team of Dutch players to become a championship team and finally bring the World Cup to the Netherlands. Cruyff is now heavily involved in enabling the next generation to enjoy sport and obtain a decent education through his (global) work with the Cruyff Foundation and the Johan Cruyff University.

> A good coach will make his players see what they can be rather than what they are. *(Ara Parasheghian, American college football coach)*

As the final step in the process of creating leadership identity, it is helpful to have something to show for it. As long as the outstanding qualities of the leader remain limited to the rare moments of actual leadership performance (to see the leader in action), the opportunities to market those qualities also remain limited to real time. In sport there are ample examples of outstanding players who have capitalized on the willingness of followers to pay handsomely for the evidence of their achievements, in the form of merchandise. We are not talking about the organizational outcomes that the leader is achieving now. This evidence of leadership will be discussed later in this chapter. In terms of developing leadership identity, we are talking about showcasing the outstanding qualities of the leader as a person. For example, Tiger Woods showcases his superior golf skills in books and on DVDs, Michael Jordan's abilities are animated in motion pictures, and Jack Welch, the former General Electric leader, has sold millions of books, telling stories about leadership "Jack style."

We have now provided solid foundations for leadership marketing activities by creating the leadership identity. The next step in the process of maximizing the impact of leadership through marketing is to actively develop leadership panache.

Leadership Panache: Charisma, Attractiveness and Taking Charge

Military strategists have known for millennia that victory in combat depends largely on the willingness of soldiers to die on the field of battle. When soldiers believe that they can entrust their lives to their leaders fighting next to them, and more importantly that the leader will be first to charge and last to retreat, they are more likely to fight to the bitter end. War heroes are those who can show the battle wounds of fighting in the front lines, the evidence of beating the odds and surviving the onslaught. During the 1996–7 season play-offs, Michael Jordan beat the buzzer with a game winning shot to win game one, he scored 38 points in game two, and despite a stomach virus that made him vomit many times before and during game five, he scored a match winning 38 points. If the leader shows willingness to suffer on the battlefield, how can their charges not follow? Of course, Michael Jordan is not infallible. He has missed important shots and he has played bad games. The important point is that of perception. Great leaders are remembered for their successful deeds.

> I've missed more than 9000 shots in my career. I've lost almost 300 games. 26 times, I've been trusted to take the game winning shot and missed. I've failed over and over and over again in my life. And that is why I succeed.
> (Michael Jordan, former NBA superstar)

Michael Jordan has won 6 NBA championships, 5 Most Valuable Player awards and was selected for 13 All Star games. He finished his career with 32,292 points, the third-highest total in league history, behind Kareem Abdul-Jabbar and Karl Malone. His 30.12 career average goes down as the best in NBA history. The world's first billionaire athlete endorsed Nike Air Jordan basketball shoes, Big Macs, Gatorade, cars for Chicago area Chevy dealers, basketballs for Wilson, lottery tickets for the state of Illinois, calendars, school supplies and greeting cards for Cleo, underwear for Hanes, and Oakley sunglasses (his relationship with Oakley included a seat on the board). Jordan's alignment with Wheaties was so strong that the cereal's manufacturer, General Foods, printed a special edition Wheaties box with Jordan and the Chicago Bulls on the cover. When the Bulls won the NBA title in June 1996, Michael Jordan Wheaties boxes were in supermarkets within hours. Of course, Wheaties needed Jordan more than he needed them. The brand's share of the ready-to-eat cereal market was only 1.6 percent and the idea of having to do without Jordan must have been a nightmare for General Foods.[5]

Jordan's marketing agent once commented: "We haven't packaged Michael Jordan, we have done a good job exposing who he is and what he is to corporate decision makers. Once they saw what he was firsthand, the rest flowed from there."[6] It was clear from the beginning that Jordan was a made-for-the-media athlete. He had natural ability to communicate, provide intelligent answers to questions, and delicately handle awkward situations. The 1984 Olympic gold medal enhanced Jordan's image as an all-American kid, and unlike other Olympic heroes, his star continued to rise. Jordan's visibility was a key factor in reversing the declining fortunes of the NBA in the 1980s and when Nike and Jordan developed the first Air Jordan basketball shoes, Jordan advised his former roommate at the University of North Carolina to "get some Nike stock, they are going to make a shoe for me, these Air Jordans, and someday it's going to be worth a lot of money."[7] The Nike director of design, after releasing the Air Jordan No. 6 observed: "One of the things about Michael Jordan is we can take incredible risks in the product because his wearing them validates it. The fact that Michael Jordan is wearing this plain-toed shoe will make it all right for a lot of people."[8]

> Perception is reality. Remember it is not what you say or how you say it, but rather what is heard that is important. *(Ian Gray, American football coach)*

Even after his inevitable retirement in 2003, Jordan has remained an attractive spokesperson for many companies and their brands around the world. Although Jordan lost the principal platform from which he addressed the public, he will not fade into obscurity. It is assumed that when athletes stop playing, the endorsement power will dramatically fade because they are no longer in the public eye. In Jordan's case that has been rather different. He transcends the game he played and is going to be very much in the public eye for years to come. Jordan's current corporate (endorsement and business) involvement includes companies such as Electric Arts, Gatorade, Hidden Beach Records, MCI WorldCom, Michael Jordan Automotive Group, Michael Jordan Celebrity Invitational, Michael Jordan Flight School, NBA Videos, Jordan Brand, Jordan Cologne, Oakley, Sara Lee Corporation, SportsLine, the Upper Deck Company, Wilson Sporting Goods, and his chain of restaurants: Michael Jordan's Steak House, Michael Jordan's 23.sportcafe, Jordans, and One Sixty Blue.[9]

There is no better example of leadership panache in sport than Michael Jordan. Jordan has proven to be a master of exposing his flair, élan, flamboyance, style, elegance, and confidence to the world. All these characteristics made him into one of the world's most attractive personalities. The marketing of Michael provides plentiful examples of developing leadership panache, or, how to make leaders as attractive as possible for the people they have to lead.

Respect and Panache

Once leaders have earnt the respect of those they have to work closest with, they can use this as the base for wider marketing communication about their leadership qualities. Although the 1992 US Olympic dream team consisted of megastars such as Larry Bird, Charles Barkley, Scottie Pippen, and Magic Johnson, they all acknowledged Jordan to be a leader. Jordan was never afraid to let others shine (and score) if they were in a better position. In business this equates to leading from the front, but dedicating victories to others, who will in turn repay this with respect.

> When I played with Michael Jordan on the Olympic team, there was a huge gap between his ability and the ability of the other great players on that team. But what impressed me was that he was always the first one on the floor and the last one to leave. (Steve Alford, referring to playing in the last amateur US Olympic basketball team in 1984)

As politicians know, a public image reflecting respect is the ultimate expression of leadership panache. By the summer of 1993 Michael Jordan had begun to develop serious image problems. After leading the US dream team to an Olympic victory and then his Chicago Bulls to an unprecedented third straight NBA title, Jordan was the focus of unpleasant rumors regarding selfish behavior, aloofness, and serious gambling problems. Then, late in the summer of 1993, tragedy struck. Jordan's father James was found murdered in his car. The nation mourned with Michael. Scarcely two months later, in the midst of major league baseball's playoffs, Michael Jordan stunned the world by announcing his retirement from basketball. The news was so startling that even President Clinton took time out to give a statement of support. In the space of three traumatic months, Michael Jordan's public opinion ratings had gone from questionable to sky high.[10] It requires little imagination to consider the impact that the continued loss of public respect would have had on Jordan's ability to act as a product endorser. A lack of respect will debilitate the ability to lead.

Leadership Evidence: Marking and Marketing the Performance

Tiger Woods, Michael Jordan, Michael Schumacher, Kobe Bryant, and David Beckham were the top five on the Forbes.com Athlete Celebrity top 100 in 2003. The top females in the list were tennis players (the Williams sisters and Anna Kournikova, who no longer plays professional tennis) and all were in the top 25. The list is based on what celebrities are being paid, combined with their level of exposure on the web, television, and in the print media. However, a new entry in the 2003 list was Annika Sorenstam, the best female golfer in the world who earned a LPGA (Ladies Professional Golf Association) tour record of $2.9 million in the 2003 season. Tennis players receive massive amounts of media attention, largely because the majors (Australian Open, French Open, Wimbledon, and the US Open) are broadcast as mixed events for television purposes, that is, the male and female draws play in the same two-week ratings time slot, effectively sharing the mass market exposure. In other words, it is relatively easy for female tennis players to receive significant media attention compared to their golfing colleagues, who continue to be relegated to non-prime time broadcast slots. This makes Sorenstam's entry into the Forbes.com top 100 a truly remarkable feat.

Although Serena Williams has made some noise about joining the men's tour, or at least to play against the men, Sorenstam has not only talked the talk, she has actually walked the walk. After winning more that 50 LPGA titles, she argued that it was time to test her skills against the much longer hitting men on the PGA tour. Sorenstam's PGA appearance at the Colonial has been hailed by many. It was good for Sorenstam, for the Colonial, for the PGA tour, for the LPGA tour and for golf itself. The pressure that she put herself under to perform was incredible. Fellow LPGA tour player Kelli Kuehne argued:

> A lot of us are concerned about her want and need to play on the PGA Tour when we have the LPGA as our women's tour. Annika doesn't think she has anything to lose, but she's looking at it from her perspective. She's not looking at it overall, to help grow the women's game. She has a lot to lose and nothing to gain. My concern is if she plays poorly and misses the cut, it will take women's golf back a couple of steps.

In the lead-up to the event, PGA player Kenny Perry observed:

> She's going to have Tiger Woods' media. I'm anxious to see how she handles all that. I don't think she really knows what she's getting into. If she could play with no media, just a regular tournament, I think she could do well. But when she sees all the attention, she's going to realize this is a special moment.[11]

Pick your target and trust your aim. *(Annika Sorenstam, professional golfer)*

However, irrespective of the pressure on Sorenstam that most PGA tour players will never come close to experiencing, most media pundits and LPGA and PGA colleagues alike agreed that Sorenstam was the picture of grace under pressure. She showed composure, dignity, class, and sportsmanship, characteristics that were hard to detect in the critics who tended to be dismissive about the effort. Some of the top PGA players even decided not to play in the tournament.

Sorenstam also exhibited her tremendous skills as a golfer. Her precision off the tee and her long iron accuracy were the envy of many professional male golfers. Unfortunately, extreme nerves hampered her short play in the tournament. By day two, when her putting had smoothed out, nerves were finally getting to her off the tee. However, the two days that she played should elevate Sorenstam to the superstar status she deserves, and bring legions of new fans to the game. According to fellow Swede PGA player Jesper Parnevik: "She played amazing. I guess we have the Shark, the Tiger and now we have the Superwoman."

In an interview with Joel Schuchmann, Sorenstam commented on the pressures of competing in the event:

Schuchmann: "You were saying earlier in the week that you were not out to prove anything by your performance and your appearance here. What do you think you showed today to people who were curious about what you would do here?"

Sorenstam: "I don't know what those people think and saw. Personally I came here to test myself. I know what I got to work on. I got an afternoon to work a little bit on it. But I'm very proud of the way I was focusing and proud of the decisions I made and that I stuck to them. And that's why I'm here. I want to see if I could do it. That's all that matters to me."

Towards the end of 2003 Sorenstam competed against Phil Mickelson, Fred Couples and Mark O'Meara in the Skins Game. After holing only the eighth eagle in Skins Game history, she led for much of the round before a late surge by Fred Couples on the final few holes put her in second place. She marked her performance and the media were all too happy to market it for her.[12]

> Take pride in yourself. Be your own person. Don't do things because everyone else does them. Don't be part of the crowd. Dare to be different. Never be afraid to stand up for what you believe to be right, even if it means standing alone! *(Jack Lambert, NFL linebacker)*

Linking the Leader to the Performance

Part of the process of marketing the evidence of a leader's ability is in creating an association between them and the winning performance. We argued earlier that the leader inspires a shared vision, achieves this vision by challenging the common process, enables others to act, but at the same time is a role model who offers encouraging support to individuals and groups. Looking at what Sorenstam has achieved in her profession, and her challenging of professional conventions, makes her a role model for and leader among her peers. For leaders in the business environment, this is no different. One of the roles that leaders have to play is that of the "spokesperson" for, or on behalf of, the organization. It is our contention that in order to successfully market organizational performance, this performance first has to be marked (stated, outlined), ideally by leaders because they are in the best position, to sell the achievement. In other words, there is nothing wrong with leaders, in the first instance, strongly linking positive performance to themselves by implication of their success. This link will provide a range of opportunities to further share the glory with others.

In Sorenstam's case, the rest of the team are her fellow LPGA tour players. Although some of her tour colleagues were skeptical about her decision to play with and against the men, the LPGA as a collective of professional female players were unequivocal about sharing in the success of Sorenstam. They stated on their website that Sorenstam's participation and success at Colonial "garnered unprecedented worldwide interest and media attention." It is good for the game of golf and it is good for an underexposed women's sport.

It is a well-known principle in celebrity marketing that the drawing power of the famous person is partly based on the opportunity the public have to vicariously live the celebrity's life. In the case of leaders, this means that they are effectively sharing their success. At this stage of providing leadership evidence, leaders should be turning their attention to thinking about the best ways of using their own celebrity to improve the profile and perception of the company. Golfing enthusiasts' support for Sorenstam's participation was great, golf as a sport generated substantial extra exposure and golf fans around the world, male and female, debated the pros and cons of females participating in male events.

Overall, Sorenstam's participation provided a huge service to (female) golf fans around the world. It is very likely that her leadership has motivated many young girls to pick up the clubs. Business leaders can learn from athlete celebrities when it comes to talking to the customers (fans), in the process implicitly dedicating victories to them. Very few business leaders are capable of taking customers beyond the financial results of the company. The customer needs to know about the "how" and "why" of the company's operations and the leader needs to showcase the passion that the company's employees are putting into producing the organization's products – all in the name of sharing success and satisfying the fans: "We do it all for You, the Customer! Because we could not have done it without you."

As we explained in the previous section, the public at large is becoming an increasingly powerful voice of support or opposition. This public will have no interest in a major bank posting another multi-billion dollar profit. They are more likely to ask "What's in it for me?", and only those leaders who have thought about and acted on their corporate social responsibilities will have the answers. Sharing positive performance with the public at large is about the impact the company has on providing a sustainable natural environment, the contribution it makes to eradicating social problems, or in general terms, giving back to the community at large.

There are very few star athletes who have not set up their own charities or, indeed, are supporting a range of social causes. We have already mentioned Michael Schumacher's donation of US$10 million to the tsunami relief fund and another good example is Norwegian Johann Olav Koss. Winner of four speed-skating gold medals at the Winter Olympics (one in 1992 and three in 1994), he is now the CEO of Right to Play, an organization that funds and delivers sport-based development programs around the world. Koss argues that sport harnesses a power unknown to other forms of aid. For example, he recalls how a group of children who lived in a war zone picked up a soccer ball rather than the weapons offered to them by the local warlords. He feels that team sports can offer children who have nothing else left in the world a sense of belonging and community. Koss has made it clear that leaders who fail to communicate and commit to the big picture will ultimately fail to stay in favor with the fans.[13]

> If anybody has an interest in promoting the positive role and potential of sport around the world it is the companies which benefit so much from the spending power of the sports obsessed youngsters of the developed world. In some respects payback time is approaching and, on this occasion, everyone will be a winner. *(Johann Olav Koss, Norwegian speed-skating gold medalist)*

Leadership Exposure: Sharing Celebrity with the Rest of the World

David Beckham is perhaps the most well-known sports celebrity in the world. His platform is, of course, the world game, but his superior talent while playing football is only part of his celebrity. Beckham positioned himself as a fashion icon quite early in his career, changing his hairstyle every couple of months and regularly adding to his body tattoos, each of them telling the rest of the world a story about David Beckham the person and the brand. His rise to megastar status was also helped by marrying former Spice Girl Victoria (Posh Spice), although most media commentators agree that it benefits the celebrity status of Posh more than David.

On the field Beckham was instrumental in the success of Manchester United, playing 397 matches and scoring 86 goals. He was the centerpiece of the team that won the treble (English Premiership, FA Cup and Champions League) in 1998, and has been hailed by some commentators as the owner of the best right-foot cross in the game. Search engine Google rated Beckham as the most sought-after sport celebrity online, and paparazzi photographers are as likely to catch him at a movie premiere or fashion shoot as at a post-match press conference of his current team Real Madrid. When he arrived at the club in 2003, Real's president was happy to admit that although the club bought David because he was a very good football player, he was well worth the US$41 million price tag because sales of Beckham-branded Real merchandise would bring in a multiple of his transfer price over the period of his contract.

Real management also realized that Beckham would be an important tool to break open the Asian opportunities, particularly in order to sell games into the lucrative Southeast Asian television market. Although vilified for his red card behavior during a World Cup match in 1998, which cost England the game and led to the team exiting the tournament, Beckham returned strongly to captain England to the 2002 World Cup and the Euro 2004 quarter finals.

Among Beckham's handsomely paying corporate sponsors are companies such as Pepsi, Adidas (who have developed a David Beckham brand in preparation for the 2006 World Cup in Germany), Police sunglasses, Vodafone, and Gillette. David Beckham's star would not have risen as high as it is now if he had not been an excellent football player, but there is no doubt that he has successfully used the power of the mass media to his personal advantage. David Beckham is the benchmark for leadership exposure. He has used the marketable components of his football leadership in combination with his physical features to maintain and even increase his "metrosexual," international celebrity status.

> ... an icon of his generation, adored by millions across the globe, who has brought hope to his nation where there was once despair ... and Nelson Mandela. (Guardian *Newspaper, describing a meeting between David Beckham and Nelson Mandela, the former president of South Africa*)

David Beckham shows us that in order to become a global celebrity, a leader has to offer something distinctive and attractive to the marketplace. It is therefore no coincidence that we have placed leadership exposure as the fourth element in the leadership marketing blueprint. Before a leader can be exposed to the rest of the world, they need to ensure that their leadership identity is fully developed, unique and attractive. A leader with panache also needs to collect and communicate evidence of good leadership in order to enhance their credibility. When this is achieved, the leader can be packaged as a unique celebrity proposition. Beckham's celebrity proposition is based on fashion more than football. His constantly changing hairstyle and appearances at A-list events ensure that magazines and newspapers expose him favorably on a continuous basis. This in turn makes him an attractive medium to communicate to mass markets, hence his enormous endorsement power.

For leaders of a sales team of no more than five people, the principles remain the same. As the blueprint suggests, it is a matter of determining the objectives of the team within the larger organization and ascertaining which internal workers and external customers the leader needs to be exposed to in order to enhance the opportunity for sales success of the team.

For the leader of the sales team, the best platform may well be face-to-face meetings with representatives of potential accounts, or weekly sessions with his or her team members. Leadership celebrity in regard to the latter remains restricted within the boundaries of the organization, whereas frequent meetings with potential clients take a more external approach to leadership exposure. The platform for exposure is driven by the communication medium, and, in the case of small team leaders, may be restricted to the leader themselves, whereas in case of David Beckham, the mass media are the principal means of communication. Beckham's platform, as discussed earlier, is the football stage.

This platform is chiefly driven by the electronic and print media. In addition, Beckham's sponsors create more specific platforms to further their own commercial objectives, such as Adidas in creating a Beckham-specific Adidas brand. In turn this new platform will enhance Beckham's overall celebrity profile. The small team leader can create his or her own platform as well. Writing a monthly newsletter or initiating a half-yearly sales conference are examples of communication methods that can help to expose the leader to the leadership target markets. It is advantageous for the leader to recognize, however, that team members go through a process of accepting them in the same way that consumers come to accept a product.

> I've worked too hard and too long to let anything stand in the way of my
> goals. I will not let my teammates down, and I will not let myself down.
> *(Mia Hamm, US women's soccer team)*

The acronym AIDA in the strategic marketing communication process stands for attention, interest, desire, and action. It represents four sequential steps of buyer readiness and underpins the type of communication that is best suited to move potential customers from merely being aware of a product to being ready to buy it. From the perspective of celebrity marketing, this sequence can be a useful guide as well. The model represents the four stages of celebrity readiness, where the emerging leadership celebrity needs to gain the attention of the target audience, who then need to be fed more specific details that will turn interest into a desire for celebrity information. Celebrity admiration (rather than action in the buyer readiness sequence) is achieved when fans or the public want to emulate the celebrity. It is unrealistic to expect public admiration if insufficient marketing communication efforts have been put into the preceding phases of celebrity readiness.

Even if the individual in question is the leader of a small sales team, they cannot expect to be accepted unless first they generate some attention, interest and desire (to lend support) first. David Beckham has generated attention because he plays football very well, but is considered interesting because of his positioning beyond football. Beckham knows exactly what his desirable characteristics are and has used different media platforms to communicate these characteristics in order to become a globally admired leader in his sport and a celebrity in his own right. For Beckham, being a leader on the field of play was not enough, just as for some corporate leaders, like Donald Trump and Richard Branson, success in business is not enough. It is a misconception that high-profile leaders such as Beckham, Trump and Branson are just media savvy. They are not merely good at using the media to their advantage; they strategize, analyze, and plan. It is no accident that Beckham has a stronger international media profile than Ronaldo and Donald Trump's face is better known than that of Bill Gates.

Leadership Longevity: The Stuff of Legends

Six years after becoming a professional golfer in 1954, Arnold Palmer shook hands with a young businessman called Mark McCormack and joined as the first client of the International Management Group, now the largest athlete representation company in the world. Born in 1929, Palmer literally grew up on a golf course, in a house that was located on the 6th hole of the Latrobe Country Club course. He went on to win the Masters four times, the British Open twice and the US Open once. Overall, Palmer won 92 tournaments by the end of 1997, 61 of which came on the USPGA tour. Under the guidance of his business manager McCormack, Palmer championed the development of licensing and endorsement agreements which have become standard in sport business. He was also perhaps the first individual global sport brand in history; numerous companies have been created in his name or have created campaigns centered around his image. As it is stated on Palmer's website, from time to time, these trademarks and logos are updated to correspond to market trends and mirror specific products or services.

Palmer co-founded the Golf Channel in 1995, and currently there are over 100 separate Arnold Palmer licensing and endorsement deals in over 30 countries and nearly half of them pertain solely to Japan and Southeast Asia. Through many different markets and methods of distribution, the brands are successfully licensed and sublicensed throughout Asia.[14] In 2004, at the age of 75, and having survived prostate cancer, Palmer retired from playing competitive golf with his 50th appearance at the Masters in Augusta. The following overview merely touches the surface of Palmer's continued involvement in the world of charity and corporate business:

- President of Arnold Palmer Enterprises
- President and sole owner (since 1971) of Latrobe Country Club
- President and principal owner of Bay Hill Club and Lodge
- Member of the board of directors of Laurel Valley Golf Club
- Member of the board of directors of the Arnold Palmer Golf Company
- Chairman of the board of the Golf Channel.
- Palmer Golf Course Design Company
- Arnold Palmer Golf Management Company
- Arnold Palmer Golf Academy
- Charter member of the World Golf Hall of Fame
- Member of the PGA Golf Hall of Fame
- Member of the American Golf Hall of Fame
- Past honorary national chairman of the March of Dimes Birth Defects Foundation
- The Arnold Palmer Hospital for Children and Women
- Lifetime Achievement award, PGA Tour, 1998
- Donald Ross award, American Society of Golf Course Architects
- Patriot award, Congressional Medal of Honour Society.

Arnold Palmer continues to feature in the Forbes.com Athlete Celebrity top 100, which is an important international measure of celebrity status, earning power and exposure. The Palmer brand has proven to be timeless. Having been at the peak of his sporting prowess during the early 1960s, when he won 29 tournaments between 1960 and 1963, to remain one of the most recognized and valued athletes in the world almost 50 years later is a truly astonishing accomplishment. Palmer has become what very few can say: a larger than life legend of the game who is a benchmark for leadership longevity.

Johan Cruyff envisioned a new future for football long before others saw it. Michael Jordan was aware of the potential value of Nike shares well in advance of the traders at the NYSE, and Muhammad Ali was the best and knew it years before he defeated George Foreman in the rumble in the jungle. More than 40 years after celebrating the most successful period in his sporting career, Arnold Palmer has proven that his name represents the real value that was generated as a result of a triumphant career in elite sport. Perhaps more importantly for the purposes of this chapter is the power of marketing a leader for their longevity. The point of this last section is that only the leaders who manage to turn their unique vision into long-term reality will be remembered in perpetuity. Not because it is terribly important to be remembered after death, but because leadership longevity is evidence of sustainable success. Sustainable success is what every organization strives for.

> Vision without action is a daydream. Action without vision is a nightmare.
> (Japanese proverb)

The Symbology of Leadership

Creating a culture of successful leadership can be linked to the tangible and intangible manifestations of organizational culture, as outlined at the beginning of this chapter. Symbols of leadership success are relatively easy to identify, and include photographs, trophies, books, and films that each tell a part of the success story. In sport these symbols are quite overt. In business, more pretentious examples of symbols of success include lavish corporate headquarters or sport stadia that are designed expressly to showcase business or club success. We all know that to enter an impressively designed and decorated building raises our level of admiration and expectation. It symbolizes success and offers implicit evidence of great leadership. Legends in the world of sport all have, without exception, built their own personalized brands in order to link their name to commodities or service products. The associative power of a legendary brand transfers significant value to the product that it is linked to. All legendary leaders have in one way or the other created tangible proof of their achievements.

Arnold Palmer's heroic status has not only come from success on the golf course but also from overcoming adversity in his personal health struggles more recently. The custodians of the sport of golf use heroic storytelling particularly well in their lead-up to broadcasting the majors. For example, the organizers of the Masters at Augusta obsessively protect the history, tradition, and stories about the few golfers who have been good enough to win this tournament of tournaments. They know that the success of Augusta largely depends on the myths of the heroes who win. After all, without heroes it is just another golf course. For leaders to be admired, they must be able to convey stories of struggle and success. Over time, these stories become myths, which in turn become engrained in the psyche of players and spectators; employees and customers.

The world of sport is full of rituals. In Australian Rules football, for example, dedicated club members prepare a huge banner with a message of support to the team prior to every match, and hold up the banner for the team to run through it when they enter the arena. It takes the fans hours to prepare the banner, and the team seconds to tear it apart, but it is considered an essential ritual prior to every match. Directly after the match finishes, the winning team's club song is played in the stadium, for all fans to join in singing. Television is allowed in the locker rooms of the winning team where the same ritual is performed by the players in front of a national television audience. Equally, at the Masters, the leader at the end of day four is presented with the Green Jacket by the previous year's winner. This ritual is carefully scripted (for television) and has become the ultimate ceremony in golf. In business the rituals of leadership can be quite diverse, ranging from massive company organized events to carefully scripted activities. Corporate retreats, annual getaways, Christmas parties or training programs can all become collective rituals that reinforce leadership longevity.

The most important element of leadership longevity lies in cultivating and instilling values. It is hard to imagine that a leader will become a legend based on symbolism, heroism, and powerful rituals only. What leaders will be remembered for is what they have done to the hearts and minds of people in the long term. Once again sport can offer the lesson. Cruyff was not only a general on the field, only satisfied with the very best of his recruits, he also took a moral stand. His leadership brand has been developed on superior quality expectations and social morality. Much the same can be said about Muhammad Ali, whose fight against injustice in many walks of life is inseparable from his prowess in the ring. As is the case with the legends of sport, if they are good only in their sport and do not care much about what happens beyond it, it is unlikely they will receive the long-term respect of the public. Diego Maradona was one of the greatest football players the world has ever seen, but his aggressive, undisciplined, drug-influenced behavior has ensured that he will never be considered and respected as a leader in society. Surely Cruyff would never approve of the "hand of God." Similarly, for business leaders, it will remain hard to become a legend if the only thing that can be remembered about them is business success. A valuable business leadership brand is dependent on socially responsible and responsive leaders: visionary leaders who can see beyond the bottom line, leaders who think about the impact of business beyond tenure.

> The most important decision I ever made in my career was to live my life in sports as honestly and ethically as possible. Never having compromised my values allows me to look back on my life with no regrets and feel satisfaction in what I was able to accomplish. *(Greg LeMond, cyclist)*

Post Game

In this chapter we have argued the importance of marketing the leader. We consider the act of marketing leadership to be a necessary addition to the ways in which leadership can be made more effective, although this does require "thinking outside the ball park." In this age of mass media communication and the increasing power of global media conglomerates, it is critical for leaders to harness that power on behalf of their organizations. It is in this area that sport offers a key lesson. As a mass consumption product, leaders in sport are much more attuned to using the media to their advantage.

American presidents have always known the power of leadership marketing and successful candidates have successfully used the media to their advantage. In business, this may partly be the reason to engage in leadership marketing, for example at the top of large corporations where the battle for leadership succession can become fierce. However, the main reason for leadership marketing from our perspective is to become a better leader in the job. That is, to make clear to organizational members and customers what it is that the leader stands for.

All the sport examples used in this chapter have suggested that the preferred leadership response is one that leads to "celebrity." To be(come) a leadership celebrity therefore is not a superficial achievement, but rather an indication of successful inspirational communication. If the leader is successful in formulating the appropriate message and selecting the most suitable platforms and mediums, and organizational members are aligned towards aspirational objectives, then successful leadership marketing will invigorate and build trust among followers. It will enable the captain to lead the team to victory in the final match of the season.

> A rooster crows only when it sees the light. Put him in the dark and he'll never crow. I have seen the light and I'm crowing. *(Muhammad Ali, Olympic gold medalist and former world heavyweight boxing champion)*

Notes

1 Correspondent's Report, ABC National Radio Australia, reporter: Kirsten Aiken, Sunday 16 May, 2004.
2 Excerpt from Correspondent's Report, ABC National Radio Australia, Sunday 16 May, 2004.
3 Correspondent's Report, op. cit.
4 G. Hofstede (1991), *Cultures and Organisations: Software of the Mind*, McGraw-Hill, London.
5 D. Hay (1996), "Jordan Plays the Money Game", *The Sunday Age*, May 26, p. 18.
6 J. Naughton (1992), "Marketing Michael, the Making of a Commercial Superstar", *Washington Post Magazine*, February 9, pp. 11–29.
7 W.C. Rhoden (1993), "High Stakes: Low Sense of Values", *The New York Times*, July 21, B11.
8 D. Shilbury, S. Quick and H.M. Westerbeek (2003), *Strategic Sport Marketing* (2nd edn), Allen & Unwin, Sydney.
9 http://jordan.sportsline.com.
10 W.C. Rhoden, op. cit.
11 Excerpt from http://golf.about.com/cs/annikasorenstam/a/colonialquotes.htm.
12 Excerpts from http://golf.about.com/od/2003pgacolonial and http://www.lpga.com.
13 K. Roberts (2002), "Sport's Helping Hand", *Sport Business International*, November, pp. 24–5.
14 Excerpts from http://www.arnoldpalmer.com.

CHAPTER 8

Staying Ahead of the Game: Developing Leaders for the Future

> *Luck is what happens when preparation meets opportunity.* (DARRELL ROYAL, NATIONAL FOOTBALL HALL OF FAME MEMBER AND FORMER UNIVERSITY OF TEXAS COACH)

Nearly 37 years ago and with little more than a smattering of English, a fistful of money, 21 inch biceps and the American dream, Arnold Schwarzenegger arrived in the United States. He would fulfill that dream and in so doing turn his hand to a range of leadership challenges, all of which have so far proven successful. Schwarzenegger's approach to leadership reflects some of his early lessons as a professional bodybuilder, characterized by discipline and training but also with what some have viewed as an overmasculinized and Machiavellian spirit of competition. Perhaps as much as anything, an objective view of Schwarzenegger's career reveals a man capable of developing himself as a leader in ever escalating circumstances.

As illuminated by some lessons from Schwarzenegger's brilliant sporting career, this chapter examines the future of work, sport, and society and provides the basis for organizations and managers to understand the essential aspects of leadership in the future. Sport thinking helps in several ways toward fruitful consideration of the future needs of business leaders. First, it encourages leaders to be comfortable in uncertain environments. If the right management philosophy is in place, there is more room for experimentation and the potential emergence of genuine innovation that could not have been forced or prescribed. Secondly, the sport metaphor demonstrates the importance of constant research, development, and innovation in training and practice as a key to success, even when training time far exceeds that of the time spent in actual performance. The chapter also highlights how sport is at the forefront of technology and innovation, in order to stay ahead of the game. It concludes with a summary of aspects of leadership development that arise from the sport metaphor.

Born in 1947 in Thal, Austria, Schwarzenegger grew up in a household without modern amenities. Like many Austrian boys, he played soccer but found the sport unappealing, chiefly because he valued personal glory and gratification, the opportunities for which were too few in team sports. Trying his hand at field events in athletics, Schwarzenegger inadvertently discovered the weights room, on the suggestion of a coach advising him to strengthen his legs. In the gym Schwarzenegger found his calling. Here he learned the lessons that would shape his career. Seeking respect and admiration, bodybuilding gave Schwarzenegger a platform to bolster his self-esteem, his confidence inflating with his muscles. By the age of 16, Schwarzenegger was clear about his path in life, and that path would lead him to the United States, where bodybuilding was beginning to find a niche in the sexually charged 1960s.

By 19 Schwarzenegger had enlisted in the Austrian army, but denied permission to attend the Junior Mr Europe bodybuilding competition in Stuttgart a year later, he was forced to go AWOL in order to compete. Although jailed for a week on his return, the trip had been worth it, Schwarzenegger having been awarded the title despite having to learn how to "pose" properly on the run. The following year he won the Senior Mr Europe title, and, after finishing second in 1966, went on to win the Mr Universe contest in 1967. Realizing his deficiency was a lack of training and nutrition knowledge, Schwarzenegger decided that the only way forward was to train with the best bodybuilders in the world, which meant moving to the United States.

The move to the United States in 1968 proved to be a defining one. In Santa Monica, California, while working briefly as a road worker, Schwarzenegger spent as much time as he could with his idol, legendary bodybuilder and strongman Reg Park. With an improved knowledge of nutrition and access to the latest training techniques, Schwarzenegger won the Mr Universe title again in 1969, and suffered his last defeat ever in the highest bodybuilding competition in the world, Mr Olympia, at the hands of Cuban giant Sergio Oliva. Schwarzenegger was later to recall that it was the last time an opponent would intimidate him. In 1970, Schwarzenegger returned to win the competition, starting a six-title reign that earned him the mantle of the "Austrian oak". After retiring from competition after the 1975 Mr Olympia, Schwarzenegger made a successful comeback in 1980 to win again.

Shortly afterwards, Schwarzenegger made his big screen debut in *Hercules in New York*, the first of many films to exploit his extraordinary physique, although it did not exploit his acting ability, dubbing over as it did the heavy accent that would later become his trademark. *Conan the Barbarian* allowed Schwarzenegger to play to his strengths, and in 1984, *The Terminator* proved to be the role of his career, revolving around his imposing screen presence and mere 17 lines of monosyllabic dialogue deliberately enhanced by his robot-like delivery.

In 1986 Schwarzenegger married Maria Shriver, daughter of Eunice Kennedy, making him an in-law of the most famous Democrat family in the country. Even for Schwarzenegger, this was viewed as odd, considering he was a committed Republican and free-market capitalist. With several other popular films under his belt, Schwarzenegger proved to be the ideal figure to champion President Bush's (senior) President's Council of Physical Fitness, as chairman. Despite revelations that Schwarzenegger had taken steroids during his bodybuilding career, he showed uncommon political awareness, quickly becoming a regular visitor to the corridors of power, and cultivating a taste for more than locker room and Hollywood domination.

The 1990s was a time of fame consolidation and political maneuvering for Schwarzenegger. A string of moderately successful films were released, beginning with the *Terminator* sequel. But it was in 2002 that Schwarzenegger scored his first independent political victory, when Californians approved his Proposition 49, legislation to introduce an after-school education and safety program to be initiated and funded across the state's public schools.

In 2003, Schwarzenegger's was successful in his attempt to become the governor of California. In a large field of candidates, Schwarzenegger's profile and recognition proved decisive, and he became known as the "governator" on his inauguration in November, 2003. This was despite allegations of sexual misconduct and Nazi sympathies being thrown around during the campaign. Schwarzenegger's administration has enjoyed some initial success, with several propositions being passed that he promised during the election.

> The mind is the limit. As long as the mind can envision the fact that you
> can do something, you can do it – as long as you really believe 100 percent.
> *(Arnold Schwarzenegger, actor and Governor of California)*

Whether Schwarzenegger personifies the leader of the future is debatable. Clearly, those who worship at the altar of leadership traits and characteristics would point to his unswerving focus and driving desire for success, in addition to a textbook charisma and an almost Machiavellian results orientation. However, for those of us who view leadership as a more complex phenomenon than the possession of a few key personal features, Schwarzenegger's life as a leader might be more illustrative when viewed from the perspective of leadership development. In other words, the sport experiences he underwent during his formative years as a bodybuilder exemplify some important lessons that can be applied in the development of future leaders, and these are considered in this chapter.

First, Schwarzenegger's early experiences as a bodybuilder evidently encouraged him to appreciate the relationship between change and leadership. If, indeed, he was to become the champion bodybuilder that he envisioned, he realized early in life that he would have to constantly be prepared to change and adapt. One of the greatest challenges for world-beating athletes is sustainability. Schwarzenegger managed to win the Mr Olympia title six times during his record-setting career, an achievement he attributes to his hunger to refine his understanding of bodybuilding in all its facets, from training to nutrition and the skills of posing. For example, Schwarzenegger was the first bodybuilder to enlist the services of a dance instructor – a ballerina – to help his on-stage posing performances. Despite the fact that this caused him some unwelcome attention, particularly amongst his peers, Schwarzenegger claimed that it was essential to innovate and change; a disposition that he believes has been pivotal to his leadership development.

Secondly, education and training was fundamental to his success. Bodybuilding, perhaps more than many other sports where natural talent can come to the fore, is all about training, whereas in business, 95 percent of the time is spent in performance and only five percent (or less) is spent in training. The great lesson from sport is found in the fact that this ratio is effectively reversed. For a professional bodybuilder, training can occur twice a day, six days a week for 51 weeks in preparation for a single competition.

Schwarzenegger's approach to competition exemplified a single-minded commitment to training. But, notwithstanding his success in Austria, Schwarzenegger was still prepared to recognize his lack of knowledge. So, he made the decision to travel to the United States, where he believed some of his heroes might be able to educate him in the finer points of training and nutrition. Schwarzenegger was even prepared to travel to South Africa to train with bodybuilding great Reg Park. In his aptly named autobiography, *The Education of a Bodybuilder*, Schwarzenegger wrote:

> At the time I was just a punk, a bully, always ready to show off. I used to get in fights almost daily. Coming in contact with Reg helped me in getting rid of my behavioral problems. He was such an accomplished gentleman and it certainly wasn't difficult for me to admire him and want to emulate him.[1]

After retiring from competition, Schwarzenegger completed a BA in international marketing; he recognized the need for new goals and that vision has to be dynamic.

Sport remains way ahead of business in terms of its commitment to training, education, and innovation. However, in the past 15 years, business has started to embrace the fact that evolutionary change has all but disappeared. As a result of change being condensed into periods of great rapidity, business leaders have scrambled to embrace a plethora of fads in their haste to find an edge.

> If I was given eight hours to chop down a tree, I would spend seven hours sharpening my axe. *(Abraham Lincoln, former president of the United States)*

Thirdly, it is difficult to look at Schwarzenegger's life without being struck by his uncompromisingly ruthless approach to competition. He learned early the importance of psychology in sport, a lesson he has employed throughout his career in all its dimensions. In his autobiography, Schwarzenegger recalled the impact of watching the reigning Mr Olympia, Sergio Oliva, "pumping up" prior to going on stage. Oliva was deliberately hiding his physique until the last minute, when he could maximize the intimidation: "His back muscles were so huge that he seemed to be as wide as the hall itself! As far as I was concerned, I already knew – then and there – I would lose against him." In fact, Oliva narrowly won, but it was Schwarzenegger's last ever bodybuilding defeat. *Pumping Iron*, the cult documentary film focusing on Schwarzenegger, is a study in psychological gamesmanship, as he manipulates his chief competitor, Lou Ferrigno. Schwarzenegger's leadership approach had always been distinguished by a clear understanding of "the game" and, as Sun Tzu advocated, a keen understanding of his adversaries. On occasion, his ruthless commitment to winning perhaps went too far. When his father died in 1972, Schwarzenegger decided not to travel back to Austria to attend the funeral because he felt it would interrupt his preparation for the Mr Olympia competition.

> Trample the weak. Hurdle the dead. *(Unknown)*

Fourthly, although mired in controversy, Schwarzenegger has made a number of important contributions to community citizenship. These have included an association with the President's Council of Physical Fitness, as executive commissioner of the Hollenbeck Youth Centre Inter-City Games in Los Angeles, and as the "honorary" weightlifting coach for the Special Olympics, a role he has held for over 25 years, and for which he has worked with few media or commercial benefits. Perhaps most contentiously, Schwarzenegger has donated substantial sums to Jewish Holocaust causes, which culminated in a leadership award. Critics have argued that this has been to distance himself from his father's association with the Nazis. Nevertheless, even the most strident critic has to acknowledge that Schwarzenegger has played leadership roles in bodybuilding, community health, film, and politics.

Leadership Development Thinking

> Hard training, easy combat; easy training, hard combat.
> *(Marshal Suvorov, Russian general)*

Throwing around sport clichés is easy. After all, we can argue that sport is fast, aggressive, changeable, chaotic, complex, cohesive, and, at its best, aesthetic. But are these really the lessons we take from sport to business leadership? Do business leaders not yet acknowledge the turbulent environment, the cutthroat aggressiveness, and the need for innovation so helpfully exemplified in Governor Schwarzenegger's career? We would answer "yes and no": yes, in that most are aware of the changes that have arrived and those which are imminent, and no, in that most have not invested much thought into how these changes affect the process of leadership development. Put another way, and to conflate the chief argument of this chapter to a single point, while many likely elements of the future are well known to current and aspiring leaders, future leaders are still being prepared for leadership roles in the same ways. Thus, the key lesson from sport comes in its responsiveness in developing training methodologies that reflect innovation and the insatiable drive for competitive advantage. After all, athletes and coaches are more vulnerable than businesspeople to losing their jobs as a consequence of a poor performance, and sporting teams are typically composed of individuals with a personal investment in performance, which is more than can be said for many employees in service organizations.

Future changes will undoubtedly affect the context of leadership, but not so much its fundamental nature. The composition of leadership will be recognizable in the future, and the volume of traits and characteristics attributed to great leaders will remain largely relevant, if unhelpful. If one were to consider these recipes against the great leaders of history, the over-whelming majority would hold as much bearing to Kofi Annan as to Alexander the Great. The issue that we address is not what traits leaders must possess. There is sufficient written on the subject to be confident that everyone knows that leaders should be charismatic, possess integrity, be visionary, inspire confidence, and so on.

The more salient issue is that exposed by the leadership development Schwarzenegger received as an athlete. Specifically, he cultivated a *way of thinking,* engrained as a result of participating in elite sport, that emphasized competitiveness, change, training, education, and personal responsibility. As a result, we argue that sport provides a useful metaphor for thinking about leadership development in business, and this implies that leaders will need to be developed differently in the future in order to arrive at the same traits that have held firm for millennia. Being visionary and change-oriented have always been, and likely always will be, essential traits for leaders. The difference is that developing these traits is going to require a shift in educa-tion if the pace of current change holds or accelerates. Since sport is funda-mentally committed to performance and leadership development, as reinforced by the growing pool of talent identification programs and insti-tutes of sport dedicated to finding the sport leaders of the future, we look toward sport as an illustration of an industry worth benchmarking.

> If I had stood at the free-throw line and thought about 10 million people watching me on the other side of the camera lens, I couldn't have made anything. So I mentally tried to put myself in a familiar place. I thought about all those times I shot free throws in practice and went through the same motion, the same technique that I had used thousands of times. You forget about the outcome. You know you are doing the right things. So you relax and perform. *(Michael Jordan)*

The Age of Leadership?

Ideas about leadership and its development have changed over time. However, leadership researchers and authors have not steered completely away from their management and leadership predecessors. New perspectives of leadership often find significance in parts of earlier models. Leadership in this sense is a bit like fashion; some styles are unlikely to ever return, while others are cyclical and reflect the changing interests of society and the dominant perspectives of the times. Part of this paradox is that we may change our view of an individual or an organization depending on how and from where we view them. Thus, while context affects leadership fashion, it is also important to recognize that individuals change their perceptions of leadership as well. For example, some leadership research has implied that views of leadership approaches and styles change as a result of age, seniority, and past experiences.

While these changes are somewhat obvious, we must be cautious when speculating about the demands placed on future leaders. As we shall discuss, there is some evidence to suggest that some of the leadership aspects attributed to future requirements are just as relevant now, and vice versa. Put simply, we face the question as to whether there are some universal axioms, mottos or rules of sound leadership that may be almost timeless. The catch is, however, that they are not necessarily easy to bring to fruition, or more importantly, they may be more difficult to develop in the future, at least with current methods. Similarly, the obstacles to leadership development may have a consistent basis, such as in the difference between management and leadership.

In order to explore future leadership imperatives, it might be useful to consider several scenarios. To begin with, if we consider Jesus and his life, do we see a leader? For most modern-day Christians, the answer is undoubtedly "yes". If we view Jesus from the perspective of Herod, was he a leader or simply a criminal? If we view Jesus philosophically, that is, as the leader of a revolutionary movement whose beliefs two thousand years later are the touchstone of racial and religious emnity, do we perceive a leader or an ideologist who had no idea of the religious strife he would later create? Many people see Jesus as a great leader, irrespective of whether they accept him as a divine figure. In addition, the stories of his actions have become stalwarts of great leadership. It depends on from where and how we view him.

Less controversially, in the 2002 World Cup in soccer, Rivaldo, Brazil's key playmaker and one time deputy captain of the national team, play acted so well that it caused a referee to red card an opposition

Turkish player. After Hakan Unsai, the Turkish player, kicked a ball at Rivaldo which struck the Brazilian in the leg, he collapsed, holding his face, apparently in agony. But everything had been caught clearly on television. Rivaldo later refused to concede that he had acted inappropriately and the Brazilian press praised his leadership in reducing the opposition to ten men. Most sportspeople would think the act of Rivaldo despicable and would in no way consider him a leader. But, again, it depends on your viewpoint!

So let us accept that leadership can be viewed differently depending on our perspective. Does that have implications for how we develop leaders for the future? Not surprisingly, the answer is yes. Our modern concept of leadership suggests that we see our future leaders as coming from predominantly our middle or upper management strata. That is, overwhelmingly, those in the 35–50 age group. However, the face of the Western world is changing – and fast. By 2025, many minorities will have become near-majority populations in many countries – and minorities not just of race or religion, but age, gender, and education. Those over the age of 65 years will, in a quarter of a century or less, constitute almost 20 percent of many nations' populations. Women will predominate. In the more temperate environments, retired citizens may well constitute up to 60 percent of the population.

> He's soft and he's fat and he's wearing my clothes and he's getting too old and he was born on my birthday and I'm afraid if I stop running, he'll catch up with me. *(Nike poster)*

What this means is that modern leadership techniques, at least in the business environment, need to consider the point of view of this demographic change. After all, why are we seeking to develop programs to grow future leaders if not for those leaders to accept positions of responsibility in the corporate, bureaucratic, political, or similar world? If the future leaders cannot understand the perspective of their future customers, then they are likely to lose business, or confidence, or votes. In the business world, this concept is not confined to the retailing sector of the economy. Leaders will need to understand that an aging population may want more easily operable consumer goods; no more TVs and videos that cannot be installed without the aid of technicians or grandchildren. The aged will want more organically grown food, houses that are easily maintained, access to educational and physical activity facilities, and doctors who will make house visits. They will demand a bureaucracy that is understanding of their needs and compliant with their wishes. In the political world, the elderly will want leaders who understand their need for security, at home and in their normal environment.

Business and political leaders will need to understand that older citizens may want to continue working well past normal retiring age. Businesses will need to be restructured and leaders will need to understand, far more than in the past, the needs of the client, the customer, and the citizen. If leadership does not understand the perspective of the elderly, then they can expect the elderly to seek their own representation and develop their own leaders. Leaders will emerge from among the "grey army." They have the potential, and the wisdom, and will soon have the numbers to change the face of society. Current leadership and leader-makers had best be prepared.

The most prominent group of leadership gurus all worship at the altar of leadership ingredients. Whether it is Warren Bennis's five basic ingredients of leadership,[2] James O'Toole's characteristics of value-based leaders[3] or Stephen Covey's eight characteristics of principle-centered leaders,[4] they all take the view that leaders need to be taught certain skills and characteristics which they then live by. Do they live in a real world? In a real world, leadership means being followed and leaders remain leaders only as long as they are so perceived. Yet undeniably, as sport leaders exemplify, certain characteristics are desirable.

For courage, once more consider the story of Jim Peters told earlier, who, back in the 1954 British Empire Games in Vancouver, when competing in the marathon, neared the stadium some 15 to 20 minutes ahead of his nearest competitor. On entering the stadium, Peters, the first man to run the marathon in under 2 hours 20 minutes, staggered several times, all the time being cheered by the 30,000 strong crowd. Their cheers turned to tears as Peters, in the last stages of exhaustion, took 15 mins to struggle around the track before collapsing over the finish line. It was, however, the wrong finish line and, led off by the England team masseur, Peters was deemed not to have finished the race. No one who saw the race, however, whether in the stadium or on film, will ever forget the courage of the man who failed to finish.

For sportsmanship, consider the events of the 1956 National Athletic Championships in Melbourne, Australia. It was in a race between two of the fastest milers in the world, the world title holder John Landy, and Ron Clarke, the Australian and junior world mile holder. In the third lap, as Clarke moved to the lead with Landy at his shoulder, a third runner, Alec Henderson, tried to squeeze between the two and, in the process, Clarke clipped his heels and fell. Landy leapt over the falling body of Clarke, his spikes tearing into the flesh of Clarke's shoulder. The whole field of runners either jumped over Clarke or ran round him. Landy then did an amazing thing. He turned around, returned to Clarke's side, helped him to his feet, brushed cinders from his knees, checked his bloody shoulder, and then apologized. Clarke thanked him, told him to run and urged Landy to re-enter the race. Landy did, but not before ensuring that Clarke set off with him. At that stage, they trailed the field by some 60 yards. In the final yards, Landy overhauled the leaders to win in four minutes four seconds. Landy's sportsmanship could have cost him the Australian title and a place in the Melbourne Olympics. But it was more important to him that the spirit of sport was preserved. For that act he deserved, and gained, athletic immortality. Landy, now 75, has become the governor of the Australian state of Victoria.

> We run, not because we think it is doing us good, but because we enjoy it and cannot help ourselves. The more restricted our society and work become, the more necessary it will be to find some outlet for this craving for freedom. No one can say, "You must not run faster than this, or jump higher than that." The human spirit is indomitable. *(Sir Roger Bannister)*

Shifting Perspectives

With the coming of an immense demographic change, leadership will be seen differently. The baby-boomer generation will seek leaders who match and vigorously display their own required characteristics. The effect of this will be that leadership development programs will need to change in order to produce leaders who can successfully survive into the future. Sport thinking can be useful in several ways when applied to this imminent issue. On the surface, of course, sport seems to be obsessed with youth. While this is no doubt true, the more fundamental truth is that sport is obsessed with victory, and youth offers the highest chance for this payoff. From a human resource viewpoint, sport exemplifies the best person for the job, and since sport performance is a reasonably objective measurement of an individual's actions, invariably the best athletes come to the surface. Ironically, if the selection is based exclusively on performance, then the business lesson might be that in many instances older managers are better than younger, because they have the "runs on the board."

Six times a year the most skillful and powerful sumo wrestlers in Japan meet to compete in one of the grand tournaments. Twelve thousand people, strictly only those with the right connections, sit in the venue, while another 20 million watch on television. The sport is a national obsession, with over 60 percent of households tuning into the alternate monthly competitions, a figure that makes Western sport viewing look quite poor. For example, only 40 percent of households in the United States watch the Super Bowl each year.

As one of the country's most popular sports, it presents a spectacle of tradition, legend, skill, and sheer might. Although to the uninitiated there appears to be more might than skill involved, sumo wrestlers are actually remarkably expert in the 70 or so throws, trips, slaps, and strikes at their disposal. When sumo wrestlers have mastered these techniques and won their way through dozens of tournaments, they achieve the highest level of the sport – *yokozuna* – grand champion. Only around 70 sumo wrestlers have reached the illustrious ranks of *yokozuna* in the sport's nearly 2000-year history.

Yokozuna Masaru Hanada was a household name in Japan, admired for his tremendous performances as a relatively small wrestler of 290lbs, and for his leadership contribution toward the development of younger wrestlers. When he ended his 12-year career as a sumo wrestler at age 30, he made the unusual decision to pursue his dream as a professional American football player in the NFL. Although he got close, and was much admired in training camps, Hanada did not make it in professional football. However, it was not because of a lack of determination, strength, power, or fitness, but because he did not have a "football" brain. He was competing against men with around 15 years of game and training experience. They knew how and when to move intuitively. Although young, they were veterans of the game, and had learned how to think about performance and development. Hanada got close to being drafted based on pure physical ability, but he could not emulate 15 years of football experience, all of which had come very early in life to his high school and college trained fellow draft nominees.

With the demographic trend in Western nations toward higher proportions of senior citizens, in order for the pool of leadership talent to remain consistent, two changes have to occur. First, as we have already said, society and business will have to become more comfortable with older leaders, as their experience will be needed. Second, business leaders will need formative experiences of leadership earlier in their careers. That is why sport leaders can be so young and still manage the burden of leadership that sometimes sees them thrust into the media spotlight and placed under immense pressure. Many are able to cope simply because they received increasing exposure to leadership throughout their sporting careers. The evidence is clear that young people can assume leadership positions, and the future will demand that more do so. For Hanada, his development had not come from football, and his age precluded him from making the transition from sumo. His limitation was in knowledge.

> It is one of the strange ironies of this strange life that those who work the hardest, who subject themselves to the strictest discipline, who give up certain pleasurable things in order to achieve a goal, are the happiest men. When you see 20 or 30 men line up for a distance race in some meet, don't pity them, don't feel sorry for them. Better envy them instead.
> (*Brutus Hamilton, athletics coach*)

Knowledge is Leadership Power

The Future of Leadership is a compilation of nineteen chapters from some of the world's most prominent leadership commentators, and edited by prolific leadership author Warren Bennis, along with Gretchen Spreitzer and Thomas Cummings.[5] The book is indicative of writings on the future of leadership because it focuses on the changing nature of business, consumers, and life in general. As we have already asked in this chapter, does the changing face of the world, such as the aging population of consumers, affect the way leadership has to be discharged? For example, in the chapter, Knowledge Work and the Future of Management, author Thomas H. Davenport suggests that tomorrow's organizations will be increasingly filled with knowledge workers who will require a different kind of organization and leadership from what works for traditional industrial workers. In Davenport's view, these changes to the working population will demand the building of knowledge worker communities and supportive cultures where knowledge workers can thrive and grow. In other words, if the workforce of the future comprises an increasing proportion of thinkers compared to doers, then leadership development will need to prepare leaders for a new composition of followers. The world of sport provides a neat analogy here.

Over the past few decades as sport has professionalized, the relationship between doing and thinking has changed. More time is invested in preparation and training than ever before. Globalization and higher levels of competition have encouraged teams and athletes to spend hours not just on the training field but also in the gymnasium, heat chamber, physiotherapist's office, conference facility, and video room. It is standard practice in most professional team sports to spend several hours viewing video footage of the next opponent as well as the team's own performance. Every nuance of nutrition is considered, blood sugars monitored and tactics endlessly discussed. Professional sport has embraced a level of preparation that makes business training look underdone.

Sport leaders have an unquenchable thirst for training. Preparation is everything, and emerging leaders are encouraged to play a role as much as possible. Current sport leaders are rarely just the best players. More and more, they are the best thinkers, with knowledge of the game, tactics, cutting-edge training methods, nutrition, sports medicine and psychology, rehabilitation, and video analysis. The implication is that the preparation of business leaders in the future will need to be more extensive in order to keep track of the greater diversity of knowledge work that will take place in their organizations.

> In a world that is constantly changing, there is no one subject or set of subjects that will serve you for the foreseeable future, let alone for the rest of your life. The most important skill to acquire now is learning how to learn. *(John Naisbitt, futurist and author)*

Heptathlete and long jumper Jackie Joyner-Kersee exemplified the commitment to employ every means possible to be best prepared to perform. Her three gold, one silver and two bronze medals over four consecutive Olympic Games are indicative of not just mighty talent, but the preparation that bolsters it over 15 years of performance at the highest level. In the business world it is easy to complain that there is no time for training and education, but athletes like Joyner-Kersee have pointed out that there is no other option but to stay at the cutting edge of thinking in order to achieve sustainable success. Indeed, Joyner-Kersee's training background hardly leaves room for excuses. Hers was a sporting childhood that fell under the shadow of men's sport. When she discovered her pleasure in running and jumping as a child, she and her friends would carry sand in plastic packets from a nearby playground to her house and construct a long jump pit. Joyner-Kersee was ten years old when Title IX was passed in the United States, mandating equal access to sports for women, and she became a role model for female athletes around the country with her Olympic success.

The range of knowledge required by the business leader of the future will be far greater than any previous generation of leadership has needed. With fundamental shifts in the composition of Western populations, future leaders will have to acquire a firm grasp of their consumer's profiles, as well as an awareness of the knowledge sets of their workforce. This will be particularly troublesome because of the speed at which change will occur. In sport, knowledge is generally seen by professional athletes as fleeting – what is cutting-edge at one Olympics is often obsolete by the next. The traditional cry that weight training makes athletes muscle-bound and slow has been superseded with a generation of bodybuilder-like sprinters, so that even table tennis players and synchronized swimmers hit the gym. Similarly, the use of creatine monohydrate as a nutritional supplement has become a standard practice for most power athletes.

The half-life of knowledge is shortening in business as well. Business managers being trained for future leadership should be aware that studies are presently revealing that up to two-thirds of information presented at the beginning of an engineering degree is obsolete by the end. The figures are even worse for information technology and other technologically dependent areas of study. Little is known about the relevance of management training, but it would be a reasonable prediction that leaders of the future will need access to updated education on a regular basis. However, unlike their athletic counterparts, business leaders do not find much time away from the operational necessities of work to consider the latest developments in business thinking.

Vision and Chaos

The shift is also related to vision. According to the futurist Peter Ellyard, many business leaders possess the wrong kind of vision; one that is the domain of the manager rather than the leader.[6] The problem remains that the appointment of leaders – by definition – comes from the managerial ranks, and as a result, most leaders have demonstrated their abilities through impressive management. A future leader needs the opportunity to test him or herself now. No amount of management achievement is really sufficient to demonstrate that an individual is capable of taking a leadership position. Thus, one way of looking at the future of leadership is to acknowledge that most of the training and working activities undertaken by those in line for future leadership roles has little to do with leadership.

The overwhelming majority of management activity is centered on doing things rather than thinking about whether those things are the best for the future. Similarly, the structure of many large organizations remains rigidly hierarchical and discouraging for those with leadership aptitude to exercise their initiative. As the future structure of organizations shifts away from tightly bound roles and responsibilities, and increasingly managers are expected to demonstrate their ability to lead their teams through the twin challenges of competition and technological development, the opportunities for leaders to gain more practice will emerge. Perhaps, as Ellyard notes, one of the biggest differences between managers and leaders in the future will be in the questions they ask about the future.

Undoubtedly, for future leaders to receive the training they will require to deal with the rapidly changing goal posts of future business, a paradigm shift of sorts will be necessary. Most commentators about future leadership agree that as the speed of innovation continues to escalate, there will be a commensurate need for leaders to be masters of change, and even lead through what, by contemporary standards, we might consider one crisis to the next. In reality, as we have already observed in this chapter, the content of good leadership is unlikely to alter that much in the future. Successful leaders have always been shrewd change managers. The difference lies in the pace of change – the context in which the same old leadership traits will have to apply. Yes, leaders will still need charisma, energy, and persuasive communication among other characteristics, but they will have to exercise these powers during constant turmoil. Richard Pascale's term, "surfing the edge of chaos" is an apt description of this future, and also one that describes the nature of sport.[7]

> Self-security will be a hallmark of the leaders and exceptional organizations of the future. Self-security in an individual or a system brings a high ratio of coherence. Leaders or organizations with self-security can push power and authority downstream and develop centers of innovation and excellence at all levels of the organization. (Doc Childre and Bruce Cryer, From Chaos to Coherence)[8]

Sport leaders are comfortable with chaos and have acquired the mentality that goes with that comfort. The inherent unpredictability of a sporting competition lends itself to chaos, where there is a fine line between well-rehearsed synchronization and complete bedlam. Equally, breathtaking displays of aesthetic skill on the sporting field of play can come from apparent pandemonium where a team of individuals can blend into a collective mind with choreographed precision. Few business leaders are comfortable with the notion of the edge of chaos, but the nature of sport suggests that some of the greatest innovations can occur in this dynamic balance between structure and disorder. Interestingly, Pascale looks at organizations in exactly the same way, as complex systems that work best at the edge of chaos.[9] For example, he points out that organizations can be at risk when they are at equilibrium.

Consider this from a sporting perspective. Imagine a team that is behaving with complete control and stability. Although this sounds promising, little that is unpredictable and innovative occurs from such a position. Success in sport does not come during periods of stability, but rather comes in the periods between stability, where risk, boldness, and vision are critical. Equilibrium might be good during defense, but, as in the business world, it is not a recipe for market leadership any more than it is of a championship cup. As we discussed in Chapter 4 concerning team leadership, business structures in the future, if trends are to continue, will be flatter, with an increased emphasis on networks and virtual teams. Positional authority, as in sport, is likely to become subservient to the authority that comes from proximity to opportunity. In the words of Steve Grand, it will move from command and control to nudge and cajole.[10]

Pascale also noted that complex systems exhibit the capacity to self-organize and show emergent properties; the edge of chaos is not actually chaos itself, but a point where there is just enough control to manage the complexities of an organization in a standardized way and enough disorder to encourage new ways of looking at old problems, or invent new opportunities to pursue. Sport is a useful example of emergent and unexpected solutions to problems. The best athletes have the ability to manufacture something from nothing, but cannot do so as easily from a platform of calm control. We would not expect the footballing brilliance of Brazil to emerge from a playing philosophy emphasizing stability. Furthermore, sporting performances and organizations move toward the edge of chaos when the tasks they are faced with become more complex. Sport leaders tend to recognize that sport is a living entity and cannot be fully controlled or directed, so their efforts should be focused on stimulating an environment where innovation can occur. Like Muhammad Ali unconventionally leading with his right hand instead of a jab during the rumble in the jungle, a complex task sometimes produces an innovative solution. If the future of business is moving toward an environment more like sport, where change is pervasive and intrusive, and necessitates leadership through the dynamics of control and chaos, development activities need to prepare future leaders for a changing world.

Martina Navratilova was one of the first athletes to recognize the imperatives of a changing sporting landscape where new techniques of training were available for use in tennis. She attributes the turning point of her career, from 1981–1984 (Navratilova won 15 singles and 13 doubles tournaments in 1983, including Wimbledon and the Australian

Open) to her training regime, which had been developed in conjunction with champion basketball player Nancy Lieberman. Navratilova became the benchmarked tennis athlete, lifting weights, stretching, doing sprint training and agility exercises, supported by the latest information on nutrition. She was also one of the first tennis players to employ full-time coaches and rigorously evaluate every aspect of her physical performance and technical game. She adopted new equipment eagerly, experimented with tactical plans and maintained her serve and volley competitive advantage in a low-risk tennis environment that increasingly favored baseline strokes.

The Leadership Development Context

He went to Russia and wrestled. He studied all the videotape of Karelin's career. He saw things. Karelin was not quite so strong now. He could be gassed – if you were in top condition you could run him out of energy. He learned all these things. He was focused on beating the world's best wrestler. *(Reynold Gardner commenting on the preparation of his brother, Rulon, Sydney Greco-Roman wrestling gold medalist. Rulon Gardner defeated the Russian legend, Alexsandr Karelin. Going into the gold medal match, Karelin, with nine World Championships and three Olympic gold medals, had been unbeaten since 1987)*

Scarcely a comment can be made about the future of business without highlighting the radical escalation of technology that is currently occurring and is predicted to increase in pace over the coming decades. While it is not the intention of this chapter to provide an inventory of possible technological change – its presence and impact on business in general is assumed and was discussed in detail in our previous book, *The Sport Business Future*[11] – it is worth commenting on the nature of leadership development that will be required in order to prepare future business leaders. A possibility worth remembering is that future leaders may find themselves at the helm of organizations with different fundamental parameters from those at present. In effect, this means that tomorrow's leaders are being developed with the techniques, knowledge, and experiences of today. Of course, to some extent there is no way around this. However, as we have argued throughout this book, there are lessons from sport which can be helpful in illustrating how business leaders, both now and in the future, can adapt more rapidly to change and uncertainty as commonplace features of the business environment.

From sport we can find a myriad of examples of how new technology has been sought and embraced. These range from the revolutionary winged keel that won the America's Cup for the Australia II yacht team in 1983, breaking a 132-year American winning streak, aerodynamic wheels and bikes in road and velodrome cycling, recycling techniques developed for "green" sport facilities, nutritional supplements, architectural innovations particularly in terms of flexible use, and the predictable but astonishing incremental improvements in motor racing. Sport's lesson is simple: the difference between winning and losing is often a matter of exceedingly slim margins, and the results are unambiguous for all to see. Business leadership development programs should be designed to work toward inculcating future leaders with the same comfort with technology and experimentation that is both common and essential with successful sport managers, coaches, teams, and athletes. The evidence suggests that successful business leaders of the future will be those capable of introducing substantially more new technology than their competitors.

In addition to technology, the business environment of the future is likely to be characterized by several other features. To begin with, business leaders will have to manage the expectations of their stakeholders and the general public to be good corporate citizens, with well-established internal ethical controls, recently shown to be inadequate in companies such as Enron, Barings, National Westminster Bank, WorldCom, and the National Australia Bank. Interestingly, sport is a mixed example from this perspective, with some athletes leading the way with strong commitments to their local communities and charitable causes, but others showing little ethical dissonance about the use of performance enhancing drugs. Future leaders will be expected to create ethical cultures that begin at the senior level and are sustainable from the social and environmental perspectives as much as from the financial.

Change imposed as a result of globalization and an increase in the number of females in the workplace will bring about other cultural changes in future organizations. Leaders in the Western world will require more education about ways of doing business in other regions, particularly Asia. The impact of more females in business is unclear, but some studies have predicted that it will improve companies' use of human resources and will expand the view of how good performance is measured and rewarded. In the current business environment that is struggling with how to entice employee buy-in and retain high-performance staff, this may prove to be one of the key issues for future leaders. Moreover, as in sport, business will increasingly need leaders at all levels, rather than just at the top, to be able to navigate through endemic change. The process of finding "emergent" leaders can be expedited, however, through techniques like "acceleration pools," essentially a concept stolen from talent identification programs in sport.

The concept of acceleration pools picks up on the need for more systematic internal talent identification programs within companies. This concept has come to prominence as a consequence of a diminishing ability of companies to predict the career paths of their managers. External pressures such as the proliferation of mergers, downsizing, and restructuring have exacerbated this perception, which have, according to Byham et al., overwhelmed traditional succession planning within companies.[12] However, individuals with certain predetermined traits can be selected for acceleration pools, where their talents can be developed. An acceleration pool is a group of high-potential candidates for executive jobs who receive special learning and development opportunities. The acceleration of pool members is achieved through "stretch" jobs, special assignments, and enhanced visibility. Pool members are typically assigned mentors and have the opportunity to undertake additional training, such as university programs and in-company action learning sessions.

Along with this additional training, pool members receive more feedback and coaching than the typical manager. The obvious advantage of acceleration pools is that they add a systematized and practical dimension to succession planning efforts in a company. Learning is enhanced and progress is subject to an individual's performance; promotion is not designed to be attached to membership of the pool, but instead, the pool is designed to provide opportunities for leadership development. The use of acceleration pools as a component in corporate leadership development programs could provide a number of competitive advantages.

> I start with the premise that the function of leadership is to produce more leaders, not more followers. *(Ralph Nader, public interest activist and corporate critic)*

There are several alternatives. In the first instance, the corporate leadership development program could be the accelerated learning component of a leadership pool itself. The components of the program would subsequently reflect this positioning. For example, the program could, in part at least, fulfill the function of an "acceleration center," where strengths and development needs are assessed, and prescribed learning activities undertaken. Alternatively, acceleration pools and the concepts that are embraced within them could make up part of a leadership development program. Because managers from all levels can develop and implement acceleration pools within their own areas of responsibility, participants undertaking a leadership development program might be taught how to develop leaders using this technique. Given that mentoring and coaching are integral elements in acceleration pools, these managers would have to develop their own leadership skills in order to manage the pools and provide the requisite support. The leadership development program could also contain elements associated with coaching and mentoring. It could provide the framework for constructing the "stretch" jobs that would be used to supplement the program.

Preparing for Leadership in the Future

> Champions aren't made in gyms. Champions are made from something they have deep inside them: A desire, a dream, a vision. They have to have late minute stamina, they have to be a little faster, they have to have the skill and the will. But the will must be stronger than the skill. *(Muhammad Ali)*

While there are new developments in business and its environment, we would argue that the fundamental competencies and capabilities of leaders remain largely unchanged. That is not to say that leadership development will not need to be different from its current form. In fact, change to the business context will make the acquisition of the same stalwart traits more troublesome that ever before.

In 1987 Tom Peters published a book called *Thriving on Chaos*, which soon became a bestseller.[13] Despite the fact that this book was published almost 20 years ago, Peters' prescriptions for leadership in the future (which is now presumably our present) still seem to reflect current thinking about "new" leadership in the future. Peters' prescription of ten leadership axioms might be equally applicable in the first decade of the third millennium. In this context an axiom can be understood as a motto or rule of effective leadership. The possibility remains that one of the biggest issues facing leaders in the future may not be prediction so much as practice. Axioms and rules guiding good leadership are plentiful, and the majority of popular books on leadership are fixated with reinventing the axioms, often doing little more than introducing a fashionable new vocabulary.

It has been argued by hardened management consultants like Peters that it is the implementation phase of leadership that needs attention, and thus demands a place in any list of future issues. In Peters' axioms of "new" leadership, now almost two decades old, his "guiding premise" revolves around the ability of leaders to "master paradox." In other words, paradox or seemingly contradictory facts are part of the complexity of leadership. For example, sometimes better leadership involves empowering subordinates to make their own decisions. In this way, Peters tries to avoid the trap of oversimplification where all leadership is boiled down to a few pedestrian slogans. Consider the ten axioms of "new" leadership Peters provides:

1. Master paradox
2. Develop an inspiring vision
3. Manage by example
4. Practice visible management
5. Pay attention (more listening)
6. Defer to the front line
7. Delegate
8. Pursue horizontal management by bashing bureaucracy
9. Evaluate everyone on his/her love of change
10. Create a sense of urgency.

John Baldoni, in his book *Great Communication Secrets of Great Leaders*,[14] summarized our point when he commented that leadership skills for the twenty-first century are the same as were necessary in the twentieth. We might even predict that Peters' list may remain applicable in another 15 years. What changes over time, and will inevitably change in the imminent future, is *how* to live up to the axioms as the context of business changes. Although we cannot predict the future, there are certain trends that appear likely to continue. With these in mind, a general approach to leadership development can be formulated. Rather than summarizing the previous chapters, we have drawn out the themes that run through this book as key elements to the sport metaphor we have employed to stimulate discussion about improving business leadership.

What are some of the lessons we can learn from sport that might help frame an approach to business leadership development? Table 8.1 provides a list of ten key lessons from sport we have highlighted throughout this book that are relevant to the development of future leaders.

Table 8.1 Ten leadership lessons from sport for leadership development

Sport Metaphor	Leadership Development
1. Surfing the edge of chaos and capitalizing on complexity and ambiguity	Leadership development acknowledges the leader's role in ongoing change and periodic crises, including the introduction of new technologies. Constant evaluation of the business environment and trends. Comfort with surfing the edge of chaos, change and innovation.
2. Emergent leadership	Leadership development is deployed across all (or multiple) organizational levels to encourage leadership to emerge from the bottom up as well as top down. It should also consider the experiences of older organizational members and their contributions as potential leaders.
3. Importance of a training plan	Leadership development is systematic rather than haphazard, and forms part of an integrated long-term plan.
4. Relationships	Leadership development acknowledges the importance of the relationship between leaders and followers, including coaching and mentoring; leadership character and charisma; teamwork and collaboration; communication and leadership marketing.
5. Personal development	Leadership development places the responsibility for development on the individual.
6. Long-term winning	Leadership development facilitates thinking about sustainable competitive advantage and long-term strategy.
7. Never-ending commitment to knowledge development and training; perform as you practice	Leadership development is part of ongoing organizational life; education and training is normal.
8. Constant measurement and evaluation	Leadership development emphasizes the importance of performance management and measurement in all parts of leadership and the organization.
9. Uncompromising passion and spiritual connection	Leadership development works toward an emotional commitment to the organization.
10. Clear focus on the right goal	Leadership development encourages thinking about vision and is focused on core business issues and meeting core business goals without distraction.

Post Game

> The first responsibility of a leader is to define reality.
> (Max DePree, Leadership is an Art)[15]

To conclude, we would like to return to our opening comments about the nature of leadership for the future, and consider it from a wider perspective. With the tidal wave of demographic change bearing down upon us, leadership will require the development of new ways of thinking. These paradigms will ideally be cultivated and inculcated from the beginning of an individual's working life. Leadership training therefore will begin earlier. It may well be possible to locate and train young leadership talent in the same way that potential sports stars are found. Leadership training will start with the individual traits, skills, and abilities inherent or formed in childhood and youth. These traits, skills, and abilities are largely the product of genes and are influenced by the environment in the way they are nurtured. To individual traits and abilities, must be added the correct environment, to allow growth to occur. This requires that organizations produce a stable political, economic, legal, and ethical foundation. These characteristics of the organizational environment are also the subject of scrutiny by aspiring leaders. The correct mindset must then be added. This may be entrepreneurial, corporate or political, for example, and is dependent on the type of organization or corporate entity for whom the individual works. The creative use of individual abilities and corporate resources then needs to be developed. The individual will be continually examined and updated in his or her leadership capabilities. At each point in this sequence, the change process may need to be reviewed and intellectual growth determined. Outcomes will be stipulated at every point. In summary, the future of leadership will be focused on the measurement of individuals' development within rapidly changing organizations, also in a way analogous to sport today.

The material on leadership is prodigious. However, the number of contributors is misleading because there are few genuinely new ideas. Most repackage what is already known from well-established concepts of leadership and add a new twist. While they are frequently inventive, and sometimes innovative, few approaches are rigorous. Nevertheless, some are very appealing and convenient, largely because they are easy to discuss, comprehend, and remember. We must therefore remain vigilant about evaluating the composition of "new" leadership, when there is considerable evidence that the essential content of leadership has not changed substantially in human history. However, in contrast, the development of this content will need to be considerably different to account for the changes occurring in the business environment.

This chapter has reflected on the degree to which leadership imperatives will change in the future. This has been considered from the perspective of the changing nature of business, society, and culture. It has also discussed the inadequacies of our present approach to selecting and grooming leaders for the future. It has noted that some axioms of good leadership would seem to be robust and less vulnerable to fashion. In the main, we have made these points by using sport and the characteristics of some of its champions as a vehicle for argument. It therefore seems appropriate to finish where we began – with an extended biography.

If this chapter has preached preparation as a precondition for successful leadership development in a turbulent world, then a sport example need not venture further than American cyclist Lance Armstrong. In the cutthroat professional cycling environment, Armstrong's performances have exemplified remarkable training and unprecedented sustainability, marked by a level of tenacity and fortitude that would make any individual a leader and inspiration. In 2004, for a record sixth time, Armstrong cruised along the Champs Elysees to win the pre-eminent cycling race in the world, the Tour de France. More remarkably, Armstrong has become the most successful and renowned cyclist ever, despite the sentence delivered by an oncologist in 1996, which estimated his likelihood of survival at no more than 50 percent.

A natural endurance athlete, Lance Armstrong began his leadership and sporting development as a triathlete in his hometown of Plano, Texas. Although exceptionally talented, his love for cycling won out, and he qualified for the opportunity to train with the US Olympic developmental team in Colorado Springs during his final year of high school. His path toward leadership of both his sport and cancer sufferers began to gain real momentum at this time, when he was only 17. Within two years, Armstrong had become the national amateur champion and finished 11th and 14th respectively, in the 1990 Junior World Championships and the 1992 Barcelona Olympics.

In a now infamous ride, Armstrong's first professional race post-Olympics was a disaster, in which he finished not only last but 27 minutes behind the winner. However, he bounced back immediately and finished second in a race two days later. He would later credit his resolve to return after his heartbreaking professional debut to the grounding given to him by his mother, a hard-working single parent who had nurtured his talent and cultivated in him an inner strength and determination. The following season in 1993 was considerably better, including ten titles, of which the US Pro Championship, the first stage of the Tour de France and the road racing world championship were part. Armstrong's team was ranked in the top five in the world, and within three years, Armstrong himself was the number one ranked cyclist in the world.

Used to sublimating pain and living with fatigue as a professional endurance athlete, Armstrong ignored a growing lethargy that late in 1996 forced him to realize he was not well. Tests revealed that he had testicular cancer, which had spread to his lungs and brain. Not only was surgery imminent and necessary to save his live, cancer specialists placed his odds for recovery at less than even. Two lesions in Armstrong's brain were removed in October 1996, and he underwent aggressive chemotherapy treatment. Blood test results improved and within five months after his initial diagnosis, Armstrong gingerly began riding and training, uncertain that he would ever race seriously again. He was a changed man though, and, in January 1997, launched a cancer foundation and solidified his position as default leader and inspiration to thousands of sufferers around the United States. By September of the same year, Armstrong announced a return to racing. It was not a smooth transition, however, with few teams willing to take a risk with him. Eventually he was accepted by the United States Postal Service team.

In 1998, Armstrong began to regain his pre-treatment form, winning the Tour of Luxembourg and finishing fourth in the Tour of Holland and Tour of Spain. It was not until the Tour de France in 1999 that he made an indelible impression upon the world, however, beginning the race with a stage victory and winning the race by a comfortable margin. In so doing, Armstrong became a leader not only of his team, but also of all cancer sufferers everywhere; he emerged as a symbol of hope. Proving it was not fluke, Armstrong returned the following year to defeat the 1997 Tour winner, Jan Ullrich, and the 1998 winner, Marco Pantani, who were both absent in 1999. He has subsequently won the coveted race an additional four times.

Today, Armstrong considers cancer the best thing that ever happened to him: a rare opportunity to fully appreciate the gift of life, family, and friends. He has not been shy about assuming a leadership role either, as the spokesperson for the Lance Armstrong Foundation, which is working toward increased awareness of cancer, early detection, and survivorship. Notwithstanding what might be described as the best comeback in sport, Armstrong has become the archetypal leader, far more than an athlete, and a beacon to cancer victims sick with chemotherapy and despair. It is a leadership role that Armstrong fulfills with an uncommon passion, attributing the development of his leadership character and skills to the combined tempering of time on the lonely black tar and a stay beneath clinical, white sheets. In the words of journalist Rick Reilly: "People don't want autographs. They want to touch him because to them he's a hope machine."

> I didn't just jump back on the bike and win. There were a lot of ups and downs, good results and bad results, but this time I didn't let the lows get to me. *(Lance Armstrong, professional cyclist and Tour de France winner)*

Notes

1 A. Schwarzenegger (1983), *Arnold: The Education of a Bodybuilder*, Fireside, New York.
2 W. Bennis (1994), *On Becoming a Leader*, Random Century, New York.
3 J. O'Toole (1995), *Leading Change*, Ballantine Books, New York.
4 S. Covey (1992), *Principle-centered Leadership*, Simon & Schuster, New York.
5 W. Bennis, G. Spreitzer and T. Cummings (eds), *The Future of Leadership*, Jossey Bass, San Franscisco.
6 P. Ellyard (2001), *Ideas for the New Millennium*, Melbourne University Press, Melbourne.
7 R. Pascale (1999) "Surfing the Edge of Chaos", *Sloan Management Review*, Spring, pp. 83–94.
8 D. Childre and B. Cryer (1998), *From Chaos to Coherence: Advancing Emotional and Organizational Intelligence Through Inner Quality Management*, Butterworth Heinemann, Burlington, MA.
9 R. Pascale (1990), *Managing on the Edge*, Simon & Schuster, New York.
10 S. Grand (2000), *Creation: Life and How to Make It*, Weidenfeld & Nicholson, London.
11 A. Smith and H. Westerbeek (2004), *The Sport Business Future*, Palgrave Macmillan, Basingstoke.
12 W. Byham, A. Smith and M. Paese (2002), *Grow Your Own Leaders: Acceleration Pools*, Financial Times/Prentice Hall, New York.
13 T. Peters (1987), *Thriving on Chaos*, HarperCollins, New York.
14 J. Baldoni (2003), *Great Communication Secrets of Great Leaders*, McGraw-Hill, New Jersey.
15 M. DePree (1989), *Leadership is an Art*, Doubleday, New York.

CHAPTER 9

Conclusion: Leadership in Sport

None of us is as smart as all of us. (JAPANESE PROVERB)

This chapter provides a conclusion to this book by reminding the reader about the key attributes of sport that offer leadership lessons, emphasizing vision, emergence, preparation, relationships, personal development, sustainability, knowledge cultivation, measurement and evaluation, passion, and a goal focus. These ten attributes of sport have formed the glue for this book. We have used them in various forms and weightings in every chapter. Here, we return to them as a way of summarizing the lessons for business that a sport perspective can stimulate. We also remind the reader how these attributes have shed new light on some of the pivotal aspects of leadership activity discussed in the preceding chapters, including the leadership function, relationships with followers, leading teams, coaching and mentoring, spiritual dimensions, marketing leaders, and leadership development for the future.

We have argued that sport offers a unique metaphor for critically examining leadership in business. Starting with the need for comfort with the unpredictable nature of sport, to the importance of preparation and training and the key roles that those at the coal face perform, the best of sport can be found in the tension between chaos and control where a coaching approach offers new ways of thinking about followers.

In Chapter 2, we began with an examination of the key activities that leaders undertake. Instead of the conventional inventory, we observed that the opportunity sport thinking provides comes in revealing what should be core to a business. Although many sport organizations do pursue commercial revenue streams, they rarely get confused about the real issue, which is winning. Conversely, while business leaders may well be unambiguous in their goal of increased profitability, a better understanding of the activities core to their business is advantageous. We discussed many examples in the chapter. This is effectively a reminder of the importance of distinguishing between a means to an end and the end itself. We argued that the capacity of a business leader to do this is pivotal to their effectiveness as a change agent.

The ability of business leaders to bring about change depends greatly on the relationships they forge with members of their team. In Chapter 3, we used the sport perspective to consider the roles of the followers in the leadership equation. From sport we highlighted the importance of the commitment of followers to the success of a leader. In fact, the ability of a leader to cultivate deep feelings of emotional loyalty may be the distinguishing feature of successful leaders, the benchmark for which is found in sport. In order to achieve this, we discussed the relevance of the perceptions of personality, charisma, and tribal allegiances.

From this platform of followership and tribalism, we ventured into the significance of team leadership in Chapter 4. We used sport thinking to reinforce several aspects of team leadership and carefully examined the nature of great sporting teams, finding that there are several key business lessons, including how to approach membership, the awareness that team composition is more important than individual talent, the role of establishing a sense of belonging as the currency of meaning and as a catalyst for action, the importance of structure and specified roles, and the power of ritualization for reinforcing behavior and belonging.

To bolster the development of teams in Chapter 5, we turned to some aspects of leadership that are unique to sport, and that are gaining more prominence in the business world, namely, coaching and mentoring. We have argued that business leaders can benefit from understanding the coaching and mentoring function central to sport. Relationships are at the core. Our main premise has been that the best sport coaches in the world have made relationships with their players a priority part of their leadership approaches. We proposed three business leadership lessons that come from this coaching angle.

In the first instance, business leaders can behave as mentors for selected members of their team. Although limited in the breadth of impact, the intensity of the mentoring experience can yield significant results for its recipient. Next, leaders can play their role as a kind of coach – spotting, developing, nurturing, and encouraging talent to emerge. The final lesson for business leaders that we highlighted can be found in the strange position that sport coaches can find themselves in, caught between the hierarchy of the management team who tend to be eager to hire and fire coaches as a solution to performance problems, and the athletes themselves who tend to be sensitive and demanding. The cases we explained revealed that some tremendously successful sport coaches have shown their talents in managing these two divergent and sometimes contradictory forces. In many ways, we viewed the successful sport coach as the epitome of middle hierarchy leadership in business. They are capable of finding the harmony between the tension of short-term operational performance (the "win now" push of management) and long-term strategic demands (the development "pull" of athletes). We argued that Chapter 5 is closely related to Chapter 4, and that its lessons should be considered in light of the leadership of teams. In addition, Chapter 5 also related strongly to the personal development pressures of sport. This led us to discuss the importance of the spiritual and emotional dimensions of leadership in Chapter 6.

Chapter 6 explored the importance of personal development in the rise and prominence of leaders. It considered the psychological mechanisms associated with the emotional or "spiritual" journey that leaders have to undergo in order to create a personal maturity needed to handle the intense scrutiny and challenges that come along with leadership. Our contention was that sport provides an inbuilt personal development process, complete with the sort of confronting performance feedback that is unusual in the business world. When this self-regulatory system is in full swing, then the flow state can come about, where leaders experience the focus that can occur in rare moments on the sporting field of play. Because sport performance is so personal, and defeat is so emotional, successful sport performers have an opportunity to experience a level of personal growth in a contained and accelerated microcosm of life.

The lesson for business leaders can be found in the flexibility that sport leaders have acquired as a result of the vagaries of their "workplace". They are less encumbered by conventional approaches and can more readily accept novel solutions to problems. Perhaps the most important lesson that comes from sport for business leaders is about leading through pressure. Sport has long been assumed to be character building because of this very characteristic. The fact remains that it is impossible to become a successful sport performer without the capacity to come to terms with pressure and failure. This, in turn, provides sport leaders with a kind of emotional conditioning that any business leader would do well to possess. We have argued that thinking like a sport leader is advantageous because it tends to correct overconservatism. Business requires risk taking, performance under pressure, and even regular failure. The leader with enough personal strength to accommodate the emotional rollercoaster will be the most successful. Part of the winning formula is to know what to reveal and what not to, and when selling a leader is as important as the leadership itself.

Perception plays a pivotal role in the psychology of high-performance sport. Consider the youngest ever heavyweight boxing champion Mike Tyson. In his heyday, between 1986 and 1990, he literally terrorized the heavyweight division, as much a force in the minds of his opponents as in the ring. Then, at the peak of his career in 1990, with 37 professional wins and no losses, Tyson was knocked out by Buster Douglas, a 42–1 underdog. At this, Tyson's perception as an invincible was lost; after all if a rank outsider could knock him down, perhaps others could as well. After a spell in prison, Tyson returned with the same ferocity to begin to rebuild his image, at one point in a post-fight press conference stating of his next opponent: "I want your heart. I want to eat his children." Perhaps, unlike Muhammad Ali, Tyson was not in control of his own image, but as a leader in the boxing ring, he certainly was the beneficiary of some advantageous marketing.

Our argument in Chapter 7 was that the success of leaders is not always exclusively based on their actual performances. Much of what leaders do is unobserved. As a result, it is what leaders are observed to do that makes their reputation. We discussed the importance of transformational leadership and the perception of charisma in communications made by a leader. Business leaders can gain from utilizing the marketing techniques employed by some of sport's most high-profile performers who wield perception and imagery as key parts of their leadership arsenal. Selling it like Beckham is the key lesson.

In Chapter 8, we examined the future of work, sport, and society in order to better understand the essential aspects of leadership in the future. We concluded that sport thinking is essential to help business leaders feel comfortable with uncertainty, which appears more likely in the future. With the right underlying management approach – one that appreciates the lessons from sport – there is greater room for novel developments and the emergence of leadership throughout an organization. We also showed how the sport metaphor emphasizes the importance of preparation and training in transforming solid business leadership into performance.

These were the business leadership lessons from sport that we specified in Chapters 1–8. However, now we would like to return to the key themes that underpinned all the chapters; the glue that has held the book together. In other words, there are some aspects of sport that have a universal application to business leadership, whether considered in light of the leadership function, followers, teamwork, coaching and mentoring, spiritual and psychological dimensions, marketing, or the development of leaders for the future. In Chapter 1 we specified ten dimensions or characteristics of sport that we considered relevant to business leadership. We subsequently applied them to a range of business leadership aspects and situations, each of which represented chapters. It is now appropriate to return to these ten original dimensions and their inherent business leadership lessons, having provided our interpretations of them in each chapter, so that the reader might apply them to their own circumstances. We provide the following section as a reminder of the ten characteristics and their chief, but general, lessons.

> Having read our interpretations in the preceding chapters, the reader can now consider how the ten original business leadership lessons from sport apply to their own specific circumstances.

Business Leadership – Ten Lessons from Sport

I. Vision: On the Edge of Chaos

Two boxers slug it out in the ring. Punches fly, some are parried, others ducked or slipped and a few hit without serious damage. Then, during another flurry, one punch suddenly connects with enough force to knock out its unlucky recipient. The match is over, and spectators can only contemplate what might have occurred if only ...

The first characteristic we have drawn from sport concerns its inbuilt chaos and unpredictability. Since sport is one of the most changeable products in the world, sport leaders have to be capable of navigating the turbulence and constant crises that occur. Business leaders can learn from this comfort with uncertainty. Business leaders can improve their performances by learning to surf the edge of chaos in the same way that sport leaders do. It is in the dynamic tension between chaos and order that original solutions to problems can arise. Some of the most exhilarating moments in sport have occurred in the transition between chaos and stability, where seamless and spontaneous streams of play can emerge at any point, executed with more precision than if it had been scripted. The winner in sport is the athlete or team capable of transforming chaos into opportunity. Consequently, to follow the metaphor, the best business leaders can see beyond the indecision that accompanies disorder and uncertainty, envision the goal, and create opportunities to bring it to fruition. The lesson for business leaders is in determining the vision and understanding that chaos is normal and cannot be escaped. The best course of action is to accept it and forge a vision, allowing enough flexibility for tactical change at a moment's notice.

Sir Clive Woodward, former England rugby union coach and leader of the 2003 World Cup winning squad, is a great example of a sport leader who saw through the grey zone and envisioned what could be achieved. For Woodward, getting through the ups and downs of the English rugby performances necessitated treating the leadership of the team like a professional business. Hardly hailed as a visionary, Woodward was considered something of a crank by the media when he declared that he would make the team the best in the world.

One of Woodward's most noticeable leadership strengths could be found in his ability to hold his vision steady throughout the turmoil of tournament success and failure. One way in which he was able to lead through the uncertainty was to devise general rules that could be followed when there were no other cues available; when in doubt it was always possible to revert to a couple of key rules and principles that could be assured would lead in the right direction. For example, Woodward was aware that in the turbulence of the sporting environment, small but essential details could be overlooked. By treating the team as a business to be led, Woodward was able to deal systematically with the scores of details that eventuated, knowing that in totality they represented the difference between success and failure. Similarly, Woodward believed that success demanded a different approach. As a result, another basic rule was the encouragement of thinking differently about the game and training in order to develop innovative and lateral approaches.

Woodward's example is noteworthy for many reasons, but for us the most interesting aspect of his approach is that it blends the characteristics of business leadership with sport thinking. In this sense, Woodward's leadership is an exemplar of exactly our point in writing this book. He has taken the lessons of sport to the leadership of a team, and he rightly observed that it really did not matter what kind of team it was, as the leadership philosophy behind it is completely transferable. It is no wonder that Woodward is confident enough to imply that he could take the helm of any top sport team. Woodward's vision-dominated leadership approach provides him with the direction to overlook the vagaries of coaching life that can reduce a prince to a pauper almost in a single season. The leadership lesson for business is clear: sport thinking allows the leader to see beyond the minutiae of operational activities and focus on the vision just over the horizon, visible at first only in the mind of the leader, through a field obscured by a distracting range of choices. The leader who is comfortable with the uncertainty of this environment, however, knows what he or she is looking for and remains ready to pounce on any opportunity that will help to realize the vision.

> High-performance sport exists in the tension between chaos and order; a "chaordic" grey zone from which anything can emerge at the confluence of an unpredictable interaction between changeable variables. Sport leaders capable of seeing beyond the grey "chaordic" zone are the ones who can make great things happen.

2. Emergence: Bottom to the Top

One of the great delights of sport is that when it comes to performance, it is difficult to defeat genuine talent. It bubbles to the top, as often as not defying expectations and the predictions of scouts and commentators. The precise formula determining the composition of physical prowess, skill, psychological disposition, and coaching that yields a star remains uncertain, always subservient to an unforeseeable X factor. As we noted in the first point, at the edge of chaos, where great sport is performed, there is always the possibility of an emergent force, driving from the bottom up irrespective of how much they get paid or whether anyone knows their name.

Sport epitomizes the potential for emergent leadership; leadership emanating from the bottom up rather than just the top down. For several decades it has been fashionable in business literature to talk about the importance of workers or employees at the coal face. Their importance, we are told, is unquestioned because it is they who manufacture the products or serve the customers from which the organization generates its revenue. However, while times have changed, there is no foreseeable future in which these employees can expect to be remunerated at a level relative to those who deliver the product in professional sport. The sports industry, like some pockets of the entertainment industry, is among the few where those delivering the key services are considered the most important individuals in the organization, and are compensated accordingly. With sport thinking, business leaders can benefit from a renewed awareness of the potential for leadership to emerge from unexpected locations in the hierarchy. Part of the lesson here is in recognizing that the conditions have to be right for emergence to occur. Leaders capable of providing suitable conditions will find key team members in unexpected places. In more conventional organizations, emergent leaders will not be found until some catalytic event forces them under the spotlight.

One such incident we highlighted was caused by the air disaster on 6 February 1958, in which the core of Manchester United's team was lost. Despite the 24 deaths, one of the survivors was 20-year-old forward Bobby Charlton, to whom the on-field leadership of the team fell. Charlton was thrust into a leadership role well before he could have reasonably expected. However, he proved a tremendous leader and earned himself a place on the England team, and took Manchester United's under-experienced side to the final of the FA Cup. Charlton ultimately won 106 England caps and was awarded both European and Football Association Player of the Year honors.

Business, like sport, can experience its own crises that give rise to unexpected sources of leadership. We would hardly advocate the deliberate instigation of such crises, even if they do provide the inspiration for a new level of leaders to emerge. On the other hand, understanding that leadership resides in people at all levels within an organization is a powerful awareness if it is translated into action. This means that leaders have to be prepared to facilitate the access of individuals to the top with new sources of innovation and thinking, and once there, they must be given a voice in its implementation. A leader might even, for example, organize mentoring or other programs to help tease out this talent. This does not necessarily compromise hierarchy, but it does assume that leadership is as important at the coal face or middle management as it is at the top of an organization, as sport reminds us.

Sport also suggests that emergent leadership may be the outcome of the interaction of a group, rather than the exclusive result of an individual's efforts. This kind of emergent leadership is also sometimes referred to as distributed leadership,[1] and, as we said in Chapter 5, is the outcome of a collective set of simultaneous activity instead of cumulative action. The clear lesson for business leaders here is that new forms of leadership can be discovered from the bottom up when the conditions of work encourage collective contributions and not just directive control from the top down. In other words, as on the sporting field of play, the power ultimately should be in the hands of the players. This lesson implies that business leaders would be wise to consider opening up the boundaries of leadership, recognizing that there are inevitably a variety of skills and expertise ranges covered by different team members and at different levels of the hierarchy. The more leadership decisions at the operational level are made by experts the better.

> Spontaneous forms of emergent leadership can be encouraged by changing modes of decision making to embrace its potential. This is achieved by increasing the autonomy of teams, changing organizational structures to reduce unnecessary controls, supporting examples of informal and unexpected leadership, and providing opportunities for collective contributions to strategy.

3. Preparation: Perform as you Practice

Trial and error is not enough to make it to the top in sport. Only dedicated training and preparation can transform natural talent into elite success. In some sports the ratio between training and performance is extraordinarily high. Consider, for example, the 100 meters sprinter for whom any given 10 or 11 second performance is supported by thousands of hours on the track and in the gym. Or, what about the gymnast for whom a 60 second Olympics routine has been preceded by four years of training, six hours a day, six days a week. It may not be practical for business leaders to engage in such time-consuming preparation, but the sport thinking approach does stress the value of training as an avenue for the development of quality performance. As every coach knows, you can only expect an athlete or team to perform as well as they have practiced. Sport thinking encourages business leaders to think more consistently about training as a normal part of business activity.

Arguably more than any other type of athlete, bodybuilders win or lose depending on the quality of their preparation. Notwithstanding their inherent genetic advantages and the impressiveness of their posing routine, the whole of a bodybuilders' on-stage performance is determined beforehand in the gym and the kitchen. With this in mind, the career of Arnold Schwarzenegger as an athlete, actor, and politician is illustrative of a leader who, time after time, was reminded of the importance of preparation. From Schwarzenegger's life several leadership lessons drawn from sport thinking are apparent.

Threaded throughout Schwarzenegger's bodybuilding career was the apparent awareness that part of the training and preparation cycle is change. Not only was Schwarzenegger aware of the latest training techniques, he constantly sought new advantages that he could wield against his opponents, including a better understanding of the psychology of competition and even the nuances of dance as they applied to his posing routines. Where success can urge some athletes to believe that they have hit upon the magic formula, Schwarzenegger's career is peppered with examples of careful analysis. His reputation as a competitor may indeed have been associated with arrogance, but his actions were of humility before the training altar.

Schwarzenegger recognized that his training and nutritional regime were the only things keeping him ahead of his competitors. Given his extraordinary competitive record, including a six-year period of apparent invincibility, Schwarzenegger was clearly capable of taking the extra step in preparation. Focused, aggressive, and hungry, Schwarzenegger's bodybuilding career also shows a streak of ruthlessness that is a hallmark of successful athletes.

> Implicit in this book is the view that training must precede performance. Leaders cannot expect their team or organization to perform at a high level without carefully planned preparation. Nor can leaders expect their team to remain at the top without an ongoing preparedness to innovate, along with a redoubled commitment to training and practice, as well as a genuine hunger for success.

4. Teamwork: The Synergy of Success

Throughout this book there are examples of leadership success built upon relationships. Indeed, we devoted Chapters 4 and 5, to this fundamental lesson from sport. Even in individual sports, athletes remain the product of a team effort. However, it is in the performance of teams that the sport metaphor is so patently useful. Sport leaders must be fully aware of the importance of the relationships between team members as well as their own relationships with subordinates. The advantage of looking at the role of relationships from a sport viewpoint is that their fluid nature can become more transparent than they are in business. In businesses where leadership roles do not tend to vary, sport might serve as a reminder of the advantages of fluid relationships where a team operates best with diverse pockets of leadership depending on the situation. The obvious lesson from sport revolves around the power of synergy. As we have noted, teams constructed of the best individuals, while impressive on paper, will not necessarily outperform a synergetic team. In the same way that the best tennis doubles players will defeat a team comprising the number one and two ranked individual players in the world, a team that has become more than the sum of its parts is more dangerous than one full of individual stars.

From 1999 to 2005 (and perhaps beyond), the Australian cricket team has embodied the characteristics of a team whose leaders understand the effects of synergy. Up until 2004, the team was captained by Stephen Waugh, and since then has continued to perform as the best cricket side in the world with an historic test series victory in India, under the leadership of Ricky Ponting. From October 1999 to March 2001, the team rewrote the record books, with 16 consecutive test match victories. During Waugh's captaincy, the team also secured two World Cups.

Waugh's vast legacy as a leader of the Australian cricket team was a strongly bonded core group of players, who considered themselves accountable not only to themselves and their country, but also to their colleagues in the dressing room. There is also evidence that Waugh's captaincy emphasized a fluid leadership contribution. For example, every member of the team was a match winner in various circumstances. Each was nurtured and developed so that, when under pressure, at least one player would perform at their best. All were expected to make a contribution to match strategy discussions. As a defining trait, Waugh's leadership was distinguished when the team was underperforming. It was his capacity to change the fortunes of a match that demonstrate a leadership approach that makes the best use of the synergistic potential of strong relationships.

> Sport thinking can draw attention to the importance of coaching, mentoring, teamwork, collaboration, and communication while reinforcing malleable ideas about leadership positions. Business leaders need to be aware that synergistic teams comprise individuals who are best suited to the roles they are playing. Like "race seating" in rowing, where individuals are replaced one at a time during training, there are sometimes synergistic effects that make the team perform better with a new addition who, in theory, should not bring an improvement. Synergy in teams means performing better than the sum of the parts would predict.

5. Personal Development: Leadership from the Inside Out

The brevity of professional sporting careers offers athletes a lifetime of opportunities for personal development compressed into little more than 15 years, or sometimes more, for the best, but less than three years, on average. It is for this reason that it is not uncommon for individuals in their early twenties to be considered seasoned veterans and team leaders. Where in the business world personal success is sometimes ambiguous and generally that knowledge is confined to a handful of people, it is impossible for high-performance athletes to avoid confrontation with failure, often in a public forum. Imagine that every decision you took from behind your desk were on public display, the fodder for discussions ranging from the back page of the paper to the pub. For elite sportspersons this is a daily reality. Indeed, since many sportspeople are relatively young, they are forced to endure immense pressure, and are expected to improve with every performance. While many athletes are unable to face the pressures of the spotlight, those who endure benefit from an accelerated exposure to the vagaries of life.

In short, although some champion sporting performers show immaturity in parts of their life and in some dealings with the media, they have nevertheless developed psychological robustness on the field of play. Clearly, personal development is relative to the manner in which it is cultivated. We have not followed the traditional argument that sport builds character. However, it is clear to us that high performers have undergone some personal development that is critical to their success as leaders in sport. Equally, we contend that the sport metaphor reminds us that business leaders are also the product of their personal development, the relevant portion of which needs to be cultivated from experience in business.

One case that illustrates a degree of personal development is that of former Arizona State University and Arizona Cardinals linebacker, Pat Tillman. Although he was a star at college, Tillman was selected in the NFL draft as 226th pick for the Cardinals. Within five months, Tillman had become the team's starting safety, and in season 2000 had set a club record for tackles, in turn attracting a lucrative $US9 million offer from the St. Louis Rams. Not only did Tillman decline this offer, he also turned down a three-year, $US3.6 million contract with the Arizona Cardinals in order to enlist in the army with his brother Kevin. It was their response to the September 11 terrorist attacks. They felt as though their country was under threat and it was their responsibility to respond by putting themselves on the line. Kevin and Pat Tillman completed basic, individual, parachute and ranger indoctrination training and were assigned to the Second Battalion of the 75th Ranger Regiment, the US army's premier light infantry unit, and were subsequently deployed to Iraq and Afghanistan. Sadly, Pat Tillman was killed during a fire fight in the mountains of Afghanistan bordering Pakistan while searching for al-Qaeda and Taliban leaders. As team leader, Tillman provided covering fire against the enemy position, an action for which he was posthumously awarded the Silver Star. Subsequent reports have suggested that

Tillman was killed by friendly fire, but this possibility does not diminish his decision to sacrifice fame, fortune and, ultimately, life, for the service of his country.

While the tragedy of Tillman's death is difficult to overlook, his decisions were indicative of a man with a strong sense of duty and obligation. Whether sport developed this personal strength and loyalty, or just brought it to the surface, we will never know, but for the business leader, Tillman is more than an inspiration. Whether we agree with Tillman's values is another matter, but it is hard not to admire the conviction that drove his loyalty to the Cardinals and his country. Whatever might be thought about Tillman, there can be little doubt that to have a leader with clear values and demonstrable loyalty is advantageous.

Business leaders can draw from the sport the reminder that their capacity is measured in part by their followers on the values expressed and supported in action. Conviction and loyalty are paramount. Actions are always more powerful than words. Business leaders need to be unafraid to take positions on major issues. They need to be aware that they and their subordinates are always going to be developed in the forge of personal development.

---

6. Sustainability: Keeping the Form

Of all the measures of sporting success, staying at the top is the most respected. Setting a world record or winning an annual title, for example, may be much admired, but it is another thing altogether to emulate the longevity of a Sergei Bubka or Arnold Palmer. The competitive nature of sport means that winning even consecutive titles is a magnificent feat. Increasingly, business is subject to the same sort of competitive pressures common in elite sport. With the deepening of the global economy and pace of technological innovation, the opportunity for businesses to hold market leadership by default is diminishing. This fact is well illustrated by Peters and Waterman's famous 1982 management guide, *In Search of Excellence*,[2] wherein they profiled 43 of the best performing companies in order to determine their common characteristics. This they did, but many of those companies were faltering within a few years, and some went out of business altogether. Sport thinking encourages an awareness of competition and the need for sustainable performance, the achievement of which demands a long-term philosophy toward strategy and leadership.

Few champion athletes can legitimately claim to have been great coaches as well. Dan Gable, US amateur wrestling athlete and coach, enjoys rarefied status as both a legendary wrestler and coach, renowned for an extraordinary focus that held for over two decades. With the exception of one match, Gable was undefeated throughout his high school and college wrestling career, culminating in several national titles as well as an Olympic gold medal. Remarkable though it was, Gable's performance as a wrestler was exceeded by his success as a coach. Over 21 years as the coach of the University of Iowa, Gable achieved an unprecedented 93 percent win record, coaching 78 national champions, 152 all-Americans and four Olympic gold medallists.

One of the striking features of Gable's long career is his claim to have missed no more than one practice in 25 years. This impressive claim is a reflection of Gable's long-term view of performance. Prepared to set clear priorities, Gable was able to maintain his success through the assumption that all activity had to revolve around performance not just for the next season, but for the next ten seasons.

> Sustainability at the top of sport performance demands a long-term view of strategy. Business leaders need to set priorities that reflect a strategic intention to perform in the long term as well as in the immediate future.

7. Knowledge: Innovation as a Competitive Advantage

In a business world full of jargon and fads, the concept of knowledge management has been one of the last decade's silver bullets. From a strategic perspective, knowledge management is about making sure that the organization is able to capitalize on what it has learnt, as well as putting aside what are no longer the best ways of doing things. It is about making sure that the right things are being done in an organization. Sometimes whether this is the case can be ambiguous in business; there is always a lag between performance and the measures that express it. This feedback is less troublesome in sport, however, which in turn helps sport leaders to reflect on the appropriateness of their preparations and innovate as a result. Thus, the ability to innovate always returns to knowledge. Indeed, sport leaders are typically obsessed with knowledge and innovation in trying to find new competitive advantages over the competition. This tends to include nutritional supplements, novel training methods, and even drugs. For the business leader, this commitment to developing new knowledge as a competitive advantage is a useful benchmark.

As a benchmark in sport it is difficult to go past the performances of the Ferrari Formula One team. Their success is all the more impressive in a sport that relies heavily on the knowledge of its 800-strong team to remain at the forefront of innovation, where to do something genuinely new is comparable to the development of new technologies at NASA. The 2004 season brought even more records for the Ferrari team. The season included 15 wins from 18 races, its sixth constructor's championship and lead driver Michael Schumacher's fifth successive driver's title. In Formula One, these achievements are evidence of the best team in the sport's history, and arguably the best sporting team of all time.

Why can Ferrari dominate in a sport that changes significantly in technology and rules every year? All signs should suggest an increasing parity rather than a domination of one team over the rest. From their commitment to invest in the best driver in the world, to the design and engineering advantages orchestrated by Jean Todt, Ross Brawn, and Rory Byrne, Ferrari is the master of knowledge management. In a competitive arena that rewards innovation and punishes complacency, the Ferrari Formula One team is permeated with leaders at all levels who constantly push to develop new ways of doing things.

Sport emphasizes the importance of a commitment to knowledge development and management. Business leaders can profit from an innovation perspective as a vehicle for stimulating competitive advantage.

---

8. Measurement: Leading by the Numbers

Performance measurement in business has long been accepted as a conventional practice. However, the benchmark for performance measurement set by sport is well beyond that of the business world. In fact, no other activity in the world is subject to such intense measurement and scrutiny as sporting performance. Just about every aspect of performance in professional sport is measured in some statistical way, and those that cannot be measured with numbers are videotaped, discussed and assessed in more subjective terms. There is no escape from evaluation in sport. It is an obsession that may benefit business leaders to embrace further. Business activity is full of distractions from those operations that are core to the business. A renewed commitment to performance measurement is in the interest of business leaders if for no other reason than to ensure that the right things are being measured in the first place.

There are times when the true measurement of performance requires unusual action. After winning more that 50 LPGA titles, golfer Annika Sorenstam determined that it was time to measure herself against a new benchmark. In 2003, she competed in the Colonial PGA tournament against some of the best male players in the world. Although hampered by nerves and excessive media attention, Sorenstam showed herself to be an outstanding golfer. When asked after the event what she had achieved, Sorenstam commented that she had come to the tournament to test herself. As an athlete dedicated to her ongoing self-improvement, Sorenstam was prepared to face intense scrutiny just to gain an objective measurement of her game.

Sorenstam exemplifies many admirable qualities, as do most champion sportspeople. Amongst these, it must be acknowledged that her tenacious preparedness to test and measure her performances is one of the most impressive. Perhaps few business leaders would voluntarily place themselves, their organization or team in a situation of such vulnerability, with the simple objective of putting their competencies in perspective.

> Although business has embraced performance management as a fundamental aspect of leadership, the comprehensive approach to measurement demonstrated in professional sport offers a reminder to business leaders of the depth and frequency with which a performance can be assessed. This can extend to all parts of leadership and the organization.

9. Passion: Connecting with the Leadership Source

There can be little doubt that sport arouses an emotional intensity with which there are few parallels in the world of business. The symbolism of sport seems to transgress the rational borders of the mind, generating a kind of deep psychological bond that few brands could ever dream of acquiring. Even some of the most prominent brand names in the world, which already enjoy tremendous product loyalty, like Coca-Cola and Sony, regularly align themselves with sport to enhance their image. The passion of sport does not end with the sport itself or even a club and its heroes. As Coca-Cola understands, sport entangles other relationships, enhancing experiences with family, friends, and other fans. As a result, one of the more powerful lessons from sport can be found in the way it operates as a stimulator of emotional attachment. It is principally concerned with the attachments that permeate commercial benefits. While professional athletes may well treat their training and performances as a job, in the sense that it requires a complete and systematic commitment, they nevertheless see it as far more than merely a job. As Martina Navratilova once commented in an interview when asked about her involvement in tennis, she replied that she was not just involved, but was committed to tennis.

Of sportspeople who have generated and exuded passion, American cyclist Lance Armstrong stands out from the crowd. The record six-time winner of the pre-eminent cycling event in the world, the Tour de France, Armstrong might be considered lucky to be on a bike at all, if not lucky to be alive, after a cancer diagnosis in 1996 that gave him even odds of survival. Struck down with testicular cancer, which had migrated to his lungs and brain, Armstrong's career as a cyclist seemed certainly over. After surgery and an aggressive chemotherapy regime, Armstrong slowly improved and pulled himself back on a bike within months. He even established a cancer foundation that has since offered hope and inspiration to thousands of sufferers. Armstrong's greatest legacy to the foundation was his form on the bike, however. He won the Tour de France in 1999, and has not been defeated in the tour since. The rare passion that Armstrong holds for his sport and the passion he evokes in those who have followed his career are a result of the adversity that he has faced. Armstrong says his uncommon passion was forged by pain: on the bike and in the hospital bed.

> For the business leader, the connection that sport elicits in fans, players, and support staff is a benchmark of commitment, loyalty, and inspiration. The ability of business leaders to cultivate even a comparatively small sense of passion in individuals for their team, organization, or product is a powerful ability indeed.

10. Focus: Pursuing the Right Goals

The competitive nature of elite sport demands focus; either the right goals are being pursued or performance is compromised. As any athlete in the public eye can attest, there is never any shortage of advice on how to improve their game. While some of it may come from legitimate sources, and some of it might be sound advice, there is a great danger in acting on it. Athletes need to have the clarity and focus to avoid getting distracted by other possibilities, advice, and ideas. High performance can only be realized when an athlete takes a single-minded approach and can build a momentum toward a singular ambition. Seeking a number of simultaneous goals presents a danger of achieving none of them. Equally, in business, there are always more opportunities than resources will allow to be pursued. It is the leader's responsibility to ensure that the right goals are focused upon.

We could draw on any of the sport leaders highlighted in this book to reinforce this lesson. Indeed, there can scarcely be any theme in this book that cannot be illustrated by Michael Jordan, his six NBA championships, five NBA Most Valuable Player awards, Olympic gold medal in the original dream team and 13 All Star games, demonstrating a focus that is all the more impressive considering the immense media scrutiny he had to endure. Alternatively, consider Ric Charlesworth, one of the most successful coaches in Australian sporting history. Charlesworth's ability to focus his team on the right goals was legendary, taking them to double Olympic gold. Others like Olympic athletics gold medallist Jackie Joyner-Kersee personify goal setting, having shown her focus as a child while leaping into a home-made sandpit near her home. Finally, Japanese sumo wrestling champion, or *yokozuna*, Masuru Hanada showed enormous fixity of purpose when pursuing the unthinkable goal of playing NFL football at the conclusion of his sumo career. He would have made it, but was giving away a substantial degree of youth and experience in the game. However, none questioned his tenacity or focus.

Sport thinking for business leaders encourages clarity of focus on core business issues and meeting core business goals without distraction. As much as anything, leadership in business can be defined by the responsibility leaders hold for determining how scarce resources can be deployed toward a consistent and focused goal.

One Final Comment

We have tried to avoid cliché where possible, but the use of sport as a metaphor can lead to overused slogans and catchphrases. Allow us the indulgence of concluding with one: Leaders are doers.

It's not the critic who counts, not the one who points out how the strong man stumbled or how the doer of deeds might have done them better. The credit belongs to the man who is actually in the arena; whose face is marred with the sweat and dust and blood; who strives valiantly; who errs and comes up short again and again; who knows the great enthusiasms, the great devotions and spends himself in a worthy cause and who, at best knows the triumph of high achievement and who at worst, if he fails, at least fails while daring greatly so that his place shall never be with those cold and timid souls who know neither victory nor defeat.

(Theodore Roosevelt, 26th president of the United States)[3]

Notes

1   P. Gronn (2002), "Distributed Leadership", in K. Leithwood, P. Hallinger, K. Seashore-Louis, G. Furman-Brown, P. Gronn, W. Mulford and K. Riley (eds), *Second International Handbook of Educational Leadership and Administration*, Dordrecht: Kluwer.

2   T. Peters and R. Waterman (1982), *In Search of Excellence: Lessons from America's Best-run Companies*, Warner Books, New York.

3   T. Roosevelt (April 23, 1910), "Citizenship in a Republic", speech at the Sorbonne, Paris. Excerpt from *The Works of Theodore Roosevelt – National Edition*, H-Bar Enterprises CD rom.